Tracking Down
Ecological Guidance

Presence • Beauty • Survival

*Hope is not the conviction that something
will turn out well, but the certainty that something
makes sense, regardless of how it turns out.*

Vaclav Havel

Dedication

For Ellen, who insisted I get this done
and
For Brendan, who created it

Tracking Down Ecological Guidance

Presence · Beauty · Survival

Keith Helmuth

Chapel Street Editions
Woodstock, New Brunswick

Published by Chapel Street Editions,
Woodstock, NB, Canada
www.chapelstreeteditions.com

Library and Archives Canada Cataloguing in Publication

Helmuth, Keith, 1937-, author
        Tracking down ecological guidance : presence, beauty,
survival / Keith Helmuth.

Includes bibliographical references.
ISBN 978-0-9936725-3-8

        1. Human ecology. 2. Ecology – Economic aspects.
3. Ecology – Religious aspects. I. Title.

GF41.H44 2015   304.2   C2015-901627-4

Cover illustration: "North Hill Pine" by Gordon Hammond.

Quotations from *The Man Who Killed the Deer* by Frank Waters
used with permission of Ohio University Press.

Photograph of the author by Brendan Helmuth

Contents

Preface: "Darkness and Scattered Light" I

The Angel of History, the Storm of Progress, and the
Order of the Soul 5

First Light & Last Things: Presence, Beauty, Survival 45

Indigenous Wisdom and Ecological Guidance 69

Technology: Tool Kit and Mindset 93

The Evolution of Environmental Education 127

In the Ruins of a Faith-Haunted World 163

"There'll Come a Day" 193

Tracking Down Ecological Guidance 201

Epilogue: Down to Earth With an Eye on the Future 229

References 245

About the Author 271

Preface:
"Darkness and Scattered Light"

In 1976 William Irwin Thompson gave four lectures to mark the opening of the Lindisfarne Center in New York City that were later published under the title *Darkness and Scattered Light*.[1] With his prescient grasp of cultural change, Thompson's lectures caught the moment and mapped the probable future. "Darkness and scattered light" – what image could better capture the human situation in the latter part of the 20th century, and now in the first part of the 21st?

From the time it dawned on me in the late 1950s that industrial civilization was degrading the integrity of Earth's ecosystems, and that this trajectory was bound to end badly, I have been on a quest to understand the human-Earth relationship, and what is required to achieve an ecologically sound way of life.

Despite the environmental awakening in the 1960s, and the fact that some of this new awareness was translated into important legislation and effective public policy, industrial civilization is now, in 2014, in ever more desperate conflict with the integrity of Earth's ecosystems worldwide.

In order to advance the growth of the consumer economy, and to keep the financial system from collapsing, it is literally the case that we are systematically disrupting and degrading the biotic environments that underlie the wellbeing of all life on Earth. Our high-energy, industrial-consumer civilization is rapidly dismantling the evolutionary complexity of Earth's commonwealth of life.

A rational response to this dilemma is to say, "But that's absurd! That's suicide!"[2] Indeed it is. But by any sober assessment this is the situation of modern civilization, despite the scientific evidence that has piled up in the last sixty years on the deteriorating state of the human-Earth relationship.

The "darkness" has not abated; in fact, it has grown into such dense complexity that even those best positioned to understand what is happening are hard pressed to offer good explanations or sound guidance.[3] But it is also true that the "scattered light" is now brighter than ever, and, in some cases, has coalesced into pockets of brilliance that throw the irrationality of "business as usual" into stark relief.[4,5]

It is not irrational to wake up in the morning and ask yourself: how long can things go on like this; is there a plan B for the end of the fossil fuel era; how can we have perpetual economic growth on a finite planet; what happens when economic growth comes to an end?

Has industrial civilization, like the cartoon character, Wile E. Coyote, already gone off the ecological cliff? Are we now hanging in thin air about to experience a dramatic and unpleasant crash? Or do we expect that our technology will magically sprout wings – like the marvellous flying car, *Chitty Chitty Bang Bang* – and carry us over a sea of troubles, landing safely in another utopia of cheap energy so the growth of industrial-consumer civilization can be kept going?

Meanwhile, back on Earth, the signals are coming thick and fast. "Business as usual won't do," it won't do as a strategy for a sustainable economy, it won't do as a system of stable finance, and it won't do as a context for human wellbeing, or even survival.

More and more, economic growth is pushing past the breaking points of Earth's ecosystem, and patchwork at the breaking points won't work. When systems are broken, new system thinking is needed. The good news is, new system thinking is one of the beacons of light now scanning over the dark miasma of "business as usual."[6,7,8,9]

A few years ago I helped author a book titled *How on Earth Do We Live Now?*[10] The title was both a cry of alarm and a call to action. The prospect of catastrophic ecological, economic, and societal breakdown looms ever more ominously in the logic of globalized hyper-industrialism. The ecological guidance now firmly within the grasp of both scientific and spiritual insight must be urgently applied if this outcome is to be averted, or even just ameliorated.

The essays gathered in this book are reports from my quest to understand the adaptational mistakes now darkly shadowing the human prospect, and to gather the light of ecological guidance into better illumination. I am not sanguine about the outcome. Adaptational mistakes on the scale of hyper-industrialism have consequences that cannot be cancelled or even mitigated, as seen, for example, in the meltdown of the nuclear reactors at Fukishima, in the climate change effects of global warming, and in the hormonal chaos now being caused by the widespread dispersion of endocrine system disrupting chemicals.

My assessment of ecological guidance and the prospect of its effective application to global environmental restoration is tempered by an increasing sense that various stages of civilizational collapse are already underway, and that major strategies of difficult readaptation are in the offing. This perspective and this theme are present in the essays that follow. I am now concerned in almost equal measure with the means of ecological and spiritual resilience. I have come to understand and experience them as two aspects of the same guidance, hence, the subtitle of this book, *Presence, Beauty, Survival.*

I am keenly aware that much of what I have written is surrounded by the work of many others who have been engaged in a similar quest. In order to honour this context, and to provide access to additional material for further study, I have included numbered references in the text and listed them at the end of the book.

I have been thinking for some years of writing a book that gathered and distilled my perspective on the ecological worldview and ecological guidance. Careers in business management, teaching, farming, and community economic development have regularly pre-empted a concentrated effort in this direction. At a certain point several years ago, I realized that in writing for public presentation and for occasional publication I had, in fact, written the book I had in mind. It remained to select, edit, and amplify the material into a coherent package. This book is the result of that effort.

Keith Helmuth
Wolastoq Watershed
New Brunswick, Canada
December 2014

The Angel of History, the Storm of Progress, and the Order of the Soul

Based on a presentation made to the Southern Appalachian Yearly Meeting Association of the Religious Society of Friends (Quakers), June 10, 2005, Warren Wilson College, Swannanoa, North Carolina.

Anyone who has felt a baby being born, or had a whale come up under a boat, understands that ideas are no big deal. Ideas come and go, like rain in a ditch at the side of the road. It is a defining aspect of modernity to treat ideas as matters of utmost importance. Within that importance, however, the immanence of earth has lost its significance.[1]

-Raymond Rogers

Those who formulate policy should recognize that if humans pit themselves against the fundamental dynamics of cosmic nature, they are certain to lose...It might be argued that war and civil disorder are presently the greatest threats to the human future. One need not minimize their dangers to also recognize that attrition of the Earth's biosphere and life support systems could continue unobtrusively under conditions of peace until a point is reached at which environmental disintegration led to societal disintegration.[2]

-Lynton Keith Caldwell

Over the Amazon with the Storm of Progress

A year ago this past January [2004], under the light of the full moon, I looked from the window of a jetliner over a vast expanse of the Amazon watershed. I saw the large slowly winding main trunk of the great river gradually disappearing into the eastern horizon. Just ahead I saw the confluence of a large tributary that had begun its multi-stream course on the flanks of the northern Andes. Closer at hand, and just below, another major watercourse curled into view from under the body of the plane, and meandered for some distance on a northward course before also merging into the main body of the Amazon River.

I was not prepared for this view. I was transfixed for over an hour, taking in the slow rolling scene of the slow rolling rivers and the vast forest of this still largely intact upper basin region. I knew the route and had followed the flight path monitor closely on the overnight trip to Buenos Aries two weeks earlier. But two weeks earlier there had been cloud cover, no moonlight, and I was sitting on the side facing the Andes.

Looking far to the east I could see clusters of lights at points along the river bank signaling human settlements. Scanning closer as we came directly over the course of the river, I could also see smaller clusters of lights coming further up stream. A few lights were also dotted here and there on small tributaries now visible. These settlements rose up in my mind's eye: a fishing village here, rubber tappers there, hunters, loggers, mineral prospectors, plant researchers, all with their diesel generators pushing like demons ever deeper into the biotic integrity of the land. Indigenous peoples, resource raiders, and bio-pirates all mixed up on the leading edge of the great storm of progress.

Then the scene changed. Coming even with the great river, and looking to the land flowing north and east, I began to see rectangular outlines and distinctly different shadings in variegated blocks. Between them and through them ran arrow-straight lines of a much lighter hue, roads through the forest, and whole tracts of forest gone.

I have seen a lot of clear-cut forestland close-up, but from 36,000 feet the vast scale of this destruction was stunning. When I was earlier looking down on forestland yet intact, I thought about the communities of life that are tucked into every nook and cranny of this region. Those of nocturnal habit would now be out. Later, with the sunrise, another group of residents, adapted differently, would employ their life skills to good effect. With clear cutting, this fabric of life is blasted, smashed to smithereens. With clear cutting, the storm of progress has truly mounted to hurricane force.

Lifting my eyes to gaze one last time over the whole panorama rolling out to the horizon, another story of this land came into view – fire. To the southeast I saw a few smudges of orange flame and hanging smoke. And then due east and to the north, more fires; some small, some very large, considering the distance at which I was seeing them. The refuse of the cleared forestland was being burned, releasing large amounts of carbon from long-term storage into the atmosphere.

Here was another feature of the storm of progress; firestorms burning up the rain forest, preparing the way for the beef industry and the soybean business. I slumped back in my seat and thought about Bruce Cockburn's classic 1988 song, "If a Tree Falls." Speaking specifically of rain forest clear cutting, he sings:

Green brain facing lobotomy
Climate control centre for the world
Ancient cord of coexistence
Hacked by parasitic greedhead scam –
Take out trees.
Take out wildlife at the rate of a species every single day.
Take out people who have lived with this for 100,000
years.

If a tree falls in the forest does anybody hear?
If a tree falls in the forest does anybody hear?
Does anybody hear the forest fall?

The Order of the Soul

There is a kind of knowledge that often comes to us as a fully rounded comprehension of reality, a sense of over arching and underlying relationship that cannot be achieved by understanding an accumulation of details. Formed as we are within spheres of relationship, this knowledge is born of participation. We can call this knowledge the wisdom of the soul. Coming to this knowledge is not a matter of chronological age. It is a matter of a certain kind of experience of the world. And the earlier in life we come to this experience, the greater our chances of living within the order of the soul.

We can come to this kind of experience in delight and wonder. We can come to it in anger and agony. Wherever on this spectrum we come to this defining experience, its signal characteristic is communion, that merging of identity with the forms, presence, and process of the great world beyond the boundary of our skin and the reach of our mind.

The work of artists often moves within this range of experience. Poetry, painting, music and all the other forms and processes that spring to expression in the work of artists, often opens to communion and the order of the soul. Bruce Cockburn's song, "If a Tree Falls" from the album, *Big Circumstance*, runs the gamut of this experience, and its presentation of vision and pain had long contributed to my image of what is happening to the great rainforest of the Amazon region.

My recent, unanticipated experience of the Amazon landscape by moonlight has enlarged my sense of communion, made newly visible to me the order of the soul, and added to my knowledge of what it is that cannot be fully understood but, nevertheless, in our hope for the future, must be communicated among us. I come to the occasion of this Quaker gathering to share some of the images and some of the thinking that keeps me on track in my quest for ecological guidance.

On the Ground with the Angel of History

Whenever I have the opportunity to prepare a presentation for a gathering like this, I am drawn to issues pounding hard on the shores of faith. In recent times the range of issues and the force of events have dramatically escalated. Any number of concerns or profoundly challenging events that are daily before us could be the focus of an entire lecture.

Instead of choosing a single theme and focusing in the usual way, I would like here, however, to share with you several probes. A probe, as you may imagine, is a brief foray into a topic that opens it up for further consideration. I will, therefore, be presenting thoughts on several themes with which I have been engaged over the years as I have worked to understand the unfolding of the human story, and, in particular, the human-Earth relationship.

We are now seeing more and more clearly that there are no single focus issues, and that justice, equity, peace, and the integrity of Earth's ecosystems form a coherent framework of ethical development, economic behavior, public policy, ecologically coherent adaptation, and human betterment. In this expanded context, the juxtaposition of a series of probes is often useful.

You may be wondering about the title of this lecture. I, too, am still wondering about it. It came to me like a kind of large swooping bird that alighted on the page and refused to clear off even when encouraged to do so. I tried several other titles, but the more I looked at this one and the more it looked back at me, the more it seemed right for what I thought I wanted to say.

I have found that writing is not so much a process of recording what I think, as it is a way of discovering new images and new thoughts that would not have come to me had I not set out on the journey of writing. So with the angel of history as our guide, with the storm of progress at full pitch, and with the order of the soul struggling to keep its head above the waters of fatalism, I will try to coordinate this exploration in a way that reaches a helpful focus for living into the future. I am convinced we must choose the future as never before. We must collectively choose, design, and create alternatives to the trajectory that is now sweeping us into ecological and societal breakdown.

The appearance of such a highflying title does not come out of the blue. Many things we read or hear feed into the images that form our thoughts. And so it was that while pondering this title, I realized it had two primary sources that will help set the stage for what follows.

The first is from philosopher and cultural analyst, Walter Benjamin. Walter Benjamin was a good friend of the great Swiss painter, Paul Klee. He collected Klee's work and at one point acquired a painting titled, "Angelus Novus." In the spring of 1940 Benjamin completed a short work called, "Theses on the Philosophy of History," in which he wrote the following:

> *A Klee painting named "Angelus Novus" shows an angel looking as though he is about to move away from something he is fixedly contemplating. His eyes are staring, his mouth is open, his wings are spread. This is how one pictures the angel of history. His face is turned toward the past. Where we perceive a chain of events, he sees one single catastrophe which keeps piling wreckage upon wreckage and hurls it in front of his feet. The angel would like to stay, awaken the dead, and make whole what has been smashed. But a storm is blowing from Paradise; it has got caught in his wings with such violence that the angel can no longer close them. The storm irresistibly propels him into the future to which his back is turned, while the pile of debris before him grows skyward. This storm is what we call progress.[3]*

The second source of my title is from the song "The Future" by poet, and musician, Leonard Cohen.

> *Things are going to slide in all directions*
> *Won't be nothing you can measure anymore*
> *The blizzard of the world has crossed the threshold*
> *And has overturned the order of the soul.*

The references overlap. The "storm of progress" becomes the "blizzard of the world," and that which the angel longs to accomplish – "awakening the dead and making whole what has been smashed" – is beyond his power. The storm has crossed a critical threshold and "has overturned the order of the soul." Such are the apprehensions and the images of the artist, the seer, and the poet.

I take these images seriously because I think it is true, as Marshall McLuhan once said, artists are the early warning systems of cultural change. And I am further convinced that to understand the processes of life and societal development we must, as Kenneth Boulding has clearly shown,[4] understand the role of the "image." We must understand the way, for humans, a complex inventory of images build up into various stories, and frequently into a primal or master story that attempts to make sense of our situation in the world and guide behaviour.

Those who know the work of Thomas Berry will see where these thoughts are headed. In thinking about the human situation, Berry observes, "We are in trouble just now because ... we are between stories. It's all a question of story."[5] This may seem like a simplistic observation, but once we understand that all knowledge is built up around images, and the way images are combined into convincing stories guide behavior, we can see the aptness of Berry's observation.

The master story of Western Civilization about human domination of Earth has now ended in a destructive storm of "progress" and is no longer credible even in its own terms; it no longer provides a believable system of guidance. We are now in the process of creating a new human-Earth story that provides better guidance, but the outcome still hangs in the balance. It is far from certain that the "new story" will emerge with the speed and global reach needed to create a mutually enhancing human-Earth relationship.

Into the Storm of Progress

Seeing the Amazon by moonlight has lodged an image in my mind that is among the strongest and most deeply imprinted experiences of my life. It resides in a zone of memory that comes into focus unbidden and with great frequency. It has become one of those constant images that connect. I have always had a weakness for landscapes. I more or less fall instantly in love with new landscapes, and fill up with emotion on return to the landscapes of home. I agree with the great French novelist, Stendhal, when he says, "The purpose of home is to make the heart leap."

To be so powerfully imprinted by a landscape from over six miles in the air, and at night, is hard to account for. It is a puzzle, but a puzzle with an answer. And the answer lies in the image, and in all the prior images and the stories they compose about this region of Earth that I have had the good fortune to encounter. (The irony of my story does not escape me. My experience of the Amazon was delivered while cradled in the wings of an agent of the storm of progress – an ozone-blasting jetliner. This is not a trip we ever imagined making, but when a marriage in the family included a celebration in Buenos Aries, we hesitated not a minute in booking our flight. Such are the wonders of the storm of progress.)

When I speak of the storm of progress, I am not speaking as a Luddite, as one who wishes that technological innovation had been stopped with the water wheel and the iron tipped plow, although there are good reasons to think that might have been a wise decision. From an evolutionary point of view, from an ecological perspective, and from within the human story, it is an objective fact that the history of progress since the sixteenth century has been a storm; not "like" a storm, but an actual, objectively trackable storm – a turbulence of change, mounting in intensity, scale and scope, still cresting in successive waves of disruption and reconfiguration. The disruptions have been horribly damaging to the social systems and ecosystems that have suffered them. The reconfigurations have been wonderfully, though perhaps superficially, beneficent to those who have prospered and claimed the lion's share of the booty and privilege.

Progressive thinkers once imagined that as the storm ran its course, virtually everybody would benefit in a way that would be well worth all the disruption and suffering. The technological utopians like to call this process "creative destruction." Now that this optimistic scenario is clearly not the case, not even for those with most of the booty and privileges, a great loss of faith stalks the land. And the storm, rather than running its course like a natural storm and allowing for recovery and adjustment, shows no sign of abating. Innovation is all the rage. Innovation is expected to produce progress. But the great doubt, the great loss of faith now active in the culture, is that innovation and economic growth are not inevitably progressive.

There are forms of progress that truly advance human betterment and ecological integrity, but the forces of so-called "development" that literally decompose social and biotic resilience are now betraying many of them. This is what the angel of history is trying to say; wake up, the outcome of the human story is at stake! What is smashed is smashed, but some integrity remains – the fecundity of earth, the solidarity of human communities at their best, some good tools, and some old manuals of practice.

But who is this angel of history? If, as Walter Benjamin says, "the storm is blowing from Paradise," and the angel of history is storm driven, he is then clearly an exile, a homeless angel, a lonely spirit in a hurricane of troubles being blown increasingly beyond recovery, increasingly beyond the threshold that overturns the order of the soul. I submit that the angel of history is a mirror. In our contemplation of this figure, we are given an image of the postmodern human, a figure transfixed by the force of progress, but steadily losing the sense of wholeness and integrity, steadily losing the order of the soul. Which brings me to the next theme I wish to explore.

Angels of History and the Mindset of Domination

The first step in this exploration will be upstream into history. I want to get below the full force of the storm for a bit and take a look back toward its origin, back toward one of the drivers of the storm. This will be a small expedition into cultural archeology.

In the course of my work I recently received a book with a title that immediately commanded my attention – *An Angel Directs the Storm: Apocalyptic Religion & American Empire*, by British theologian, Michael Northcott. We have here another angel of history, but it is clear from the title, an angel of a very different sort. On investigation, I learned that this image comes from the time of the American Revolutionary War. Soon after the publication of the Declaration of Independence, a Virginia statesman, John Page, wrote the following in a letter to Thomas Jefferson: "We know the race is not to the swift nor the battle to the strong. Do you not think an angel rides in the whirlwind and directs the storm?"[6] This angel reappears in George W. Bush's first inaugural address. In speaking about the destiny of the nation, and his determination to confront all enemies with the full force of American strength, he says the struggle will ultimately be successful because it is "the angel of God who directs the storm."

We are here dealing with one of the master narratives of Western Civilization – the story of the "will of God." The history of this narrative as applied to the founding of the United States is well known and not surprising given the theological worldview of the time. What is surprising, and more than a little suspect, is that a refurbished vision of this kind is now being promoted as a way to understand contemporary world history and America's role in shaping and controlling the world economy; This is more than surprising, it is alarming.

This is especially alarming because there is considerable evidence that a significant number of players in American political life actually believe, as a matter of religious faith, that the US has become the world's victorious superpower because it is the will of God. The US, as a chosen nation, is divinely ordered to prevail until such time as the apocalypse is unfolded and the end of history is at hand.

The idea of an apocalyptic end to human history does not trouble them. From their reading of the Bible, God clearly wills this scenario. To be an agent of the apocalypse is to be doing the will of God. Reflecting on this theological mindset within American political leadership, Bill Moyers recently observed, "The delusional is no longer marginal." Those in national leadership who do not exactly share this Americanized biblical worldview, still support the policies that flow from it for military and economic reasons. The delusion is useful.

How has this situation arisen? How did it come about that the idea of the will of God became equated with an authorization for one cultural complex and its metaphysical worldview to defeat and/or dominate all others? How has it happened that this authorization also turned into a worldwide exploitation of Earth's human and natural resources in favour of wealth accumulation for the dominating culture, which, in its global hyper-industrialism phase, now threatens the biospheric integrity of the planet?

Where does this kind of idea come from? There are a number of tributaries that flow into this cultural stream, but the main trunk is easily traceable to the ancient watershed of biblical storytelling. If we turn to the story of the Israelites' invasion of Canaan, we can clearly see how the story of the will of God gave warrant in those days to a mindset of domination, and how the journey of this mindset began that eventually became a master narrative of Western Civilization.

Historically, the first codification of a single supreme deity appears in the Egyptian cultural tradition long before the tribes of Israel departed the Nile delta and wandered into the wilderness of Sinai. The ancient Israelites carried Egypt's unique religious innovation with them and employed monotheism to powerful effect as a force for tribal cohesion, and as a conquering force of divine will.

Elijah and the Victory Over Canaan[7]

When the Israelites moved to invade and colonize Canaan, the physical takeover of land and settlements was only a part of the conquest. A well-developed religious culture with diverse sites of practice also had to be defeated. The local deities that symbolized the powers and processes of the land of Canaan were not just an affront to the Israelites' supreme, invisible deity, but remained a constant and alluring temptation to the people of Israel themselves. So prone were they to turn their eyes and religious affections to the forms and process of the tangible world, and away from the abstract conception of an invisible, supremely all-powerful god, that, according to the record, the priests and prophets of Yahweh were often marginalized.

Finally, with Elijah, so the story goes, this conflict comes to a critical test. Under the leader Ahab and his assistant, Obadiah, the Israelites had apparently accommodated so completely to the worship of local deities, including Baal, that the prophets of Yahweh were living in caves, exiled away from the settlements. It was also a time of drought "and there was a sore famine in Samaria." In the third year of this period, Yahweh speaks to Elijah: "Go shew thyself to Ahab; and I will send rain upon the earth." Elijah does as he is told but Ahab calls him a "troublemaker" in Israel. Elijah fires back, "I have not troubled the house of Israel, but thou, and thy father's house, in that ye have forsaken the commandments of the Lord, and hast followed Baalim."

Elijah proposes a test and convinces Ahab to let him try it. Ahab agrees to gather all of Israel to Mount Carmel along with four hundred and fifty prophets of Baal. The people and prophets assemble. "And Elijah came unto all the people, and said, how long halt ye between two opinions? If the Lord be God, follow him: but if Baal, then follow him. And the people answered him not a word." Elijah then issues his great challenge – the setting up of competing stone altars complete with wood and slaughtered bullocks on top. The contest is for each side in the dispute to pray to their respective deities, calling for the wood to spontaneously ignite and burn the offering.

We are well acquainted with the contest, so classic has this story become in the subsequent history of biblical faith. The prophets of Baal do their utmost, to no avail. Elijah mocks them, making fun of the fact that none of their deities seem to be listening. Have they fallen asleep, he asks? Have they gone out walking and can't hear your prayers, he taunts?

When evening comes, Elijah swings into action. He builds up the altar of Yahweh. He digs a trench around it. He stacks the wood. He lays the bullock on the altar. He commands that four barrels of water be poured over the whole arrangement – bullock, wood, and altar; not once, not twice, but three times, so that the trench fills with water. Elijah makes a prayer to Yahweh, fire falls on the altar and burns, not just the wood and the sacrificed bullock, but the stones of the altar and all the water in the trench. "And when all the people saw it, they fell on their faces: and they said, the Lord, he is the God; the Lord, he is the God."

But this is not the end of the story. Elijah took no chances. He now had the upper hand with a mob force at his command. In current jargon, he had earned political capital and he knew how to spend it. "And Elijah said unto them, take the prophets of Baal; let not one of them escape. And they took them: and Elijah brought them to the brook Kishon, and slew them there."

Elijah then ascends Mount Carmel, falls to earth with his head between his knees and commands his servant to look toward the sea. Seven times he makes this command until a cloud appears and the sky turns dark. They rush back down mountain to take shelter from the storm. The rains have come. The drought has ended. The will of Yahweh has been accomplished and the reward is given.

What are we to make of this story? Those who regard Hebrew scripture as a document of singular revelation from an otherwise unknown and unknowable God have labored for many generations to draw guidance from its stories. The legend of Elijah, empowered by Yahweh, defeating the indigenous religious culture of Canaan and its worldview, has become a flagship story of monotheism as it has developed in its Jewish, Christian, and Islamic forms.

For those who see the significance of scripture within the larger context of human cultural development, the story of Elijah is no less important, but in a rather different way. Like the story of Abraham and Isaac, which signals the end of human sacrifice, the story of Elijah signals the victory of a particular structure of belief; the belief that the personal will of Yahweh is the metaphysical reality that creates, organizes and commands the world.

The work of Gordon D. Kaufman, emeritus Professor of Divinity at Harvard University, is especially instructive on this critical juncture in the origins of Western Civilization. In a variety of studies, he shows how the die was cast when Israel won the great religious struggle with Canaan, and the personal moral will of Yahweh triumphed over the powers and processes of Earth as represented in local and place-based deities.[8,9] The monotheistic worldview thus begins its long offensive against the ancient place-based, Earth-centered religious traditions. These traditions were alert to the powers of the animate Earth. They invested the forms and beings of Earth with a touch of the numinous and a sense of the sacred. The devotees of monotheism, as exemplified in Elijah, have been ruthlessly opposed ever since to this kind religious diversity and its forms of worship. This is not to say that a belief in monotheism must necessarily take this attitude or act out this intolerant role in the world, but only to say that in its historically dominant forms, this is how it has behaved.

Moral will, as personified in and derived from Yahweh, came to be seen as the only authentic metaphysical reality. The powers and processes of Earth that were symbolized in the god Baal, and in a variety of other local deities, came to be seen as without any authentic metaphysical standing.

When the story of this god and his will is reconfigured in Christian and Islamic iterations, the full force of the monoculture offensive is unleashed. In their orthodox forms, both of these religions hold they are destined to dominate and eliminate all other human cultural traditions, and have, thus, visited their competing missions on the world. Both Christianity and Islam have taken on this universalizing mission.

The unfolding dynamic of this universalizing story has become one of the master narratives of Western civilization, giving it its distinct character, motivation, and energy. Guidance within this context became progressively, and then exclusively, located within a structure of stories about the will of God – a Christianized version of Yahweh on the one hand, and an Islamic version, Allah, on the other.

To its great credit, no such mission ever tempted Judaism. Although the ethos of monotheism was intensely cultivated in the Jewish tradition, and served as both a sword and shield for tribal formation in biblical times, it did not develop an expansionist, universalizing cultural mandate, such as emerged in Christian and Islamic understandings of Divine will. Judaism remained essentially tribal.

From early times in Hebrew culture, and eventually in Christian and Islamic cultures, all models of metaphysical understanding and religious behavior are framed within the supremacy of personal moral will. From the stories of Yahweh and his intervening behavior on behalf of his devotees, through the religious warrant under which Christian Europe carried out its modern global colonization project, the imposition of personal moral will over all other sources of power, and over the forms and processes of Earth, has been the main story line of the Western tradition.

And in this story line it is important to note that this imposition of personal moral will is always characterized by male domination. Scholars of this history have shown that, in this respect, and in many others, European culture and Middle Eastern culture are "sibling civilizations."[10] Christian and Islamic cultures have their origins in the same story of the will of God in history. Islam is a constituent part of the Western tradition, a tradition that advances male domination as the expression of a singular and absolute metaphysical reality.

The Quandary of Metaphysical Guidance

I have included this story in some detail because I want to emphasize the quandary we are now in over this construction of metaphysical reality. Christian and Jewish fundamentalists have no doubt that war against their militant Islamic enemies is exactly what God wills. Islamic militants are absolutely certain that war against the Christian and Jewish infidel and apostate Muslims is the very essence of God's will. As between Christian, Jewish and Islamic fundamentalists there is not much difference on this matter of the will of God. They all hold to it as the absolute metaphysical reality of the world, as the only thing that makes sense and the only thing that matters. They are all Elijah's children. This is, essentially, a family fight – the worst kind – over resources, territorial dominance, and cultural influence.

What could be more painful? What could be more distressing? The master narrative on which the whole meaning of our cultural history hangs is now the agent of endless war at best and unimaginable disaster at worst. We can object as much as we want, we can tell the fundamentalists they have it all wrong about the will of God, but logically it won't wash. Their case is perfectly consistent with the deepest roots of the tradition. Violence, war, and even genocide are incidental matters within the scope of this history. When it comes to territory, resources, dominance, and cultural influence, personal moral will, projected into absolute metaphysical guidance, trumps compassion and justice every time.

I am not satisfied with this scenario. My probe seems to have entered a theological and cultural black hole and left me stranded in a kind of wasteland. But I have arrived at this point because I am deeply concerned about two things: 1) the deterioration of biospheric integrity under the domination of a dysfunctional metaphysical worldview, and 2) about the spiritual survival of human communities in a deteriorating biosphere. We face two catastrophes: the collapse of biotic carrying capacity within ecosystems, and the collapse of faith in the human future. The first is the loss of Earth's self-renewing biotic resilience, and the second is the loss of spiritual resilience – the blizzard of the world overturning of the order of the soul.

When I get into this kind of discouraging spiral, I feel a stop in my mind. I am not constitutionally disposed to this kind negative thinking. But I believe it is essential to understand the situation we are in if we are to work effectively to redeem it. I have spent much of my life working on the practical details of ecological adaptation, but my concern for survival has also taken me into these matters of cultural archeology and worldviews. Action requires faith, and faith requires a worldview, a way of understanding our situation in the world that makes sense to us, a believable story. When the world around us changes, our worldviews change, and we must find our bearings in a new compass setting, a new understanding, a new story.

A Blessing and a Curse:
The Natural History of a Worldview

The dilemmas of this analysis warrant careful review. A strong argument can be made for the great blessings of Western Civilization. It can be readily shown that this tradition has produced significant and lasting ethical advances in social behavior. In addition, the powerful and unique imagination of Western Civilization stands behind astounding scientific discoveries and technological innovation. This genius of the Western cultural tradition has been central to institution building, effective political administration, and great economic development.

Unfortunately, the lineage of cultural and ecological destruction that has also been sponsored by Western Civilization's historically unique worldview is a daunting counterweight to these blessings. The storm of progress is still building. The wreckage is still piling up. The order of the soul is now routinely sacrificed to the financialization of economic life and the unremitting drive of commercial commodification into every detail of ecosystem and social system functioning.

The *modus operandi* of this monoculture has shifted from an other-worldly metaphysical and religious focus to a this-worldly focus on economic growth and wealth accumulation. Globalizing the market economy on Earth has replaced evangelizing the spiritual economy of heaven, same song, different verse.

The organizational modes and operational effects of hyper-industrialism and advanced capital accumulation, driven by the mindset of market fundamentalism, are now on a trajectory of steadily increasing the risk of ecological and societal collapse. No history of blessings can offset the prospect of such an outcome.

No temporary benefit for a privileged sector of humanity can justify running the risk of crashing the functional integrity of Earth's life support systems; yet this is the threshold across which the logic of Western Civilization's metaphysical worldview has now driven the human-Earth relationship.

In order to deal with this troubling history there is a line of reasoning that says it is not fair to bring all these destructive aspects of Western Civilization into account because they are obviously the result of a failure to understand and faithfully uphold the best aspects of the tradition as first developed within the tribes of Israel, and then reconfigured in Christianity and Islam with the help of Greek and Roman cultures.

I have great sympathy for this argument. There is, in fact, a radical tradition within Christianity that grounds the Faith in a literal interpretation of Jesus' Sermon on the Mount and insists on living out a witness of peace and nonviolence, compassion and justice, simplicity of material life, and devotion to community service. The Anabaptist Reformation in the 16th century and the rise of Quakerism in the 17th century are notable in this regard. Tolstoy's writings on Christianity in the 19th century are a towering achievement in the attempt to recall the Faith to its New Testament origins and the teachings of Jesus. The Catholic Worker movement of Peter Maurin and Dorothy Day in the 20th century witnessed valiantly to recall the Church to this alternative Christianity. Although contributing significantly to a heightened ethical awareness and to the evolution of human betterment, this alternative Christian tradition did not change the trajectory of Christendom's domination story.

History, unfortunately, gives no exemptions after the fact. The cultural history that has been made is the history we have. Although we may not like it, the plain fact is the metaphysical tradition of supreme moral will has been the sponsoring agent of such cultural phenomena as the rise of Constantine Christianity, Islam's spread into Europe, the Christian crusades against Islam and Islam's response in return, European religious wars and persecutions, a holocaust of witch hunting against women, colonial imperialism in general and the genocidal destruction of indigenous peoples worldwide in particular. In addition, patriarchy, slavery, capitalism, totalitarian communism, fascism, and militarism all arise within the sanctioning ethos of the cultural tradition that imposes some version of a supreme moral will on the world.

All these events and movements emerged from a metaphysical worldview in which personal moral will is the organizing and driving force. All these movements, activities, and cultural tendencies, all these social, economic and political institutions were undertaken and came about because men believed absolutely in the rightness of what they were doing and regarded their own moral will as aligned with the will of God, the will of history, the will of the people, etc. It is important to note, by way of clarification, that "moral," in the context of this discussion, does not necessarily mean "good." It means a governing rationale, a justifying structure of belief that guides behaviour. It means that whatever action is undertaken is believed to be called for and guided by divine will, the will of history, the will of the people, duty, honor, destiny, revenge, justice, loyalty – some version of an absolute metaphysical imperative.

Even the case of Germany's National Socialist movement, and the project of cultural reconstruction, European domination, and ethnic extermination that Hitler and his colleagues undertook, was framed within the terms of the metaphysical supremacy of moral will. They had no doubt they were creating a better world, and that the destruction they employed would, in the end, produce a result that would be morally justified.

Despite the unfortunate mutations of its metaphysical mindset, one must agree that much good has been done through Western Civilization's way of understanding, organizing, and operating the world. The great storm of progress has had its blessings. But, at the same time, this history is so paradoxically disabling, so humanly destructive, and so ecologically degrading as to be mentally and emotionally numbing. Viewed objectively, it is so painful that it is almost impossible to avoid some degree of denial. We may wish to disown it, but it will never abandon us. The storm of progress will likely appear to our far descendants (if we have any) as it has appeared to many indigenous peoples – a peculiar disease of the mind, resulting in a violent, disruptive, and maladaptive episode in the human story and in the human-Earth relationship.

The Order of the Soul Overturned

What does it mean to say the "blizzard of the world" – the storm of progress – has "overturned the order of the soul?" Is this anything more than poetic hyperbole? I think it is. I think it is the metaphorical rendering of a reality that is coming increasingly into view, a reality that is coloring the human horizon in a distinctly ominous way.

From among the multiplicity of examples that could be marshaled to illustrate this societal regression, I wish to mention just one. What is the prime signal that a society has lost faith in the future, that the order of the soul on which a hopeful outlook depends is being overturned? As I have pondered this question, no sharper answer has come to me than this; the failure to comprehensively care for and support the wellbeing of children, the failure to nourish, protect, and provide for the young at every stage of growth. This is a sure sign that a societal disintegration is underway.

Societal regression in the care of children is increasingly structural. Jurisdictions that are, or are trying to become, intensely capital-driven and largely market-dominated have little capacity for the equitable care of children. Almost thirteen million children in the US live in poverty.[11] Poor children, of course, live in poor families, unless they are homeless, which is also a reality. How many more live in households just above the so-called poverty line, and on an insecure and declining income? The result for children of these high stress situations often ranges from abuse to neglect to abandonment.

This is not the place for piling up research findings, but I wish to cite one particularly egregious US policy context. Children in poverty are almost always malnourished. "Malnourished" is a euphemism for chronic starvation. Chronic starvation of the body means developmental impairment of the brain. Cognitive dysfunction, learning disabilities, and disturbed behavior are the direct result of this developmental compromise. The utter falseness of the US government's recent slogan, "no child left behind," is revealed in the defunding and dismantling of significant child nutrition support programs.[12] Kurt Vonnegut cut to the chase when he recently asked; "Can't we at least agree to share the wealth with the babies?" Apparently not; this deliberate neglect would be incomprehensible to persons in traditional and tribal societies. Modern societal regression, in this respect, is simply stunning.

The layers of social disregard that have accumulated in the US political economy are often difficult for Americans to recognize because they seem normal. But they are not normal, not in comparison with most other wealthy nations. Eliot Currie, Professor of Law at the University of California, Irvine, puts the case as follows: "We are the industrial nation with the weakest and least reliable supports for the young: we have no system of family allowances, no universal health care system, no paid parental leave to care for children, no national apprenticeship system to link school with stable and rewarding work...We have increasingly become, as two British observers put it, the land of the 'non-helping hand.'"[13]

The steadily rising rate of suicide among young people seems to me the starkest evidence that the storm progress has overturned the order of the soul.[14] Girl-on-girl violence has grown to the extent that it is now a new field of social research. Children killing children is no longer shocking news. And one final note on this that is too glaring to omit; I have, in this case, no research evidence but simply an irrepressible sense that the disrespect, indignities, abuse, violence, and killing that now flow from the war making policies and behavior of the US government are warping the psyches and trampling the souls of all Americans, and especially the young, in such a way that it is hard to see how the spiral of regression can be arrested and reversed.

Archeological and anthropological literature offers a variety of instances in which environmentally linked societal regression can be clearly seen. The history and fate of human settlement on Easter Island is perhaps the best known[15] but the story of the Ik people in contemporary Uganda is even more instructive.

The removal of this cultural group from its home territory to make way for a national park resulted in societal disintegration so complete that recovery has been impossible. Their loss of environmental security led to the breakdown of social relationships. Rank individualism, with regard to resources for survival, replaced the highly cooperative and sharing behavior of former times. The increasing failure to care for and nurture children emerged as a key element in the disintegration of Ik culture.

Anthropologist, Colin Turnbull, writes: "...the Ik clearly show that society itself is not indispensable for man's survival...he is perfectly capable of associating for purposes of survival without being social...That is how it is with the Ik. They are brought together by self-interest alone...Does that sound so very different from our own society? In our own world the very mainstays of a society based on a truly social sense of mutuality are breaking down."[16]

A little over a decade later Margaret Thatcher, Prime Minister of Britain, speaking as an advocate of neo-conservatism, declared, "there is no such thing as society." In her worldview, and in that of her supporters, the only realities that mattered were individual competing interests and the special groupings that advanced individual interests. Thus has the wind been sown, and thus is a whirlwind of societal regression being reaped.

The Temptation of Fatalism

From the evidence before us it seems highly probable that circumstances of ecological disruption, economic instability, and societal regression are now entering a stage of synergy and have landed us in a condition from which it will not only be difficult to recover, but from which it may be difficult to even see how a recovery could take place. This is a critical and fateful difference, a real spiritual danger. It is the difference between retaining the energy of faith and the mind of hope in difficult circumstances, and finding faith drained away and hope closed down when no image of a positive future can be held in focus. I do not think we have yet reached that point, but it is not hard to imagine the conditions that could trigger this kind of general psychic collapse and consequent societal regression.

Trying to understand the relationship between economics, ecology, and societal regression runs the risk of opening the door to fatalism. Trying to understand the way the ecological crisis of human adaptation is related to the Western worldview runs the risk of cultural despair. Trying to understand the way the elevation of personal moral will into a metaphysical absolute has sanctioned patriarchy, domination, and war runs the risk of throwing faith into a black hole.

Having raised these issues and run these risks, I am under some obligation to offer further navigation. I have struggled with the temptation of fatalism. I have noticed I am not alone in this struggle. I have noticed that among many people with similar concerns a kind of background struggle haunts our deliberations – a struggle between fatalism and faith.

It is not surprising that we are tempted by fatalism. The tension of the unresolvable conflict between the industrial-consumer economy and the integrity of Earth's ecosystems is very difficult to live with. The stress of societal regression and, now, of endless war, greatly compounds the problem of faith, and the maintenance of a hopeful outlook for the future.

Fatalism about the human future offers relief from this tension and stress. We literally cannot live without some kind of faith, some kind of story that makes sense of things. Fatalism provides a believable story for bad times, and it is better to have a story with a bad outcome that is believable than a story that is unbelievable or no story at all. Fatalism is a kind of faith substitute. There are, however, at least three important observations about fatalism that can be offered as an inoculation against this temptation.

First, fatalism about the conflict between economics and ecology is based on the idea that economic behaviour functions according to a universal "natural law" of self-interest governed by hardwired human behavior, and that nothing, not even the prospect of catastrophe, can alter this scenario. Within the scope of human history, the claim of capital-driven, free market economics to be a phenomenon of "natural law" is demonstrably false. Historically, the dynamic it describes is a cultural anomaly. The evidence from cultural history reveals this so-called "natural law" to be an astutely composed arrangement of property, financial, and commercial relationships that were assembled to advance wealth accumulation at the beginning of the industrial era.[17] Suffice it to say, that a great many cultures throughout history have developed economies that do not operate according to this so-called "natural law."

Relationships that were once composed for the purpose of maximizing wealth accumulation for a select group of power brokers, can be recomposed. There is no insurmountable barrier, either politically or socially, to the creation of an economy that fosters equitable access to the means of life for all people, provides for the mutually beneficial care of the common good, and establishes an ecologically coherent human-Earth relationship. Ecologically-oriented economists and community-based economic development practitioners are working in precisely this way.[18] The eco-justice movement now brings these two streams into a single flow of redesign and readaptation. The capital-driven, wealth-accumulating economy may not yield gracefully, but a strong current of ecological sanity is beginning to reshape the human-Earth relationship. Fatalism about the "iron law" of economics is undercut every time a new cooperative enterprise is launched.

Secondly, fatalism as an attempt to gain a sense of certainty about what is happening is a flawed resolution, even on its own terms. For example, if a society adopts a fatalistic worldview, and the deterioration of the human-Earth relationship and societal relationships continue as expected, it can never know for sure if this reading of the human situation was a true assessment or not. A different reading, prompting different policies and different actions may well have produced a different outcome.

This uncertainty is an important realization. Calling attention to the fact that fatalism fails the test of certainty diminishes the power of its temptation. Once we realize that human cultural adaptation to the various ecosystems of Earth is always an open, emergent process, the book on future options cannot be closed. A live current of doubt will forever disturb the comfort of the fatalistic faith and cleave the focus of its certainty. Always, at the deep core of consciousness, fatalism's attempt at certainty is compromised as we realize the human situation does not have to be this way. Things could be different. They have been different in the past, and they can be made different in the future. It's always a matter of power relationships and control of resources.

Thirdly, fatalism is a closed loop mindset, a positive feedback system. (In this case, the term "positive" means feedback that Increases the tendency to fatalism, that is, it just makes things worse.) There is simply no point in taking a fatalistic view of the human-Earth relationship or of social relationships. Taking such a view sets up a self-fulfilling dynamic that gives license to the continuation of an inequitable and ecosystem damaging way of life.

A view that holds out for positive social relationships and the growth of a mutually enhancing human-Earth relationship sets up the scenario for a good outcome. Given this inescapable self-fulfilling dynamic, why would anyone of good will choose fatalism? I am not suggesting a naive cheerfulness or a Pollyanna outlook. I am suggesting, however, that fatalism is a mug's game and that only an intransigent allegiance to human betterment within the regenerative powers of the biosphere provides a story for the future that satisfies the mind of faith. If the worst befalls us, if ecological collapse and societal regression run amuck, it will be spiritually better to go down still working for a positive outcome than to be able to say, "I told you so."

Reciprocity, Communion, and the Order of the Soul

What if the Canaanites had won the religious struggle with the Israelites, or, at least, had been able to work out a reasonable coexistence? What if the sacred powers and processes of the land had continued to be recognized as metaphysically and spiritually significant, and had continued to play a role in shaping the cultural experience of Mediterranean and, eventually, all European peoples? What if the animistic worldview – the oldest of human spiritual traditions – had been incorporated into the cultural mix that became Western Civilization? How might the history of the world have been different? Of course, we do not know, but the question is instructive.

It is not unreasonable to imagine that people and planet might have been better served in the long run by a metaphysical understanding that honored the powers and processes of Earth. It is true, the animistic worldview has often carried a load of superstition that has sometimes had unfortunate behavioural results. But the same thing can quite fairly be said of the monotheistic worldview that did win out and become the way of the West. Superstition is clearly a problematic human characteristic whether the context is animistic or monotheistic.

A part of our problem is that worldviews are mostly invisible. The observation that our history has been shaped by the metaphysical domination of personal will is likely to be met with the question: "What other kind of history is there?" This is a fair question. It is not easy to step out from under a well-ingrained worldview. An answer to this question can be gleaned, however, by noticing a significant omission in the list of problematic cultural phenomenon previously mentioned. Science is not included because it does not quite fit the mold; in fact, it breaks the mold. Science grows from curiosity about design and diversity. Although scientific thinking started out as a branch of theology, the more it grew, the less inclined its proponents were to see the world as a projection of personal will. While it is unfortunately true that much scientific work has often been swept up in struggles driven by the will to domination, the part of science we call "natural history" has not generally been susceptible to this appropriation.

Natural history not only resisted the attempt of nineteenth and twentieth century social Darwinists to co-opt it for the "natural right" of domination, but, together with its theoretical offspring, ecology, established an alternative worldview. The work of natural historians and ecologists (both theoretical and historical) has created a story of Earth and its life communities distinctly different from previous histories.

This story provides a useful answer to the question: "What other kind of history is there?" The history of Earth-process and the ever-renewing fecundity of the biosphere is a different kind of history. It is the history of the context within which all human settlement and adaptation takes place and is worked out.[19, 20, 21] It is the story of the interweaving of many relationships in continuously reciprocal ways. It is a story that includes personal moral will as an attribute of the human, but embeds the human in the ecology of Earth-process.

This is a new kind of history, a new story about the biotic relationships within Earth's ecosystems. It is a story about mutual interdependence and reciprocity. It is a story that has grown from a sense of curiosity and wonder at the embeddedness of life in the evolutionary history of Earth-process. It is a story that includes the volcanism of Earth's interior, the structure of Earth's supporting lithosphere, the surface landforms, the soil and water environments, the atmospheric envelope encircling the Earth, and the amazing diversity of life that flourishes within this thin planetary membrane. This is the context from which the human story emerges, and the boundaries, limitations, and thresholds within which human adaptation is worked out. Culture is a human variable that emerges and plays out within the ecosystems of Earth-process. This new story of Earth-process, as it is now being composed from indigenous knowledge, natural history, and Earth system science, opens the door to a reconfiguration of culture that puts ecological guidance at the centre of its orientation.

The hallmark of this reconfiguration of culture, in addition to wonder and curiosity, is *respect* – a respect that often includes awe and sometimes, quite reasonably, an element of fear. This may be thought of as the return of a higher animism.[22] Animism was never actually defeated, even in the West's most theologically sophisticated cultures. It simply went underground and now returns with the realization that Earth's environment as a whole, and in all its particulars, constitutes a living entity, or, as we like to say, a living system. With the Earth sciences and anthropology as allies, this whole-system approach raises a banner for respect and reciprocity as it aims for an ecologically coherent and mutually beneficial human-Earth relationship.

This is not, strictly speaking, a new story. For a very long time the so-called, non-historic, Earth-centered cultures of the world have been telling metaphysical stories about the powers and process of Earth's environment, and about the human-Earth relationship, based on the experience, understanding, and practice of reciprocity. This worldview, once condemned by monotheism as superstition, can now be understood in scientific terms as a reasonable representation of Earth's functional reality and of the human-Earth relationship.[23][24]

We can easily imagine that ancient Earth-based metaphysical traditions began when what might be called a "soulful" quality emerged in human experience. We might picture this as a growing disposition to step back just a bit from the immediate flow of sensations and events into an open space of imaginative contemplation. As this experience developed, a sense of the human as an interwoven presence among the powers and processes that permeate the world must have further enhanced the sense soulfulness. Thus, the human-Earth relationship in its most fully rounded development carries the sense of an interior reality, the sense of a characteristic spirit and particular power within all the forms that make up Creation.

This primal experience of Earth's landscapes and life forms underlies the development of human spiritual awareness and the growth of that interior sensibility we call the soul. As Thomas Berry repeatedly points out, we have the kind of spiritual sensibility we have because we have emerged from and have been shaped by the kind of planet on which we have developed. To underline this observation, Tom Berry was fond of asking (with a twinkle in his eye) what kind of spiritual sensibility would humans have if our species had developed in a moon like environment?

Consider the forestlands and open plains, the deep valleys and high mountains, the flow of rivers and the beauty of lakes, the vast oceans, the fluorescence of plant life and all manner of animals; consider fire, atmospheric storms, earthquakes and volcanoes; reflect on the great sun-filled cloud-piled skies of day, and the star-filled beauty of night; consider the moon – that ever-changing body of soft light, companion of longings and dreams. All this, along with the evolution of domestic, place-based, social relationship and a widening sense of solidarity, has drawn out human consciousness into the particular configurations it has taken.

From the beginning, all these aspects and processes of Earth have been the formative context of neurological, cognitive, and emotional growth of the human. The perceptual and cognitive skills and the emotional repertoire we have as humans has been shaped and conditioned – literally created – by this very particular kind of world. This world, with all its hazards and unaccountable eccentricities, yet displays a consistent pattern of renewal we recognize for its integrity, and a coherent pattern of relationships we recognize as reciprocal. Out of this history of development we have come into a sense of the order of the soul that is aligned with the integrity and reciprocity of Earth's whole commonwealth of life. This is not surprising. We are citizens of this commonwealth. The order of the soul has a home. This home is now in urgent need of respect and much better care.

Worldviews in Transition

The transition in which, hopefully, we are engaged, involves stepping back from the metaphysical supremacy of personal moral will, and its ideologies of hierarchy, domination, and submission that have brought the human-Earth relationship to its present state of incoherence, and skewed societal relationships into highly damaging forms of competition, greed, and inequity. The endless theological and ideological struggle to interpret and rearrange the guidance function of this heritage has lost its credibility.

The transition in prospect is to the widely shared growth of an ecological worldview in which a sense of emergence, presence, interdependence, communion, reciprocity, cooperation, and continuous learning inform and guide both the human-Earth relationship and human-to-human relationships. My guess is religious traditions of all stripes will remain credible to the degree that they shift their focus to the ecological imperative of the human-Earth relationship and the eco-justice imperative of human solidarity and human betterment. This can be thought of as a shift to the ethic of "right relationship."

Understanding this transition can be difficult and even threatening for religious orthodoxy, and a closer look may be helpful. If metaphysical understanding is now moving beyond the supremacy of personal moral will and into a sense of whole Earth reciprocity, does this mean, in plain language, that Nature replaces God as the focus of spiritual experience? For some folks this may be the case, but it is not the conclusion to which this narrative necessarily leads.

The idea of Nature is a cultural story that human experience has composed to makes sense of the Earth environment in the same way the story of Yahweh was composed by the Israelites to make sense of their tribal history. Seeing Nature as a God substitute runs into the same difficulty that has befallen the story of Yahweh. Nature is a concept that has arisen within our cultural history. It served as an integrating story for some time, but now, in its "orthodox" rendering, no longer covers the way we experience and understand the powers and processes of Earth. The story of Nature is not adequate to the reality of Earth. Nature is an abstraction, which, as we know, is readily manipulated by ideology and advertising. What we are actually dealing with in our quest for ecological guidance and in our work for ecologically coherent adaptation is the functional reality of Earth-process and the human-Earth relationship.

I think it fair to conclude there is no God substitute. The Hebrew god, Yahweh, was born into Western cultural development in a particular and unique way.[25] The story of Yahweh (or Allah) is a reality of the history of Western cultural and religious life, a matter of heritage. There can be no substitute for cultural heritage. It is what it is for each of us, and we all deal with it in one way or another until we reach an accommodation that is coherent with the unfolding awareness to which we have come.[26]

However, the experience of the ineffable and the numinous remain. This kind of experience rounds out and broadens the awareness of relationship. With open-minded, soulful attention, this awareness becomes a fully rounded sense of presence. A sense of presence is at the heart of what engages us with the life of the world in all its particularities, and with the human-Earth relationship in general. I think what we really need to know is not the metaphysical answer to the mystery of Creation, but how to reformulate the human-Earth relationship in ways that keeps faith with the literal ground of our existence – the biotic integrity of Earth.

Our human situation at the beginning of the third Christian millennium requires not just an expansion of generic environmental awareness, but a fully rounded ecological consciousness that brings the sense and practice of cooperative reciprocity into every strand and loop of behaviour and enterprise. With human solidarity as our compass setting, and a close reading of Earth-process as our guide, human settlements can achieve a certain harmony within the integrity of Earth's biotic community. We have clear models, both past and present, on which to build.[27, 28, 29, 30]

The Experience of the Divine and the Ecological Worldview

Our religious life, our spiritual survival, and the fate of the human, now hang on our engagement with this encompassing task, the task Thomas Berry calls "the great work."[31] We are, perhaps, in a situation that both mirrors and reverses the story of the ancient Israelites. We are looking, as it were, into the land of Canaan, the landscape of Earth's biotic integrity. The prospect, however, is not one of invasion and domination, but of a mutually enhancing human-Earth relationship. The sense of guidance that is growing around this vision is not unlike that of a new revelation, perhaps even a new sense of the Divine. This new revelation and its sense of guidance are emerging in a down-to-Earth way that can enable us to become ecologically readapted citizens within the integrity of the whole commonwealth of life.

We may not have an adequate name for this new sense of the Divine, and that's probably a good thing. A little caution is in order after several millennia of such certainty, and the unfortunate results of this mindset. There is a real danger that if the ecological worldview is superficially grafted onto the mindset of certainty, cultural and political life could veer, as Murray Bookchin has eloquently and repeatedly warned, into a kind of "ecological fascism."[32] Rather than clamping onto a new sense of metaphysical certainty, authentic ecological guidance fosters a fully rounded mindfulness of Earth-process, a new sense of presence and beauty, a response of respect, cooperative reciprocity, reverence for life, and an ethic of right relationship.

Whether this new sense of the Divine, and its collective behavior, will emerge in the current and rising generation is a troubling question. On the face of it, the prospects do not seem hopeful. It seems likely a great fling of human aggrandizement, and a great behavioural sink of societal regression are yet to be played out. But, at least, we are now at a point in the human situation where the options are clear. Either the processes of cultural and economic life become infused with the ethos of cooperative reciprocity and ecological coherence,[33] or the trajectory of unlimited economic growth, inequitable capital accumulation, intense competition, wasteful consumption, and resource wars will continue to grind Earth's ecosystems and social systems into breakdown and collapse.

There can be no doubt, however, that in the long run the powers and processes of Earth will prevail. At what cost to our society depends on the adaptive stance we take. If we can shift our collective focus to the human-Earth relationship, and build the discipline of cooperative reciprocity into every level of this relationship, we will have a better chance of redeeming our economy from its renegade status, and, perhaps, give our society the prospect of a much longer and more equitable run than is currently in view.[34, 35]

At some point down the road, we may imagine the angel of history will find a resting place under a great tree by a clear flowing stream. The storm of progress will be a painful memory now recounted now in sad songs. Nearby, children will gather armfuls of flowers from the woodland meadows and the domestic gardens on their way to the pavilion where citizens from the surrounding region will soon gather to honour the Order of the Soul in the Great Commonwealth of Life.

As we gain skill in making this great transition, we may be pleasantly surprised to find ecological guidance and the presence of the Divine, pivoting into a single focus. In the simplicity and clarity of this revelation we may pause and wonder why it has taken us so long to find our bearings.

First Light & Last Things:
Presence, Beauty, Survival

Based on a presentation made at Sierra Friends Center, Nevada City, CA, September 30, 2006

Here I recaptured the former beauty, a young sky...The
memory of that sky had never left me. This was what in
the end had kept me from despairing...There the world
began over again everyday in an ever new light. O light!
This is the cry of all the characters of ancient drama
brought face to face with their fate. This last resort was
ours, too, and I knew it now. In the middle of the winter
I at last discovered that there was in me an invincible
summer.

Albert Camus[1]

The first effect of cloud study is a sense of presence in
storm process. Weather does not happen. It is the visible
manifestation of the Spirit moving itself in the void...
Hardly anybody takes account of the fact that John Muir,
who knows more of mountain storms than any other, is
a devout man.

Mary Austin[2]

To the Range of Light and the Bristlecone Pine

When John Muir first ventured into the high country of the Sierra Nevada, he was especially struck by mountain light. John Muir was a person of clairvoyant openness to the experience of landscape, and the extraordinary quality of light in the high Sierra ushered him into a profound experience of presence. He called these mountains "the range of light" – a name that has entered the language of landscape and now has deep resonance for all those touched by the experience of this California high country.[3]

Two months ago, on repeated mornings, I sat on a second story deck overlooking the town of Bishop, California in Owens Valley watching the first light reach the high peaks and snowfields of the central Sierra Nevada range. The presence that accompanied those times of mountain light has stayed with me. In one sense it is as clear as the light itself, but in another sense it is teeming with a caravan of associations. This caravan starts with John Muir and then moves to Mary Austin, Kenneth Rexroth, and Gary Snyder – all poets of mountain light. In addition, the haunting figure of Ishi joins this caravan. Ishi, the last of his tribe, lived on the western slope of the Sierra Nevada – a story to which I will return.

We had come to Bishop to visit the Bristlecone Pine, to make a pilgrimage into the presence of the oldest living creatures on Earth. But another focus of this pilgrimage was the presence of Julia, our twelve-year old granddaughter. This weeklong adventure was a gift to her at a time of transition; a time when the holistic learning of childhood is still prominent, but the details and complex significance of all the relationships that make up the world are rapidly coming into view.

Ellen and I were eager to revisit the Sierra Nevada region and we recruited my brother, Harlan, into our traveling party. From his many years as a highly observant cross-country truck driver, and an avid reader of history, he was well versed in the geography and geology of the American landscape. With his store of geographic and historical knowledge, he was an ideal traveling companion for us all, but especially for Julia.

Visiting the Bristlecone Pine was the primary focus of our trip and accomplishing this lifted us into an elevated state of body and soul. The Bristlecone Pine Forest occurs above 10,000 feet on the cresting plateaus and upper slopes of the White Mountains that frame the eastern side of Owens Valley across from the Sierra Nevada. From these heights, the view of the Sierra range to the west is spectacular. To the east, we gazed into the desert land of "basin and range" country. To the south, beyond the flow of still more shimmering ridges and hidden canyons, lay Death Valley. While my body had a little trouble at this elevation, I am happy to report that my soul experienced no hesitation. Soaring is the soul's natural response to presence, and in the presence of the Bristlecone Pines soaring was the order of the day.

The sun had set behind the Sierra when, after our first day with the Bristlecone Pines, we turned from the mountain road onto the valley highway and headed north toward Bishop. The White Mountains were shading into a blue-gray twilight. I pointed out that the Patriarch Grove, where we had spent most of the day, lay on the far side of the two most prominent peaks coming into view – Sheep Mountain and Campito Mountain. Julia looked up at the mountains and said, "Really? We were up there? All the way up there?" I said, "Yes, that's where we were." There was a long pause, and then she said in a hushed voice; "It makes me feel so small."

I heard this expression, considered the experience from which it arose, and tucked it away in special memory.

The next morning on our breakfast deck we laid out the maps, of which we had collected a good variety. To the south, the Sierra led on to Mount Whitney, the highest point in the range. Late in the day, from this direction, we would see dark curtains of rain sweep down the steep eastern face of the mountains and walk in airy columns up the edge of the valley. To the north, the upland terrain led to Tioga Pass and the road to Yosemite country – the spiritual lodestone of John Muir's mountain experience.

We discovered that a day trip from Bishop over Tioga Pass, through the Tuolumne high country, and on to Yosemite Valley could easily be accomplished, including a visit to the Tuolumne Sequoia Grove. Our pilgrimage would now encompass visiting the largest creatures on Earth, as well as the oldest. Although I had seen these same trees fifty-seven years before – when I, too, was twelve years old – I was again struck into a kind of speechless awe as we entered the grove and came face to face with the first of these immense and towering trees.

This day trip included a stop at Tuolumne Meadows, for which Julia had a secret plan. She took off her flip-flops and began a light footed run across the gently sloping meadow toward the Tuolumne River that, at this point in its journey, was a meandering stream of liquid light matching the air around us. Halfway across the meadow she stopped and called back; "Grandma, bring me my flip-flops." What looked to the eye like a soft meadow of grasses and low flowering plants had a ground surface of gravelly granite worn down by weathering from the ancient mountaintops around us. We caught up with her, finished a lovely walk to the small river, and spent an hour out of time exploring its gravel bars looking for special stones.

She told us that when we had earlier been studying the map, and heard me speak enthusiastically about stopping on our journey at Tuolumne Meadows, her imagination went to the "Sound of Music," and the image of Julie Andrews dancing out over the great meadow, arms outstretched, flinging her song into the luminous air of the Austrian Alps. It was the word "meadow" that prompted her plan, and, although the gravelly soil of the Tuolumne was a surprise for her tender feet, she had reenacted this famous scene with aplomb. The image of our granddaughter dancing over the green and flowered meadow now plays in my memory like the vivid scenes of my own childhood.

We had planned our trip around a visit to the Bristlecone Pine and to now have the Sequoia added to our experience gave our pilgrimage an even more fully rounded sense of presence. From the open mountaintop light of the Bristlecone terrain to the deep forest light filtering through the Sequoia grove, the reality of a multi-layered presence was unmistakable.

There is a particular presence in the form of each tree; there is a wider presence in the larger forest environment, all of which arise for us from the plenitude of Earth. And this is just a consideration of trees and forests. Think of what needs to be added with regard to a still larger experience of presence – the whole world of animals. And indeed, animal encounters graced our experience of Owens Valley and its mountain regions. Julia kept a logbook of the trip that included wildlife sightings. Of particular note was a coyote that passed so close to us we could see the distinctive look of its face. And then there were the twin fawns that emerged from under cover on the slope of Tioga Pass only a few yards below our roadside lookout point. Unmistakable presence, unaccountable beauty, unfathomable light!

Julia was sitting with Harlan on the return flight to Birmingham, Alabama. As the plane descended toward the city, she said to him, "The rolling green hills of Birmingham look so friendly. It's as if they're welcoming me home." My heart leaped when he later told me this; for now it seemed to me that not only had the mountain lands of California provided a new sense of landscape, but a new sense of home had also come into place. New eyes were seeing the green hills of home with new affection. What more could I have hoped for from this trip? No matter how much we may travel, it is love for our home place that is needed to preserve the beauty and health of the living Earth.

Old Growth Air

As you might have guessed by now, I have a passion for trees and forestland. When it came time for Ellen and I to retire from the farming business, and pass our farm on to another family, we retained a seventy-acre tract of forestland. My attachment to trees and forests still has real grounding. I have always felt that trees were elders providing a kind of continuous silent teaching and good companionship. I have a place where I can go, sit under two hundred-year-old hemlocks and ponder our responsibility to the Saint John River watershed. In my study of trees and the literature of forests, I have found some especially interesting information that documents the human-Earth relationship in amazing and significant ways. Here is one example.

In June of 2005 I attended the Annual Meeting of Friends Association for Higher Education at Haverford College. If you have been to Haverford College, you probably know that the campus is something of an arboretum with an abundance of lovely old trees. During a break between the Annual Meeting sessions, I retired to the base of an ancient oak and began reading a new book I had brought with me – *Teaching the Trees: Lessons from the Forest*⁴ by Joan Maloof. The first chapter, "Old Growth Air," tells the story of the author's visit to the last remnant of old growth forest on Maryland's Eastern Shore. There are times in reading when a particular piece of information or stroke of imagination stops me in my tracks and I have to close the book and follow my thoughts. This was one of those times. A story within the author's story sent me into an extended reverie; the story goes like this.

In traditional Japanese culture there is a practice called "shinrin-yoku," that translates into English as "wood-air bathing." The practice of visiting old growth woodlands to "bathe" in forest air, has long been known in Japan to produce good health effects. Now we might think of this in terms of general spiritual uplift or psychic rejuvenation, but it turns out that something of a more holistic nature is occurring. For example, Japanese researchers have discovered that when persons who are diabetic go wood-air bathing, their blood sugar drops to a better level of balance.

These findings are stimulating further research. Whole research symposia are now being held in Japan on the health benefits of wood-air bathing. This is what they have found; trees continuously exhale a range of volatile chemical compounds and forest air is, in this respect, a very different environment than non-forest air. The human body, as we know, is highly receptive and highly reactive to organic chemical compounds. So when we go for a walk in the woods and say, "Ah, that was refreshing," we are likely responding to the tangible effect of being molecularly embedded in the chemical environment of the forest.

Researchers in the Sierra Nevada have recently found one hundred and twenty naturally occurring chemical compounds in mountain forest air, only seventy of which had been previously identified. Isn't it interesting to think of the great sea of relationships in which we are embedded, to which we are biochemically adapted, and about which we often have an intuitive sense of response? Wood-air bathing – a stroll among the trees – is one such response. This strikes me as exemplary of the human-Earth relationship at its best.

Think of what it would mean for the design of human settlements, social life in general, and economic adaptation in particular if so simple a practice as wood-air bathing became a high level priority. From the standpoint of the present political economy, and a way of life keyed almost entirely to resource exploitation and the accumulation of wealth, such a priority seems quaintly bizarre. I suggest, however, that the destruction of woodlands and forests that has historically rampaged across this continent, and is still going on, is far more bizarre. I can imagine a time, an economy, and a way of life in which this rampage ceases, the restoration of wooded landscapes begins, and wood-air bathing becomes a wide spread practice of health maintenance. For example, good urban design and town planning of the future would make sure that significant groves of trees were within easy walking distance of all residents.

Attunement & Guidance

Practices of attunement are central to guidance. We cannot do without some form of this process. Ceremonies of all sorts offer attunement and provide guidance. For example, in my tradition, the silent Quaker Meeting is a practice of attunement that often results in guidance. For traditional Wabanaki people, the first light ceremony is focused on attunement and guidance. Informal and spontaneous ceremonies are often among the most powerful experiences of attunement; here is an example.

Many years ago I spent several periods of time in Mombasa, Kenya's coastal city. On my first arrival, the municipal architect, a long time city resident, told me about an informal ceremony the Indian community in Mombasa observed each month in the park on the bluff overlooking the Indian Ocean. He knew my work included cultural studies and thought the event would interest me.

I paid attention to his information, and sure enough on the appointed evening, a little before dusk, a leisurely flow of people began moving along the city streets toward the bluff. Eventually, a large but unusually quiet group of city residents gathered under the trees in the park, all facing eastward toward the ocean. Some folks had brought folding chairs, some had blankets for sitting on the ground. Children collected in little groups. Some folks had food baskets and were sharing an evening meal. Quiet conversations were barely audible. Time that seemed out of time gathered the scene before me. Sunset light faded in the west and the darker hue of twilight rolled in abruptly as happens in the equatorial zone. Suddenly, an expression of delight, a kind of drawing in of the breath rose softly from the whole assembly – the leading edge of the full moon had become visible on the horizon of the Indian Ocean!

We all remained quietly gazing as the luminous orb steadily gained height and spread its moon-path over the sea. Slowly, as the night both darkened from the sunset and brightened from the moonrise, the participants in this informal ceremony began to pick up their chairs, blankets, and food baskets and make their way back down the hill to their homes in the city. Although there were hundreds people departing the park, the sound I remember is the rustle of flowing garments and the soft flop of thong clad feet. I had often viewed the rise of the full moon in good company, but never before had I felt communal attunement to cosmic beauty in the way that was present in this gathering.

All cultures have practices of attunement. Frequently they are formally constructed and conducted as religious practice. What interests me, however, and what strikes me as far more significant, are the informal practices of culture that create a kind of unconscious attunement, the kind of attunement that informs the routine practices of everyday life, attunement we don't often think about because that's just the way life is. Imagine growing up in a community that has a spontaneous, informal ceremony of attunement each month around the cosmic beauty of the moonrise.

Practices of attunement generate a sense of guidance. All cultures have them, but there are dramatic differences between and within cultures on what kind of attunement is fostered and what kind of guidance is generated. For example, some practices of attunement enhance the human-Earth relationship and others do not. If we do not think about this, and do not consciously choose practices of attunement that result in good guidance, we will likely fall into practices of attunement that, for some reason, seem alluring but then lead to whatever guidance is implicit.

Think, for example, about the aura of attunement created by devoted attention to big time sports events. Thousands, even millions of folks channeled into the spirit of winner take all competition, aggression, and often violence. Think about the enculturation of young folks, for example, into NASCAR racing. Consider the attunement that accompanies such events with regard to the culture of automobiles and the ethos of power, aggrandizement, competition, and domination, not to mention the excitement of great crashes and the ritual acceptance of an occasional sacrificial death. Think about the attunement surrounding the culture of video games. Think, too, about advertising in general, and about what is now called "branding" – the imprinting of commercial logos into the psyche in a way that guides personal shopping behaviour. By way of shining a light on this perverse attunement, ask the question: if the persuasive voice of advertising fell silent, what would people want?[5]

A key factor for our species is revealed in these considerations. Both individually and collectively the human condition is one of great plasticity. The human is a highly malleable species. We have great latitudes of adaptational response. This is both our genius and our curse. This is the context of both our goodness and our evil. It matters a great deal, therefore, with respect to guidance, how we allow ourselves to be influenced, how we direct our attunement.

The attunement-guidance continuum is a fundamental and pervasive process that shapes and directs human malleability. Within a certain range of options we can quite deliberately choose our attunements. Attunement to the beauty of Earth in all its various forms and processes is a program, as it were, of the human condition. We are highly malleable, but we are not a blank slate. We have come into the world bearing the imprint of our origin. We come from the Earth with Earth impressed grooves of attunement ready for recording, and with the potential for making a harmonious contribution to the music of life.

The Light of Presence and Presence of Light

Religious and philosophical language often have well-developed metaphors for expressing the experience of light. Light is a central motif in talking about presence, and about the presence behind presence. This is not as obscure as it may seem, nor is it necessarily mystical. It may be mystical, but that is something that happens to some people. Presence is actually the plainest thing in the world if we are truly awake, if we understand, as Thomas Berry never tires of pointing out, that Earth is a communion of subjects, not a collection of objects.

When coyote passes so close we can see the expression on her face, we are in a situation of presence. When the tall walking rain comes over the mountains and down into the valley it is a situation of presence. When I meet Paul Stone, a Paiute artist, in his Bishop studio, and he tells me he really doesn't know how he makes the images that inform his work, and then adds, "It's the gift of the Creator," I am in a situation of presence multiplied.

All around his workshop are paintings, drawings, and carvings emblematic of his culture and its profound attunement to the creatures and landforms of the Owens Valley region. Every item, every piece of creative work is a real presence. In conversation, the artist is ever concerned that we recognize the wellspring, that we meet the source, that we honour the presence behind presence. He sees his work and the world around him from which it comes in a certain light – the light of presence and the presence of light.

In considering the experience of light, it is helpful to start with the immediate reality of ordinary daylight, the reality of the relationship between our eyes, the sun, and the world around us. From the beginning of human experience, this Earth, with all its various landforms and life communities, has been the context in which consciousness, reflective thought, and spiritual sensibility have developed. The reality of ordinary sunlight in which this whole story unfolds, is clearly our underlying and overarching context, the context from which all our experiences and expressions of light arise.

There is a tendency in some forms of spiritual thought to see the human as a kind of container into which an extraordinary form of consciousness has been poured by a divine source from somewhere beyond the world. While this view has a certain appeal as a way of explaining human uniqueness, it has only speculation to support it, and its effect is often to produce a sense of aggrandizement, alienation, and carelessness about the world around us. It is true, in the scheme of things, human consciousness seems quite extraordinary, but that may be only because we have such a limited understanding of whales wolves, and honeybees – for example.

The fact that human cultures have, from time to time, created ways of life that are spectacularly at odds with Earth's ecological integrity, is not good evidence that our intelligence is a superior endowment from a higher realm. All the evidence places human emergence within Earth-process. Earth-process has been forever bathed in and nourished by the cosmic reality of sunlight. Sunlight is the catalyst of consciousness. Consciousness is the signature of presence.

We awaken in the presence of the world's plentitude. The presence of light and the light of presence shines across the entire range of our experience from the first hints of dawn, through the weave of all our relationships, to the final clarity of the soul at rest in the sunset. The soul that is centered in the plentitude of Earth's relationships has the reality of presence and the guidance of beauty close at hand.

First Light Guidance: Before the Metaphor

So much has been written in the literature of spiritual consciousness about the place of light and the experience of presence that I do not imagine saying anything here that adds to the richness of this tradition. What has come to me, however, is a kind of sidebar that makes, if I may say so, an illuminating connection.

In the part of the continent where I am at home, traditional Wabanaki people, have a ceremony celebrating the coming of the dawn – the first light ceremony. Although other First Nation peoples also practice this ceremony, it seems to have special significance for the Wabanaki. Perhaps the first light ceremony has a special potency for the Wabanaki people because Mount Katahdin is a sacred site, and its high peak is the first spot, each morning, touched by the sun in this region.

A few years after becoming acquainted with the first light ceremony, I was engaged in a study of seasonal affective disorder (SAD syndrome), otherwise known as winter depression. In the course of reviewing the research on the relationship of light exposure to the onset and treatment of winter depression, I encountered an interesting fact; research findings show that exposure to dawn and early morning light has a uniquely characteristic effect with regard to alleviating seasonal depression.[6,7,8] Compared to light later in the day, early morning light produces the beneficial effect needed in a shorter time at lower intensity. Apparently light exposure in the early morning hours triggers a higher level of bioactive response.

Why this should be the case is unknown. But we do know that every bodily function, including those that are responsible for emotional and mental states, are directed and regulated by chemical signals produced in the part of the brain called the hypothalamus. The hypothalamus functions in response to the flow of light coming through the eyes. It is literally the case that every cell in the body is directly affected in its function by the ebb and flow of light. As organisms we have emerged within the diurnal rhythms of day and night and our entire state of being, including the mental and emotional states that cradle our spiritual life, are keyed to this reality.

Light, as defined by its utilization in the body, is a nutrient; it is an essential component of biotic functioning. In this context, to say that light is also spiritually nourishing is not just a metaphorical statement. It is a precise description about the unity of body, mind, and spirit. The intuitive sense of the importance of light that has been carried within human development and spiritual experience, probably since the beginning of conscious reflection, has, since the 1970s, been given a map of the pathways through which this unity is created.[9] The scientific information on this relationship does not replace its intuitive grounding, nor reduce spirituality to biochemistry. The effect is quite the reverse; biochemistry now folds into the overall holistic relationship. Light is, indeed, the Circle of Creation in which we abide, along with the whole commonwealth of life.*

---

*A recent book by Daniel Chamovitz, the director of the Manna Center for Plant Biosciences at Tel Aviv University, provides further information about the central role of light in biological functioning, and on the surprising way in which plants and animals are linked in their relationship to light. He writes: "My interest in the parallels between plant and human senses got its start when I was a young postdoctoral fellow at Yale University in the 1990s. I was interested in studying a biological process specific to plants and not connected to human biology. Hence I was drawn to the question of how plants use light to regulate their development. In my research I discovered a unique group of genes necessary for a plant to determine if it's in the light or in the dark. Much to my surprise and against my plans, I later discovered that this same group of genes is also part of the human DNA. This led to the obvious question as to what these seemingly "plant-specific" genes do in people. Many years later and after much research we now know that these genes not only are conserved between plants and animals but also regulate responses to light in both!" (*What A Plant Knows: A Field Guide to the Senses.* 2012. Scientific American/Farrar, Straus and Giroux.) This book makes clear that the expression, "the kinship of all life," is not a metaphor.

The first light ceremony stands as a remarkable practice for human wellbeing. Imagine all those generations of Wabanaki people, as well as others, who, around the fire circle, have offered their prayers of gratitude to Creation, and then faced into the dawning of a new day. I suspect the recent scientific information about the benefits of such practice would be met with a tolerant smile, and perhaps the teasing comment; "Sure took you guys a long time to figure out how the Creator works." Nor should it come as a surprise that light, the central metaphor of our spiritual life, is the reality that truly unifies body, mind, and spirit.

The Intimation of Last Things

Turning now to the second area of this exploration – the horizon of last things – I want to address the sense of foreboding I hear increasingly expressed, and that I share with those who are carefully considering the likely prospects of the human future.

First light and last things; where are we on the spectrum? Are we on the dawning horizon of a shift in the human-Earth relationship toward ecological sanity, or is our high energy, high-tech adaptation careening madly into a crash of last things? We hear less and less environmental discourse these days that includes the old line about "acting now before it is too late." Climate change changed all that. The now measurable slowing of the Gulf Stream in the North Atlantic, the release of methane from the thawing tundra and deep-sea hydrates, and the implication of these trends continuing, is beginning to sink in.

The burning of fossil fuels is steadily increasing. The worldwide destruction of forestland continues. The people who know about species extinction are ringing all the alarm bells they can, but the capital-driven growth economy continues to bulldoze and "develop" the ecosystems on which bio-diversity depends. Widespread distribution of hormone disrupting chemicals is setting up a biotic meltdown scenario, a holocaust-like effect on biotic integrity.[10] Researchers working in this area of biology are extremely alarmed. I need not extend this litany.

My consideration of these ecological circumstances and their intimation of "last things" comes up sharply against what I think of as spiritual survival as well as physical survival. Our current high-tech adaptation could come apart at the seams at any time, it could snap, it could flip into chaos with the disruption of major life support systems. Living with this kind risk requires thinking about "last things." Not that some semblance of life won't go on after a breakdown of essential systems, but that the ending of a reality to which we have been accustomed entails a sense of "last things." This kind of situation is often played out at a personal level with sudden death, fires, floods, business failure, family breakup, mental illness, dementia, etc, and that is difficult enough. Imagine the difficulty when the scale and scope of overwhelming change affects a whole community, an entire region, or, in the case of climate disruption, large parts of the whole world. Thinking about "last things" on the scale of life support system breakdown is almost beyond imagining. But if we don't think about it, we will be ill prepared to cope. If we do think about it, and run test case scenarios in our imaginations, we will at least be somewhat mentally and spiritually prepared to act strategically in response to breakdowns that may occur.

This kind of thinking is not my natural mental habitat. I am a partisan of the "first light" story because I have no doubt that paying close attention to presence and beauty activates ecological guidance and, thus, our potential for survival. But, at the same time, I see no way of being a responsible person without thinking hard about "last things," thinking about what may be required of us on the other side of any number of momentous or even catastrophic changes.

I have paired the "first light" story with the intimation of "last things" because I want to focus here on what I think of as spiritual survival. The work of physical survival in the midst of catastrophic change is one thing - we generally rise to the occasion as best we can, but the "best we can" has a psychic or spiritual background that can make a crucial difference on whether and how we rise to the occasion. I have a strong sense that paying close attention to spiritual survival will be critical for the whole spectrum of re-adaptation that is likely coming up. In my study of response to "last things," I have found no example more captivating and instructive than the story of Ishi, the last of his tribe.

The Trauma of Last Things and the Strength of Beauty

In the realm of last things and overwhelming change, the story of Ishi has a unique place. Ishi was the last surviving member of the Yahi people whose home place was the ridge and canyon country of the Sierra Nevada foothills below Mount Lassen in California. On August 29, 1911, Ishi walked into the town of Oroville and was given shelter and protection by the sheriff. He was in bad shape. His whole community and all his family had been hunted down and killed by the settlers and gold prospectors invading the region. He had kept hidden and on the move to remain undetected, but without family and community, and with the constant threat of being found and killed, he was unable to secure adequate food and was slowing starving. He was the last of his tribe left alive in the world.

Ishi was passed into the care of anthropologist, Alfred Kroeber, who provided for his recovery and made a residence for him in the California Museum in San Francisco. This is a well-known story, thanks to Theodora Kroeber who published the book, *Ishi in Two Worlds*, in 1961.[11] This work of popular anthropology has become a classic. Less well known, however, is the novel she also wrote about Ishi and the life of his small hidden community in its last years.

On one level this is a story of genocide, a story of the complete and intentional destruction of a distinct people by the settlers and gold prospectors of California. On another level it is the story of Ishi and his adaptation to a new and strange situation after the disaster. The most striking aspect of this story is the fact that, although Ishi saw all the members of his family and community die as the result of the settler's incursions, he had no heart for revenge. He bore no trace of bitterness or hatred. He exhibited a demeanor and conducted his relationships with others in a way that was described by those who knew him, as of the highest humanity. This is hard to explain. How could Ishi possibly come through the most horrific experience of last things imaginable without deep psychic wounding, without damage that would manifest in disabling ways, and without resentment and hatred toward the people who had destroyed his people and his world?

We will never know the full answer to this question, but I have found some hints in Theodora Kroeber's novel, *Ishi, Last of His Tribe*.[12] The author was thoroughly familiar with the Yahi worldview and the cycle of stories that supported and expressed Yahi culture. She weaves these stories into her novel in a way that I find particularly instructive to my question. The novel begins in the years just prior to the disruption and collapse of Ishi's world, a time when the cycle of life still proceeded according to the seasons and still included the ceremonial recounting of Yahi Creation stories.

On the night of first snow, Grandfather tells the Yahi Creation story with Ishi and his girl cousin, Tushi, acting out the role of two main characters. The story starts in the time of gods and heroes when Earth is fished up out of a great ocean by the god Jupka. Jupka, together with the god Kaltsuma, then prepare Earth in all ways needful for the life to come. The time of gods and heroes draws to a close and they begin to transform themselves into all the animals, birds, and fish of Earth. Jupka and Kaltsuma take sticks from the buckeye tree, blow smoke across them and these sticks become the first people. Quoting from Kroeber's novel, the story continues:

Kaltsuma taught these first people to flake arrowheads, to make bows and harpoons, and to build houses. From him they learned to hunt and fish, to make fire, to cook and many things besides. Said Kaltsuma to them day after day, "Do this and this and this as I show you, and teach those who come after you to do the same."

Jupka taught the first people the meaning of the moons and the seasons and what work and prayers and songs and dances belonged to each moon. He also taught them something of the nature of men and women and the rules belonging to the wowi and the watgurwa [the women's house and the men's house]. From Jupka they learned about death and the Land of the Dead, and all matters which had to do with the Yahi Way. Said Jupka, "Listen and remember all I tell and teach you now. In your turn, teach these things to your children and your grandchildren. Then in time to come, the people will always live in warm houses; their baskets will be full of salmon and deer; there will be peace within the village, and between neighbors up and down the streams, with the creatures of the air and water and brush. The people

*will not forget their Gods and Heroes nor their teachings.
In the moons to come it will be as it is now."*

*Jupka's and Kaltsuma's work was now finished; the time
had come for them, too, to transform themselves, leaving
the World to the Yahi people.*

And here is what these Creator gods choose to do:

*"I, Kaltsuma, Maker of Arrows, choose to become a little
rock lizard. My hide will remind the People of flint, gray
flint on top, blue and yellow and white flint underneath.
I will sun where the People sun and they will stroke me
sometimes with a soft blade of grass."*

*"I, Jupka, choose to become a many-colored butterfly. The
women will weave the pattern of my wings into their
finest baskets. And when I flutter over the hillsides in the
time of green clover and the New Year, I will remind the
People that the world is dambusa* [beautiful, gentle] *and
its Way a good Way."*

The extraordinary thing about this narrative is that the chief
gods turn themselves into lowly creatures that are always at hand,
always present. And all the other gods and heroes give themselves
into Creation so Earth will be just the kind of place needed by
the People for a good life. This Creation story is the founding
narrative of Yahi culture. Comparing the Yahi Creation story
with the Biblical Creation story provides a telling insight into the
significance of worldviews.

The significance of the Yahi story as a founding narrative for a
worldview and way of life includes the following elements. 1) The

fundamental powers of Creation do their preparatory work and provide the skills and teachings needed for a good human life. 2) The full responsibility for continuity and maintenance is then given to the People. 3) The primary gods of Creation become forms of common life that continue in immediate and intimate relationship with the human. They each become a real and continuing presence in the world. One reminds the people of the technical means of survival, and the other of Earth's plentitude and great beauty.

Picture for a moment this sense of reality, this blending of the domestic and the cosmic, this way of life attuned, in all its ordinary details, to the overarching cycle of the seasons. Picture, as well, the sense that Earth and all it provides for a good life comes as a gift. Imagine that in stroking a little rock lizard with a soft blade of grass as it rests in the sun, you are enacting a story that has come from the beginning of your People. Imagine gathering acorns in a basket in which the beauty of your world and its way of life is woven into the design. Imagine a world and way of life that continually gives rise to a sense of beauty. Imagine living in a way in which beauty is the dominant perceptual experience. Imagine this sense of beauty as a pervasive presence, as the light in which life moves ever forward through the seasonal round. All this, in one sense, was lost to Ishi in the destruction of his community and culture. But, in another sense, he carried the essential strengths of this worldview with him through wrenching change and readaptation.

When Ishi walked into the town of Oroville, leaving his home place behind, it might reasonably be expected he would have been a man broken in spirit. But such was not the case. From all the descriptions of his subsequent demeanor and behaviour, he clearly remained a centered and fully intact person. Photographs taken at the time he appeared in Oroville show a figure suffering from malnutrition, but with aware and watchful eyes. As he came under the care of Alfred Kroeber, and a home was made for him at the Museum, he amazed those around him with his powers of observation and quick learning. But most of all, it was his profound sense of dignity, his unfailing kindness in relationships, and his cheerful demeanor that was most often remarked on by those who knew him.

How could this be? How could Ishi have suffered the most devastating loss possible for a human being and remain, not only a centered, well balanced, and fully functional person, but a person imbued with the highest and best qualities of humanity? Ishi remained highly reserved in matters of person, and, thus, we cannot really know his inner life in a way that answers this question. But we do know, through the agency of stories, about worldviews, and the way they center and focus strength and meaning. Through the knowledge of Yahi stories and the Yahi worldview that Theodora Kroeber brought to her writing, and through her poetic intuition, we may catch a glimpse, below time and beyond thought, of what it was that sustained Ishi in his humanity and provided guidance through deep crisis and great change.

The glimpse we may catch, and the awareness that may emerge from this contemplation, brings us to a worldview that centers the soul in Earth's beauty and is suffused with the reality of presence.

We may have hard times to come. Who can tell what disruptions, or even severe dislocations may occur? Whatever happens in this regard, the effect should be to re-enforce the centrality of the human-Earth relationship and our focus on ecologically sound adaptation. If we are centered in right relationship, and if we live in communion with the commonwealth of life and the larger arc of Earth's plentitude, we will have the reality of presence and the guidance of beauty to keep us upright and functional in the work we now have to do, and in whatever work is to come.

Indigenous Wisdom
and Ecological Guidance

Frank Waters and the Hopi Way

Based on an essay written for the South Dakota Review (SDR) in 1964, but not published. John R. Milton, founder and editor of SDR, , was kind enough to inform me he was preparing an article of his own on Frank Waters for the journal. He also told me he had circulated my essay to his class on Western literature at the University of South Dakota and it had generated a lively discussion.

In the beginning, we were told that the human beings who walk about on Earth have been provided with all the things necessary for life. We were instructed ... to show great respect for all the beings on this Earth. We are shown that our ... well-being depends on the well-being of the Vegetable Life, that we are close relatives of the four-legged beings. ... We give a greeting and thanksgiving to the many supporters of our own lives — corn, squash, beans, wind, rain, and sun.

...We walk about with great respect, for Earth is a very sacred place.
     The Hau de no sau nee(Six Nations Iroquois)[1]

*We were contented to let things remain as the Great Spirit
made them. They were not; and would change the rivers
and mountains if they did not suit them.*

Chief Joseph of the Nez Perce[2]

When Henry David Thoreau died in 1862, his sister, Sophia,
reported that among his last utterances was the word "Indians."[3]
At first thought, it may seem odd that a man who knew death was
near should be thinking of something so seemingly extraneous.
But that thought reckons without the man. As Thoreau's health
began to fail, his attention turned more and more to the life and
history of the American continent's first inhabitants. He began to
collect material for a book on Aboriginal peoples.

What kind of book Thoreau would have written is difficult to
say, but judging from his lifelong effort to "front only the essential
facts of life" we may suppose it would have had a direct bearing
on this quest. As he lay dying, the essential facts of life must have
been preeminent to him. The fact that Indians figured in his last
thoughts indicates the strength of interest and sense of connection
that goes beyond the strictly historical or anthropological.

Many other students of culture before Thoreau were drawn to
a strong interest in Aboriginal life. Some missionaries spent more
time learning the customs, language, and stories of Aboriginal
cultures than they did preaching the gospel. European poets and
novelists without any direct experience of Aboriginal culture
committed to print lengthy accounts of Indian life. The roots of this
fascination with the Aboriginal are deep in Western Civilization,
going back to at least 4th century (BCE) Greece and 3rd century (BCE)
Rome. Beginning with African cultures, European social thought
used a perspective on so-called primitive societies as a comparative
method of cultural reflection.

With the European discovery of the "new world," the Indian replaced the African as the focus for the primitive, and the idea of the "noble savage" was born. The tradition of the noble savage, as a standpoint from which to critique civilization, gained a considerable and respectable currency in early modern Europe. In colonial North America, however, it gained little footing and appears only as a minor literary theme and in the work of a few radical social thinkers.

With the work of Henry Lewis Morgan[4] in the mid-1800s, interest in Aboriginal culture entered a new phase, and the considerable literature of North American anthropology is the result. At the same time, the tradition of the noble savage underwent an important change. With Emerson, Thoreau, and Margaret Fuller, the uncritical praise of Indian life and virtue, that had previously been characteristic of those fascinated by Aboriginal cultures, turned into a kind of holistic truth seeking about human nature and the effect of culture on human development.

Thoreau would have preferred to let the Indian people live as they pleased, but realized that the European invasion had thoroughly disrupted Aboriginal cultures. Even so, he hoped to study the Indians so closely as to know the "basic principle of their existence." Emerson and Fuller saw in Indian people a wholeness of spirit, a unity of thought and action, and a harmony with Nature that, they believed, Europeans must also achieve if the promise of their civilization was to be fulfilled.

Most Americans, however, saw nothing to admire in Indian life and no place for a consideration of Aboriginal culture ever gained a foothold in the American Dream. Indeed, the steady displacement of Indian communities was taken as confirmation of the settler's innate superiority. The predominant understanding that came out of the European encounter with Aboriginal culture was the doctrine of "savagism." This doctrine held that in the developmental scheme of things the Indian was in the "childhood" stage of the species, and had either to grow up into the civilized "maturity" of European culture, or perish.[5]

Although some variant of this doctrine is still present in the minds of most North Americans, it can hardly be regarded as a satisfactory summation of either the European/Aboriginal encounter, or the meaning of Indian experience. One hundred years of American anthropology has added considerable perspective to a wider view of Native American life. However, it has rarely led to that deeper reflection on culture in which values, ideals, goals, and concepts of human nature, along with lifeways in general, are raised for open and serious evaluation.

Anthropology, as a "social science," is not comfortable with the questions this kind of evaluation tends to ask. Most anthropologists go to some pains to avoid any association with the supposedly discredited concept of the noble savage. However, in times of crisis these questions and this deeper kind of evaluation come inevitably into focus, as Aboriginal peoples well know, and as the rest of us are now discoving. Thus, the conviction that European civilization has the opportunity for learning something of profound importance in its ongoing encounter with Native Americans continues to find advocates.

Since the early 1940s, Frank Waters has been the most eloquent and authentic voice for this deeper view of Aboriginal life and culture. He has been closely associated with the Hopi people of the American Southwest for much of his life and has written a number of seminal books based on his learning from this long experience. The books of Frank Waters on the Hopi bear the marks of a man wholly involved with the lifeways and the environment of these people. He has not fallen victim to the curious notion that objective detachment and analysis yield the best understanding. He has, instead, entered into the world of the Hopi to such a degree that his own perceptions, values, and patterns of thought reflect a distinctly Hopi sense of reality.

In writing about the Hopi, Frank Waters is always clear about his position as an outsider. Yet, it is also clear from his work that he has not held back from allowing the ceremonial life of the Hopi, and the ambiance of primal mystery that envelope their ceremonies, from entering and profoundly shaping his life and thought. Frank Waters' understanding of Hopi culture was so well regarded that when a group of elders decided their Road of Life should be recorded, they asked him to help them compose the *Book of the Hopi*.[6] Since this written account of the Hopi way was to be directed, in particular, to those Hopi who were now outsiders in their own community, as well as to the non-Native world, the shaping of the work needed to be done by someone who fully understood the crisis of modern culture in both its Indian and non-Indian contexts.

Frank Waters had already published *Masked Gods*,[7] a major treatise on Navaho and Pueblo ceremonial life, and, in addition, several novels, set in the Southwest, that were built around a keen sense of crisis in both traditional and modern cultures. In both *Masked Gods* and *Book of the Hopi*, his writing evokes the myths and ceremonials to such a degree that his experience of their powers cannot be doubted. He records the ceremonies and ritual dramas as a participant-observer, as one who has profoundly experienced the reality of the mysteries bodied forth.

In Frank Waters' portrayal, the central and organizing reality of Hopi life is a sense of total participation in all aspects and levels of the great surrounding world; a world that includes not only plants and animals, lakes and rivers, clouds and rain, and all manner of landforms, but the energy, beauty, and presence that informs all things. The entire natural landscape is felt to be a kind of great homeplace and all the inhabitants a kind of great family. While various life forms and landforms each have their distinct qualities and energies, they are, at the same time, understood to be mutually interdependent aspects of a whole Earth presence.

The seasonal round to which Hopi culture is attuned, integrates their working and ceremonial life into a cosmic perspective. They experience the world as a patterned process that requires a certain kind of participation in order to keep the harmony of life in good order. The Hopi understand their role in the process of world maintenance to be unique, yet, at the same time, perfectly integrated with all the other energies of the great surrounding environment that also have their Earth maintenance work to perform. If any fail in their given function, all are affected. Interdependence is the focus of their worldview. Reciprocity is the manner of all relationships. Ecological is the pattern of consciousness.

The fact that there can be no human life without the supportive presence of plants and animals within the whole Earth environment is a kind of biological baseline that Western thought has only recently begun to appreciate. For the Hopi, this knowledge has always been the central fact of their existence, a felt reality pervading every aspect of their lives, a reality giving richness and depth to their myths and ceremonies, and a profound significance to their daily activities.

For example, in their origin myths, animals help the People as they journey through the Three Worlds of emergence. Animals and plants figure centrally in the ceremonies and without them Hopi and pueblo life would be both physically and spiritually impossible. Plants and animals are experienced as creatures that stand on Earth in their own right. They are seen as a kind of extended family of beings who have also been given a share of Earth. To use plants and animals for survival is, therefore, accompanied by a sense of ceremony, a sense of request, permission, and reciprocity.

Although Frank Waters deals at length with these matters in *Masked Gods* and *Book of the Hopi*, it is the story told in *The Man Who Killed the Deer*[8] that most dramatically and succinctly evokes the Hopi worldview and its social process at work in the life of a pueblo community. In this 1942 novel he tells the story of a young man who had been taken away to a boarding school, and, now returned, neglects his ceremonial responsibilities. He thus lives like an outsider on the edge of the settlement. In portraying this and related conflicts, Frank Waters reveals the nature of Hopi consciousness in concise and dramatic detail.

The story opens with the young man, Martiniano, killing a deer out of season in an area of forestland controlled by the Federal government, and without ceremonially granted pueblo permission. He is arrested by Federal officers, and, in the process, beaten by police, an overall bad situation. A pueblo council meeting is called. The meeting begins with the burning of pungent cedar. Tobacco is handed around and smoked with deliberation. (All quoted material from *The Man Who Killed the Deer* as referenced.)

> *Now the silence, impregnated with smoke, seemed thicker, heavier ... As each man threw away his stub, he leaned*

*back against the wall and drew the blanket up around his
head. They might have been settling in for a long sleep.
Then suddenly, the talk. Slow, measured, polite and wary.
(p. 19)*

The Governor of the pueblo introduces the matter at hand.
Then both of Martiniano's companions tell of the incident.
Silence. Then Martiniano tells his story. Silence. Finally, the talk
begins again, starting from the simple facts: a deer killed out of
season; a Hopi man arrested; a fine to pay. The talk then develops
in ever widening circles around these facts. The man was born
in the pueblo; although he has failed to respect his ceremonial
responsibilities, and has been repeatedly warned, yet no person
is single and alone. The pueblo is involved. Still more questions
are raised. It is a matter of the land. The mountain where the
deer was killed is Hopi land, land that was never relinquished
nor legally obtained by the government. What will come of this
continued usurpation of sacred Hopi land? This matter of sacred
land involves the ceremonies and the whole life of the pueblo.
There is the matter of the deer, killed without its ceremonially
granted permission, without proper ritual awareness of the way all
that is living flows together. The issues widen, the considerations
deepen, centering down into the essential facts of Hopi life
and consciousness. The speaking stops, silence continues the
communication. Frank Waters then characterizes the silence.

*Silence spoke, and it spoke loudest of all ... There is no such
thing as a simple thing ... Nothing is simple and alone. We
are not separate and alone. The breathing mountains,
the living stones, each blade of grass, the clouds, the rain,
each star, the beasts, the birds and invisible spirits of the
air – we are all one, and indivisible. Nothing that any of
us does but affects us all.*

*So I would have you look upon this thing not as a separate
simple thing, but as a stone which is a star in the firmament
of earth, as a ripple in a pool, as a kernel of corn. I would
have you consider how it fits into the pattern of the whole.
How far its influence may spread. What it may grow into ...
(p. 27, 28, 29)*

A council meeting is not a discussion with a vying of wits, an
exercising of eloquence, or a testing of wills. It is, instead, the elders
of the pueblo laying out a matter of common concern; it is the
submitting of a problem and themselves to a process that moves
beyond a summing up of opinions; it is a process that surrounds
the matter before council with a continually widening context
and draws a coordinated sense of response out of the speaking
and silence. From the perspective thus gained, clarification and
resolution emerge. This is not to be confused with simplification
or the end of conflict. In this case, it is a deliberation that aims
at an outcome appropriate to the wellbeing of the communal
situation rather than a judgement issuing in the punishment of
an individual.

*A council meeting is a strange thing. The fire crackles.
The candle gutters. And the old men sit stolidly on their
benches round the walls. When a man speaks they do not
interrupt. They lower their swathed head or half close
their eyes so as not to encourage or embarrass him with
a look. And when the guttural Indian voice finally stops
there is silence. A silence so heavy and profound that it
squashes the kernel of truth out of his words, and leaves
the meaningless husks mercilessly exposed. And still not
a man speaks. Each wait courteously for another. And
the silence grows around the walls, handed from one to*

> *another, until all silence is one silence and the silence has the meaning of all. So the individuals vanish. It is all one heart. It is the soul of the tribe. A soul that is linked by that other silence with all the tribal councils which have sat here in the memory of man.*
>
> *A council meeting is one-half talk and one-half silence. The silence has more weight, more meanings, more intonations than talk. It is angry, impatient, cheerful, but masked by calmness, patience, dignity. Thus the members move evenly together. (p.21)*

This is a description of ecological consciousness in a social situation. This consciousness emerges most clearly around the communication that takes place on nonverbal levels. It pulls the council meeting into a keen awareness of context and allows decision and action to be based on the mutually created sense of the group. Radical dissent rarely arises in Hopi society due, in part, to this method of decision-making. No one who is attuned to the traditional basis of pueblo life, and shares its mode of consciousness, will cultivate a position of dissent. It is this ecological mode of consciousness, this way of structuring social life, which enables the pueblo community to "move evenly together."

Martiniano is an outsider in his own pueblo. He is regarded as a troublemaker. He has been away to the white man's school and has not participated in the ceremonials since his return. He and his wife are shunned, discriminated against and not allowed to pass the winter in the comfort of the common dwelling. Martiniano's life is bitter and empty. He complains to his friend Palemon, who points out that Martiniano accepts no form of life and so remains suspended without faith. Palemon tells him:

You too have a greater body, your form of life. It is not mine,
for our old ways you reject, nor is it the Government's, the
white man's, for you reject it also; but you must have one.
(p. 76, 77)

Palemon's words take root. Martiniano actively searches for a
new faith and comes to take the "peyote road." For some time the
peyote religion has been growing within the pueblo. It has been
adopted from tribes who live on the high plains and is defended
by its adherents as the new "Indian church" that is come to give
power and unity to all Native peoples in their resistance to the
encroaching white civilization. The kiva leaders and pueblo
elders are hostile to the new religion and bring the matter to a
head by raiding a peyote service, breaking it up and confiscating
participants blankets. Another council meeting is called and
the peyote way is "put on trial" through a comparison with the
traditional Road of Life. At the end of the meeting, the common
voice of the elders, as portrayed by Frank Waters, provides a
statement that serves to illuminate the Hopi's mode consciousness
from yet another perspective.

> *Now our dances, our races, out kiva ceremonials – how*
> *can we speak of these that are a part of us? That is all*
> *we can say. The corn plants sway in the summer wind,*
> *stretching out their arms for rain; thus we dance. The*
> *young men hurtle down the race-track, one after another,*
> *giving life back to Our Father Sun for his race, so it will*
> *be returned to them, and both endure. And in our kivas*
> *we strive to perpetuate the wisdom of those Old First*
> *Ones who had their rising as we. Will the day come*
> *when Father Sun no longer has strength to make his*
> *journey overhead, when men forget their arisings? Then*

we will have no need for our dances, our races, our kiva ceremonials. We can say no more about this thing which we are.

But this Peyote. It too creates a faith. That is good, that which creates a faith. But what is this faith? It is a road that leads to a better world: this you say. The Peyote Road. Is this the road we should take, travelers dressed in American clothes? How is it we can forsake the four-fold world of which we are a part?

From the fire element of the first world we hold the heat of animal beings. That of air gave us the breath of life. That of water produced our life-stream, our blood. And from that of the earth we derived the solid substance of our physical forms. From each of these worlds we have had our successive emergences. We are all that we have been.

So we ask: what kind of religion is it which would refute that which we are; that falsely subjugates the body, inflames the mind with dreams and leads away the spirit?

Now something else. What is this better world to which the Peyote Road would entice us?

Through all our previous arisings we have slowly emerged from formlessness to separateness. Now we must return again to the formless, to the boundless, to the undivided. From the world of the physical to the world of the spirit which transcends them. But with the consciousness of their non-separateness... That is our new emergence. We are all that we shall be.

*But this Peyote Road to a new world and a better world.
It is not an arising. It leaves one world behind. It returns
the traveler to it once again. How can this be? Can we
cast away part of ourselves, either going or coming? It is
an illusionary journey, a dream.*

*There is only one world of which we are all a part: Our
Father Sun, Our Mother Earth, the birds of the air, the
trout in the waters, the corn plant and the living stones,
ourselves.*

*We are all that we have been. We are all that we shall
be. Shall we leave reality for illusion? Shall we strive for
what we already have?(p. 132, 133, 134)*

The essential distinction here is between a fragmenting faith
and a faith that integrates every aspect of life into a unified and
sustaining process. The traditional Hopi Way is not an add-on kind
of faith, something to seek and strive after, but simply a whole,
encompassing way of life. Similarly, ecological consciousness
is not something to be called into service at particular times for
particular purposes; it is a gift of insight, vision, and adaptation
that structures and coheres an entire way of life.

To speak in detail of the development and maintenance of the
Hopi's mode of consciousness is beyond the scope of this discussion,
but there is one experience within the culture that is particularly
formative in this regard – the instruction and initiation of boys
in the kiva ceremonials. Frank Waters' experience of Hopi life
was such that he is able to portray something of this journey. As
a father takes his twelve-year old son down into the kiva to begin
his period of instruction, he seeks to quiet the boy's fears with the
following words:

*Hush son! You are in the womb of Our Mother Earth.
You will be here many days, many months, a long time.
You have entered a child. You will be reborn from here a
man. Then you will know why it is you must stay. Let
there be no more whimpering, no more questions, son...
You are in a womb: In it the eyes the nose and babbling
mouth do not function. The knowledge that will come to
you is intuitive truth of the spirit, the quiescent wisdom
of the blood, transmitted through senses you do not use
outside. The pulse of the earth throbs through these walls
which enclose you; the embers there reflects the heat of
its glowing heart; that little hole runs into the center of
the world, into the lake of life itself. Remember you are
in a womb, child.*

Frank Waters further constructs this fatherly monologue
and in so doing gives expression to the reality that underlies and
nourishes Hopi life.

*Listen son. In your mother's womb you were conceived.
From an individual human womb you were born to an
individual human life. It was necessary, it was good. But
individual human life is not sufficient to itself. It depends
upon and is part of all life. So now another umbilical cord
must be broken – that which binds you to your mother's
affections, that which binds you to the individual human
life she gave you. For twelve years you have belonged
to your lesser mother. Now you belong to your greater
mother. And you return to her womb to emerge once
again, as a man with no mother's hold on him, as a man
who knows himself not an individual but a unit of his
tribe and part of all life which ever surrounds him ...*

You must be taught the laws of all life whatever form it takes: the living stones, the breathing mountains, the tall walking rain, as well as those of bird, and fish, beast and man...

You will perceive his kinship to all living creatures of these four kingdoms of fire, air, water, earth. Not only his chieftanship over them, but his responsibility to them.

But through all these truths will run one great truth: the arising of all individual lives into one great life, and the necessary continuance of this one great life by the continual progression of the individual lives which form it. (p. 115, 116, 118)

At the end of the initiation period, the boys – now young men – begin their participation in the ceremonial life of their community. The dances, songs, races, and mystery plays can be understood on a variety of levels (see *Masked Gods* and *Book of the Hopi*), but underlying all interpretation is their function of maintaining the Hopi's sense of participation in the whole panorama of life across time and throughout the sacred spaces of Creation.

In Frank Waters portrayal, the Hopi has an understanding of life with which they are satisfied. It has come to them from the Old First Ones and there is no question of improving on it. The traditional Road of Life has given them everything they need. It nourishes and sustains the People in a high desert land. To live well in the beauty of this sacred place requires careful alignment with the pattern of the seasons. With hand technology and a sensitive attunement to modest regional resources, the Hopi have traditionally engaged a way of life that has sustained their settlements for many centuries past.

A pervasive sense of gratitude, rooted in an upwelling response to the beauty of the land and its plenitude of life, is at the core of the Hopi worldview. The story of the Hopi is the story of a people who, through a profound sense of Earth's goodness, created a deeply settled, spiritually nourishing culture, centred in presence, and beauty.

Only when people live steadily in an attitude of fundamental affirmation can they express themselves richly and positively in song, dance, and ceremony. The Hopi narrative and ceremonial tradition expresses a full range of poetic and spiritual gifts. The Hopi way of life nourished and sustained an anciently enduring people, until an alien, invasive culture, driven by a quite different reading of the world, came ominously over the horizon.

Frank Waters has been a longtime and persistent voice for the conviction that Western Civilization has something of profound and crucial importance to learn from the Hopi with regard to survival. This learning is profound because the questions arising in the comparison, deal with our basic orientation toward natural and social environments. This learning is crucial because there is now legitimate doubt that Western culture, energized as it is by the values of domination, exploitation, and aggrandizement, and organized according to a technological conception of reality, can survive the logic of its own premise.

The only non-Hopi who figures significantly in *The Man Who Killed the Deer* is a long time trading post operator, Rudolf Byers. He has a genuine appreciation and respect for the Hopi people and their way of life, yet he realizes that nothing can be done to prevent the devastating impact of modern civilization on their ancient culture. He is a man of critical intelligence who attempts to formulate the meaning of Hopi life in relation to his own culture.

The reflections that follow can be taken as Frank Waters' own view of the matter.

> *Byers thought of the world of nature as the white man sees it: the sparkling streams and turbulent rivers as sources of potential electric power; the mountains gutted for the gold and silver to carry on the commerce of the world today; the steel and iron and wood cut and fashioned, smelted, wrought and riveted from the earth to bridge with shining hulls the illimitable terrors of the seas—a resistless, inanimate world of nature to be used and refashioned at will by man in his magnificent and courageous folly to wrest a purpose from eternity. And yet what did he really know of the enduring earth he scratched, the timeless seas he spanned, the unmindful star winking at his puny efforts.*
>
> *And he thought again of the world of nature as the Indian had always seen it. The whole world was animate—night and day, wind, clouds, trees, the young corn, all was alive and sentient. All matter had its inseparable spiritual essence. Of this universe man was an integral part. The beings about him were neither friendly nor hostile, but harmonious parts of the whole. There was no Satan, no Christ, no antithesis between good and evil, between matter and spirit. The world was simply one living whole in which man dies, but mankind remains. How can man be lord of the universe? He is equal in importance to the mountain and blade of grass, to the rabbit and the young corn plant. Therefore if the life of one of these is to be used for his necessity, it must first be approached with reverence and permission obtained by ritual, and thus the balance of the whole maintained intact.*
> *(p. 284, 285)*

These contrasting orientations could not be more distinct. The cultural style of the "white man" is exploitive and manipulative, while the Hopi's is adaptive and participatory. European exploitation produces competition, injustice, alienation, and exhaustion. Hopi adaptation produces cooperation, mutual support, sharing, and resilience.

The Hopi legacy, as portrayed by Frank Waters, and in the terminology I have been using, is the wisdom of ecological consciousness. This wisdom includes the following: 1) a sensitive awareness of the subtle interrelationships of all beings with each other and with the whole Earth environment; 2) a full consideration of context with regard to the wellbeing of all creatures, and the wellbeing of all Earth's life communities in general; 3) a steady orientation of affirmation for all life and an attitude of humility and gratitude for the support and sustenance received from the commonwealth of life; 4) arranging the details of living in such a way that something is always given back to the communities of life, that a state of reciprocity is maintained with the communities of life on which we depend.

At no point in his writing does Frank Waters imagine that Western culture can simply appropriate the social and ecological values of Hopi culture. If Western culture is ever to mature into a fully rounded ecological consciousness, it must come from an authentic developmental process that reconfigures values, priorities, and behaviour from within the resources of the culture itself. Frank Waters does hold up the possibility, however, that through a process of cultural cross-fertilization a kind of hybrid civilization may be created that combines the social and ecological wisdom of Aboriginal peoples with the technical proficiency of Western culture. This theme, which surfaces strongly at the end of *Masked Gods*, flows through all Frank Waters' work.

At the end of *The Man Who Killed the Deer*, he gives voice, again through Rudolf Byers, to deep reflection on the cultural crisis in which we collectively find ourselves. Traditional Aboriginal cultures are increasingly suffering the disintegrating impact of modern civilization as all judgment and decision-making are bent to technological and commercial imperatives. Modern Western cultures are now so socially fragmented, alienated from the Earth, and beholden to an economics of exploitation and domination that it is difficult to see how the development of an ecological consciousness can find a true rooting. Perhaps because he recognizes the depth of this problem, Frank Waters brings his novel to an end with a lament by Rudolf Byers, a lament which, however, rises into a vision of spiritual insight. And it is in this potential insight, this possible spiritual enlightenment, that he suggests the full dimensions of ecological consciousness may be awakened.

> *The brotherhood of man! It will always be a dreary phrase, a futile hope, until each man, all men, realize that they themselves are but different reflections and insubstantial images of a greater invisible whole.*
>
> *There are those who have eyes and cannot see, who have ears and cannot hear. They are blind, they are deaf, they have no tongues save for the barter of the day. For which of us knows that awakened spirit of sleeping man by which he can see beyond the horizon, hear even the heart beating within the stone, and speak in silence those truths which are of us all.*
> (p. 285, 286)

Postscript: 1999

In the time since this essay was written (1964), various forms of ecological consciousness have become somewhat effective in the defense of natural and social environments. Our society has advanced further with regard to a collective ecological worldview than I would have predicted, but with much less effect than I would have expected from such an advance.

At the same time, the economic and cultural forces that are decomposing the biotic integrity of Earth's environments have vastly increased the scale and intensity of destructive operations. The polarization between environmental preservation and environmental exploitation is intense and will likely become even more so. The outcome is far from certain, but it appears the forces of maximum environmental exploitation and unlimited economic growth are still in the ascendancy.

Aboriginal communities across the continent continue to suffer the disintegrating impact of modern commercial civilization. However, within various communities there has also been a resurgence of interest in preserving traditional culture and lifeways. The modes of thought and feeling, the practices of council and ceremony, and the values traditional to Aboriginal life are gaining strength despite the inhospitable context of the dominant Euro-American culture.

In addition, a steadily increasing interest in the worldviews and values of Aboriginal peoples has now emerged in a variety of ways. Long haired youthful seekers, radical anthropologists, human rights advocates, eco-justice workers, homestead economists, mainstream environmentalists, deep ecologists, Creation centered Christians, born again pagans, and a whole raft of poets are among those who make up what begins to look like the hybrid culture Frank Waters envisioned. While a big chunk of this interest must be discounted as fad and another chunk as the expropriation of Indian culture and identity by white man's acquisitiveness, there remains, nevertheless, a substantial element of participatory understanding and mutually beneficial support for the renewal of traditional Aboriginal values and life-ways.

Something of the cross-fertilization Frank Waters hoped for is taking place. Whether the influence of this new spiritual and cultural ecology can advance sufficiently within mainstream North American society to reform economic behaviour away from endless growth and toward a conserver economy is the momentous question of the hour. Whatever the outcome, the wisdom of the Hopi, here reflected in the discernment of Frank Waters, is a fundamental contribution to the ecological consciousness of our time.

Second Postscript: 2013

Since 1999, both the positive and negative factors noted above have dramatically increased. The ecological worldview is now pervasive. It is no longer possible to think intelligently except in ecological terms. Reactionary elements that still think domination is a winning game for the human-Earth relationship are shrill and ludicrous.

On the negative side, however, economic behaviour and public policy are still in thrall to economic growth and maximum resource exploitation – especially energy resources. The economy continues to plough ever deeper into Earth's ecological integrity with disastrous results for biodiversity and climate stability. However, since 2008-2009 a new perspective on this behaviour has emerged and it looks more and more like a system in failure.

It now seems entirely possible, indeed, likely, that the capital-driven economy and the market-driven consumer culture will suffer either a catastrophic collapse, or a steady loss of functional capacity. Either way, we are certainly living in shaky, high-risk times, and nothing really effective is yet being done at the level of public policy and broad societal change to prepare for the endgame transformation that will attend the playing out of either scenario.

At this time, we have a confused picture. The hybrid civilization Frank Waters hoped for can be seen in bits and pieces here and there. There is a gaining momentum of ecological consciousness, but it is far from being the societal and public policy platform needed for positive transformation, or even survival. A polarization within North American political life has made it difficult to see a convincing route to transformation.

Frank Waters lived until 1995, long enough to see his beloved Four Corners country suffer the "resource curse." The worst face of industrialization moved in and began strip-mining coal to power the lights and air conditioners of distant cities. In the last chapter of his last book – *Of Time and Change*[9] – he writes:

> *Implications of the industrialization of the...Four Corners... have spread farther; they include the entire Southwest. And they reflect a marketplace ideology leading to a worldwide despoliation of land, waterways, and the atmosphere.*

> *Yet we still have time to learn from our pueblo and Navajo neighbors that the living earth is a font of spiritual energy as well as a source of physical energy. The Cosmic energy is the same, viewed differently by those taking either an intuitive or a pragmatic approach to its*

totality. Reconciliation of these two modes of thought, with the realization that matter and spirit comprise one undivided whole, has yet to come. When it does, it will surely embrace the ancient wisdom and spiritual beliefs of the first native societies in the Four Corners. (p. 272)

Technology: Tool Kit and Mindset

Based on a lecture given to the Carleton County Forum at the Community College in Woodstock, New Brunswick, January 25th, 1988. A number of factors, circumstances, and emphasis of analysis have changed since 1988, which could have been updated for this publication in 2015. For example, climate change has now become a more critical issue. I have chosen not to revise the text, but to allow it to remain as it emerged when written. Likewise, I have not added references where I might have done so. Instead, a bibliography has been included in the references.

In the twentieth century it is usually taken for granted that the only reliable sources for improving the human condition stem from new machines, techniques, and chemicals. Even the recurring environmental and social ills that accompanied technological advancement have rarely dented this faith. It is still a prerequisite that a person running for public office swear his or her unflinching confidence in a positive link between technical development and human well-being and affirm that the next wave of innovations will surely be our salvation.

Langdon Winner

From late Neolithic times in the Near East, right down to our own day, two technologies have recurrently existed side by side: one authoritarian, the other democratic, the first system-centered, immensely powerful, but inherently unstable, the other man-centered relatively weak, but resourceful and durable.

Lewis Mumford

The opportunity to inaugurate this community lecture series is an exciting privilege. I use the word "exciting" with some reluctance because it is one of the most overused and misused words of our time. But despite my hesitation in contributing to the word's overexposure, I can use no other. I am moved by a genuine sense of excitement when I contemplate a continuing forum of this sort for the presentation and discussion of ideas rising from local contributors and contributing to the life of our local culture.

Becoming Mindful of Technology

I wish to speak tonight on a complex of themes so heavy with history, so densely interwoven, and so intimately connected with every waking moment of our lives as to require a whole series of lectures for adequate treatment. However, having been given this opportunity, I will try to lay down the broad outlines of my topic and probe some of its critical issues. But first I want to begin with a two stories.

In 1969, I travelled with an English cattle rancher, Gerard Casey, to a remote area of his 16,000-acre holding on the northwest flank of Mount Kenya in East Africa. He wanted to show me something he knew I would be interested in seeing. The season of the long rains was just past. The land in that area was now as green as it gets, a sort of rejuvenated, translucent, shimmer of green against the ancient dusty earth. We came, at last, to an open rise of land dotted with high arching thorn trees at the upland edge of the great rolling plain that extends northward from Mount Kenya to the Turkana region and on to Ethiopia and Sudan. It was a day on which the clouds that commonly cluster around the top of Mount Kenya had dispersed, and among its cragged peaks the mountain's snowfields and glaciers were easily visible, glistening in the brilliant equatorial sun. Nearby, a glacier fed stream ran swift and full down the incline of the land. The water, still cold to the touch, carried a cloudy signature of finely pulverized minerals scoured from the mountain by the glaciers.

The trail we had been following came to a wide place in the stream, clearly a long used place of refreshment for wildlife. My host told me the place had a name, Sirakowi – "zebra water." The name was from the Masai tongue, but the Masai people had moved on to the Amboseli and Kilimanjaro region long ago. We had come to see something long predating the Masai. A short distance from the small river, three rounded cairns, several metres high, had been constructed by past inhabitants of this storied land. The adjacent open area, perhaps a third of an acre, was covered with irregular fragments of black volcanic stone. Stones of a regular and characteristic shape were scattered among the fragments. We were standing in the middle of a site that had been used for the making of stone hand axes. The black volcanic stone found here had been a suitable material from which to create the pear shaped hand axes of the type archaeologists classify under the general name of Acheulean. The whole hand axes left behind among the fragments had likely been discarded as inferior specimens of the tool making process.

Gerard Casey told me that no professional archaeological work had yet been done on this site, but it was estimated to date back at least 40 to 50 thousand years, and possibly hundreds of thousands of years earlier. As I stood holding a hand axe, hot with the sun of all those years, I looked up at Mount Kenya and thought about those perpetual snowfields. I looked out over the dry plain below and thought about the ancestral chains of thorn trees and giraffes linking the ones I could see before me. I thought about the human skill that fashioned this hand axe out of the land. I thought about fire and of how likely it was that early humans, here in East Africa, obtained it from the edge of volcanic outfall. I thought about how fire and metallic ore had much later been brought together. I thought about how metal tools were thus forged and began another epoch in the human story. I thought about the pass to which we have come from such creative and highly skilled beginnings. From that reflection, I was swept forward in imagination with a rush, through the whole history of human technology and into the tangle of convenience and catastrophe in which we are now enmeshed.

Something new came to me as I stood gazing at the mountain, holding a tool that had once been held by an ancient human ancestor. I had long pondered the origin and development of technology and its increasingly problematic effects in recent times. From John Ruskin to William Morris, from Thoreau to Gandhi, from Ralph Borsodi to Scott Nearing, from Lewis Mumford to Buckminster Fuller, from Lynne White to Marshall McLuhan, from Gary Snyder to Wendell Berry, from Paul Goodman to Ivan Illich I had been searching for an understanding of how a heritage of such ingenuity, and often of such benefit for human wellbeing, was now opening into the prospect of ecological and human catastrophe. Standing on that black volcanic soil on the northwest slope of Mount Kenya with a stone axe in my hand, I knew I had come, in a sense, to the end of my quest.

The path of technology and human adaptation, starting from the hands and minds of those stone workers, spread out before me. I saw clearly that it was not just in the imagination or in the tool, but in the imagination/tool interaction that the twists and turns of adaptation, both beneficial and detrimental, must be traced. Although I had a clear sense of the logic driving technological development, I was in no sense reconciled to its inevitable momentum. I had, instead, come to an understanding of technology as a tool kit and of the need for ecologically guided discrimination around the development, selection, and use of tools. I could see that the worldview emerging from my experience and studies, and from my quest to understand the human story, was now moving into a life orientation that speaks to a kind of faith and practice.

I later had a similar experience on a family camping trip in Vermont. Ellen and I had spent the day with our two young sons, Eric and Brendan, exploring stone walls, catching salamanders, and watching water bugs on a pond at eye level, our noses just above the surface of the water. I had made two child size bow and arrow sets for Eric and Brendan. The sheath knife I used to make them had been given to me years before in a junior high school Christmas gift exchange. The blade, re-sharpened over and over, had been honed down by more than a third. I had years of use and affection invested in that tool.

In the late evening, I walked from our campfire among the tall pines to the edge of the open meadow to look at the sky swirling with stars. Two deer bounded down the hill. I thought about the day's activities and all the things our sons were learning. I thought about the bow and arrow set my older brother made for me when I was about their age and the care he had taken to select and cut perfectly straight sticks for arrows. I sat down on the rear bumper of the Volkswagen that had carried us to this lovely place, and again had the experience of being swept through the whole history of technology, right down to this favourite car sitting silently on the edge of the Vermont woods. Once again, I saw the whole panorama of technology as a heritage of useful but often very dangerous tools. I tell these stories at the beginning of this lecture because I want to underscore the importance of seeing our relationship to technology through the concept of a tool kit.

The Technological Mindset as a Mental Harness

Perhaps the most obvious characteristic of our relationship to technology is ambivalence; we really love it, we are often frustrated by it, we sometimes hate it, we may even come to fear it. If we are thoughtful observers, as distinct from passive consumers, we know our toasters may be powered by a nuclear reactor or a coal fired generator. We know our motor vehicles spew noxious and increasingly lethal levels of contamination into the atmosphere. We know the habit of eating nonlocal out of season foods is the opposite of energy conservation. We know that our fast food burgers are raised on the ashes of rainforests. We know that many of the synthetic chemicals employed at home, on the farm, in the shop, in the office, and in industry are not biodegradable and are accumulating to toxic levels in the atmosphere, in animal bodies (including our own), in the soil, and in surface and ground water. This list could go on and on, detailing the myriad ways the technology of high-energy industrial-consumer economies interlock routine habits of behaviour with complex, far flung, outrageously wasteful, and destructive patterns of resource exploitation. A degree of apprehension is not inappropriate. There is a current joke that sums up this situation: "If you're not paranoid, you must be crazy."

The technology of domestic life in the contemporary industrial-consumer economy is now of such interlocking complexity and of such high-energy resource requirements as to seem beyond the ability of individuals or households to significantly modify. When we add the technology of the workplace, be it forestland, farm, ocean, shop, factory, mines (including fossil fuel extraction), schools, hospitals, retail, service institutions, research labs, etc., we arrive at a truly monolithic creation. So much of human life is now encapsulated within this industrial artifact, and so much of our imagination captured by the accomplishments and projections of technological innovations, that it is hard to see how anything other than more of the same could possibly have a future.

Behind this techno-monolith, behind the glossy façade of business as usual, there is, however, a growing sense of apprehension. No matter how much we love our high-energy technology, no matter how convenient it seems, no matter how much our society's wellbeing seems to depend on continued technological and economic growth, we now know, or should know, that a monumental miscalculation has been made. There is no longer any doubt that high-energy industrial-consumer civilization is steadily dismantling the life support system of the planet. Quite aside from the regularity of accidents that damage specific environments, the normal ongoing processes of industrial production and consumption are making Earth increasingly less habitable for the natural diversity of life forms. There is a strong sense of the bizarre in all this. If it were simply a matter of a massive volcanic eruption throwing a biosphere changing amount of particulate matter and greenhouse gases into the atmosphere, we could shake our heads and say; "Mother Earth has really put the screws to us this time." But, in the reality of our present circumstance, we have to *scratch* our heads and ask; "Why are we doing this to ourselves and to the only home we have?" This is the question that has caused some folks to wonder if the human species is possessed of a fatal flaw, perhaps a fundamental disconnect between technological ingenuity and adaptive intelligence.

There is a fatalistic worldview that seizes on the idea of humans as a flawed species. This conclusion enables individuals and even whole cultural groups to arrive at a firm explanation for our ecological dilemma. If you off load this dilemma on God or the Devil or fate or history or even on the evolutionary process, you can avoid responsibility for doing anything to improve human adaptation. Adopting this tragic flaw scenario may provide a certain kind of mental and emotional relief but it is an abdication of intelligence and the poisoning of responsibility. I have encountered this tendency in conversations with many people and even within myself. Thus, I am particularly concerned to bring this fatalistic worldview into the open so it can be seen as a thoroughly unworthy stance. At the same time, however, I must admit there is something so baffling about our technology driven, high-energy trap that the sense of a flawed species is not easily put to rest. Nuclear arms technology is bad enough as a self-constructed trap, but we can at least imagine the conditions that would allow getting out of that one, as recent events have hopefully shown. Getting out of the fossil fuel addiction trap is much more difficult to imagine.

In an effort to understand the character and consequences of high-energy technology, some critics have come to speak of autonomous, runaway, or out of control technology. These expressions derive from a justified fear of technological encroachment on human functioning. But it is not so much that technology is taking us where we don't want to go, as it is a matter of not being able to go anywhere or do anything without the assistance of complex high-energy technology. It is not so much a matter of technology defining an environment and forcing us to live in it, as it is a steadily evolving redefinition of what it means to be human and have a good life. Technology is now a worldview, a mindset, a complete way of understanding human action.

Control of damaging technology in the environment is not a particularly difficult problem. It consists mainly of shutting down the damaging machinery and toxic processes. The deeper difficulty with this is that all contexts of conviction and action are increasingly conditioned by high-energy industrial-consumer technology.

We are passing from the ability to see and use technology as an inventory of specific tools that are part of the way we fit into our various ecosystems, to the view that technology is the system into which we must fit, the adoption of a complete technological mindset. Once technology becomes a mindset, it is difficult to call into play the discrimination needed to shut any of it down, even when it is clearly damaging.

The feeling of an autonomous technology is the external projection of an internal process. We can turn off the machines whenever we wish. What we cannot turn off is what is happening in our minds and bodies through our being conditioned by a technologically dominated environment. In these conditions, technological rationality colonizes the intuitive programs of the mind-body system. The real problem of control, the area where technology is out of control, is in the mind and body, in the eclipse of our biospherically based, evolutionary imprinted heritage – both genetic and epigenetic – by the ideology of technique. The signature of this eclipse is the feeling that what we suffer most from is a lack of measurement, analysis, and efficiency. The technologically colonized mind has the feeling that we should, above all, keep working to get measurement, analysis and efficiency right, and keep pushing this logic and its application to higher and higher levels. Now it can be argued that technological rationality is itself an intuitive program of the mind, and I would not object; I think this is correct. But, at the same time, I would point out that it is only *one* of a complex of programing loops that make up full human functioning, and that its imperial-like colonization and domination of mental and emotional space is unbalancing and pathological. We are now very close, it seems to me, to ferreting out the illusive human flaw, and it is not a flaw of the species but a flaw of culture. This point will be discussed in detail later on.

Technology is not just the machinery, the electronics, and the chemistry available for use in the environment, but the conceptual organization of both individual minds and the collective social mind. With this technological colonization of the mind, critical perspective tends to disappear. The mind, instead of surrounding technology with questions of value and consequence, and providing guidance and precaution, is itself surrounded by the logic and biases of technology and made over into a confirming accessory. The mind becomes another tool in the armoury of technological conquest rather than a source of discernment, discrimination, and seasoned judgment.

For example, the motor vehicle system has come to occupy our consciousness with the force of a natural phenomenon. How could it be possible to do things any other way? We cannot even begin to see how it might be possible to live without this system. It has become an invisible technology, a complete mental harness. To suggest we might come to live without personal motorized transport, or even significantly reduce our reliance on it, makes one seem odd and out of touch with the "real world." Yet we know, or should know, that with every turn of an ignition key, with every firing of an internal combustion engine, the real world of the biosphere suffers an insult. The cumulative effect of these of millions upon millions of daily insults, is to drive headlong into atmospheric toxification of disastrous proportions.

The urban haze phenomenon, which on a south wind now covers New England and Atlantic Canada, is generated in no small part by the motor vehicles of the densely populated Mid-Atlantic coast that start up each morning, not to mention the ones that run all night. The Trans-Canada Highway that runs through the Saint John River Valley just three miles from my homestead farm, is a main transport link between the Atlantic Region and the rest of the country. In the last fifteen years, the volume of truck traffic has increased several-fold and that high-energy haze is now appearing in the Saint John Valley without benefit of a south wind. On otherwise crystal clear mornings a band of dirty haze, quite distinguishable from the natural mist and fog, now hangs over the valley. If we take the health of the biosphere, or even just human health, as a governing norm, it is the motor vehicle system that is out of touch with the real world.

And so I come to end of my first major point: The importance of re-engaging technology as an inventory of tools that must be subjected to critical discernment with regard to their positive and negative effects on the health and integrity of Earth's ecosystems. This involves reversing the invasion and colonization of our neurological systems by the somatic and psychic effects of high-energy industrial-consumerism. We do this by grounding our minds and bodies in the real world of Earth's ecosystems and the way they actually function. We do this by taking in hand the tools that enable us to do the real work of ecologically sound re-adaptation.

Tool Kit and Ecological Adaptation

Everyone has a tool kit. We all surround ourselves with a variety of domestic and vocational tools. These tools may be broadly classified as directly activated and indirectly activated. Directly activated tools include all manner of hand and foot operated devices, such as knives, forks, spoons, pots, pans, dishes, scoops, tongs, baskets, scissors, chisels, hammers, spading forks, shovels, hoes, pumps, axes, saws, ladders, clothes, footgear, chairs, tables, desks, beds, hammocks, rowboats, canoes, skis, bicycles, roller skates, scooters, skate boards, walking sticks, canes, musical instruments, writing instruments, paint brushes, and kites, to name just a few. This category also includes structures and landform layouts that we put in place and which then need only periodic attention to fulfill their function. Here we have, for example, fences, walls, clotheslines, paths, roads, ditches, canals, dams, ponds, spring-boxes, gardens, orchards, cultivated fields, woodlot plantations, and buildings of all sorts.

Turning to indirectly activated tools we can identify three sub-categories:

1. Tools activated by the metabolism of other animals, such as, wagons, buggies, sleds and ploughs;
2. Tools activated by gravity and geothermal energy, such as waterwheels, windmills, gravity-flow water systems, and sailboats;
3. Tools activated by the combustion of biomass or fossil fuels, and by chemical or nuclear reactions; this includes all the devices of external and internal combustion, such as fireplaces, stoves, steam engines, firearms, chainsaws, motor vehicles, bulldozers and other earthmovers, airplanes, space rockets, and all the tools powered by electricity. These are all just examples.

The entire history of human development up until the last two hundred or so years occurred within the context of directly activated tools and the subcategories of 1 and 2 of indirectly activated tools, plus fire (external combustion) and firearms. Firearms date from the second half of the thirteenth century CE. I will be the first to admit that my categories are not precise. The design of our mental grids never quite stabilizes the raggedness of the world. For example, the use of fire is a high-energy technology in any application and has probably been in human hands even longer than the stone hand axe. Yet, an obvious developmental horizon of enormous consequence was crossed when the explosive potential of hydrocarbons was contained within a mechanical device and the internal combustion engine was created. With the introduction of the internal combustion engine, the long slow swell of human cultural development powered by wind, water, sun, and muscle became a tidal wave of resource exploitation that is still building and is now washing over the planet at full bore.

Electricity is a special case since it can be produced by a variety of technologies, including water and wind powered machines, solar converters, biomass and fossil fuel combustion, and with steam produced by nuclear reactors. Electricity is perhaps the preeminent example of the need for ecologically governed discernment and discriminating choice in the development and adoption of technologies. Derived from ecologically benign technologies, electricity can be a sustainable convenience. Derived from environmentally damaging technologies, electricity makes us all accomplices in the degradation of ecosystem integrity.

Paul Goodman used to say that if he could choose an environment most to his liking it would be the Middle Ages with electricity. That image certainly provides food for thought. We are accustomed to using electrically activated tools in close association with internal combustion engines. We experience the whole range of labour saving, convenience oriented tools as a cultural package. But the options for electricity production and application make its use subject to a high degree of household and industrial choice. For example, electricity can be separated from the massive use of fossil fuels. It is quite possible to envision a comfortable, socially rich, and dignified way of life from which internal combustion engines have virtually disappeared, but in which electricity is still a major component. While it is true that utilizing electricity may currently mean buying into large dams, nuclear reactors, or the burning of coal, petroleum, and natural gas, it doesn't need to remain so. It can mean low-head hydro, wind generation, and, most promising of all, solar electric technologies. It is also possible to live a good life using no electricity at all, as the Amish communities have long demonstrated.

At another level, a story told by Lewis Mumford, the great cultural historian of art and technology, illustrates the opportunity of technological discrimination. For most of his working life he composed at a typewriter. As he tells it, his handwriting was so dreadful no manuscript typist could be expected to decipher it. In his late 70s, he realized that if, for some reason, he were without access to a typewriter his work, as a writer, would come to a halt. The thought of being dependent on this machine spurred him to master the skill of legible handwriting. By trading a complex tool for a simple one – a typewriter for a pen – he greatly enlarged the range of his compositional freedom.

When I first took up market gardening, I had not the slightest doubt I needed the best tiller available for effective weed control. The Troy-Bilt tiller people had done a number on me and I ordered up their famous machine. Some years into this vocation, however, I discovered that my old, high-wheel, push cultivator is actually better for weed control. The tiller works well for preparing large garden plots for planting, and for turning under cover crops, but, when it comes to cultivating, the rotary tiller tends to bury the weeds. In a short time, the roots are re-established in the moist aerated soil and the unwanted plants are soon pushing up sturdy new growth. The hand cultivator tends to uproot weeds and lay them out to the withering power of the sun. The use of the hand cultivator takes only a little more time, does a much better job, and enables me to loosen the soil within inches of the garden plants without putting them in mortal danger, as does the sometimes lurching tiller. Bringing the tiller into action requires checking the oil, topping up the fuel, inspecting for loose bolts and leaking seals, and then walking it from the barn to the worksite. It is noisy, heavy to handle, and spews noxious fumes directly into the area from which I must draw my next breath as I follow it doggedly row after row. With the hand cultivator, I simply pick it up at the point of last use and proceed directly to work. It is quiet, easy to use, and does not foul the air.

There are farmers who still prefer horses for doing certain kinds of work, even though they have tractors, because it is the best way to get that work done. The Amish, of course, have stuck to horse farming and have prospered. There are commuters who prefer cycling because it is often the best way to travel through urban areas. Solar technologies for space and water heating are easily incorporated in new construction and added to existing structures. Composting technologies for domestic, farm, and municipal use are ready and waiting. These are just a few examples of tool kit evaluation and choice that build toward ecologically sound adaptation.

Now it may be argued that as ecologically sound as these low-energy tools are in use, their manufacture almost invariably requires exploitation of material and energy resources that do not conform to a strict rule of benign impact. This is certainly true, and I am not suggesting that human settlement and economy can operate without some degree of environmental exploitation. The human use of the Earth, no matter how carefully designed and respectfully executed, remains, as far as we understand it, firmly within the second law of thermodynamics. It may be, that from the standpoint of the cosmos nothing is really lost and that entropy will be redeemed if and when the expansion of the Universe reaches its apotheosis and then falls together in preparation for another cycle of evolutionary expansion. But for us, for now, the conversion of energy and material resources from useable to unreusable is unavoidable. This, however, is no reason to say; "Oh well, if that's the case, let's go for maximum convenience and wealth accumulation while we can." On the contrary, the reality of our ecological situation argues for an ethic of modesty, prudence, and the maximum conservation of resources, at least if we care about the human heritage we pass on to our descendants.

I have used the terms "high-energy" and "low-energy" with regard to human adaptation and here is the place to define how I am using them. Low-energy adaptation does not necessarily mean meagre energy and material use. It means minimizing energy and material *loss*. An ecologically sound economy may well use a fair amount of energy and material resources, but lose very little into unreusable forms because the processes on which it depends are mostly within the context of solar-metabolic transfer and recycling. High-energy adaptation means high levels of energy and material loss through dependence on processes that do not involve recycling and instead simply convert energy and material resources from usable to unreusable forms. A farm that operates on solar-metabolic energy transfer and organically enhanced soil fertility is an example of the former. A farm that operates on fossil fuel energy and synthetic fertilizers is an example of the latter.

The petrol burned in our internal combustion engines does not simply go away, as we have regretfully come to know. It continues to hang around but in forms that are not only no longer useful to us, but, as they accumulate past certain thresholds, are damaging to our health and to that of Earth's whole life support system. When fossil fuels are burned, they are converted to polluting gases and particulate matter that are lost to us with regard to any future use. Fossil fuels are a onetime deal. In contrast, when horses eat oats and hay, they not only provide useful energy, but also create quantities of manure that is immediately reusable by the bacteria that thrive in healthy soil and on which the whole of life depends. The idea of energy conservation does not mean to use as little as possible, but to draw whatever amount we use, as far as possible, from the solar-soil-water-plant-animal-soil recycling system. This is the way the biosphere works.

There is bound to be a certain loss in the manufacture and maintenance of tools. Entropy does not take a holiday even for the manufacture of bicycles and solar collectors. The best we can hope for is to confine that loss to the creation of tools that enable us, in all other respects, to lead lives of ecologically sound adaptation. The Earth's ecosystems are immensely resilient. If our exploitive activities were confined to the production of tools for ecologically sound living, our species would have a much longer run prospect, and, in the words of Wendell Berry; "Have much less to be forgiven."

Projecting an optimistic scenario for the future of civilization is not an easy task. Despite the cheerful talk of U.S. President Reagan, faith in progress seems to be fading fast. Even Mikhail Gorbachev, the chief spokesperson for the most rigidly progressive of all modern faiths, Soviet Marxism, now warns of grim times ahead and of the radical difficulty of a reasonable survival. He recently spoke of "defusing the time bomb planted deep inside mankind's existence by history." This time bomb can be clearly identified with the rise of a political economy that holds the Earth to be nothing more than a resource bank for the convenience, profit, power, and entertainment of the human species. The exploitation of fossil fuels, in particular, is the time bomb that has gone off, the consequences of which are now adding up on the negative side of the environmental ledger. From the perspective of the loons, the turtles, and the sequoias, fossil fuel exploitation is but an evening flash. For the human species, this euphoric experiment in extravagant living is likely to be capped by a discipline of difficult readaption.

I realize such thoughts tend toward the feeling of a flawed species. But to indulge this feeling is to be further colonized by the logic of technological determinism – the ideology that industrial-consumer civilization is the only worthwhile adaptation available. The study of anthropology gives the lie to this fixed idea. The perspective provided by the study of pre-industrial cultures is a good antidote for the technologically colonized mind. There appears to be nothing at the species level that argues convincingly for an adaptational flaw. The genetic program of the species may have its vagaries, but it is in the programs of culture that we have gotten ourselves crosswise with the integral functioning of Earth's ecosystems. With this in mind, I want to identify three programs of culture that are major flaws with respect to ecologically sound adaptation.

Unhitching a Mental Harness

The technological worldview involves three mental harnesses that entrain both thought and feeling:

- the idea that technology is ethically neutral and that it is only human use that makes it a positive or negative force;
- the assumption of an inherent natural order of passage for ideas, techniques, and tools from up-to-date to out-of-date;

- the belief that a law of inevitability governs technological innovation.

Together, these three harnesses combine into an ideological imperative of inevitable technological progress. I will discuss each in turn.

Devotees of progress are annoyed by the suggestion that technologies are not ethically neutral. It's as if all those mean looking Harley-Davidson motorcycles somehow helped conjure up the Hell's Angels, or that the mere existence of helicopter gunships caused Americans to become agents of fiery death in Viet Nam. In the United States one frequently sees the bumper sticker, "Guns Don't Kill People, People Kill People." There is a strong feeling that technology is neutral and that moral disposition cannot logically be attributed to machinery.

While superficially appealing, this view does not make sense from the perspective of cultural evolution. Those who take this view seem to think that technologies just pop into existence from some Platonic world where they have, in principle, been patiently waiting for the right moment in human history to make their appearance. This is, in fact, the way most people experience technology. Hardly anyone thinks of creating tools themselves. It's all in the hands of research and development teams and manufacturers. New technologies just appear and it takes a bit of determined research and reflection to trace out their cultural and motivational roots.

Marshall McLuhan never tired of stressing the point that all technologies are extensions of the human body – extensions of its abilities and capacities. It is because technologies are extensions of the structural, energetic, and processing features of the human organism that they cannot be regarded as neutral. Technology is neither an autonomous world with its own evolutionary program, not is it a collection of potentialities waiting in a kind of design space to be activated by human agency. It is, rather, an extended body – an extended cultural body – and, as such, has the tendencies and biases of culture built right in.

I am willing to exclude the imputation of moral character to tools, but, by any reasonable assessment, I think, we must insist that all technologies are *biased*. For example, the technology of firearms is biased toward killing or injuring living organisms. That is the only thing a rifle is good for aside from being used as a club. Down-filled sleeping bags are biased toward cold weather camping. The first sea-going ships were biased toward global exploration. Farm tractors are biased toward working more land with fewer farmers; the bigger the tractor, the fewer the farmers. Bulldozers are biased toward landform alteration. The factory system, when first developed, was biased toward high-density industrial region housing. Flush toilets are biased toward ignoring the composting value of digestive residue. Private motorcars are biased toward high mobility. The combination of transcontinental superhighways, sleeper cab trucks, and refrigerated trailers are biased toward concentrating North American lettuce production in California.

Now it may be argued I am only saying various technologies *allow* certain behaviours and courses of development. But this assumes the tool is passive, that it is not an extension of the human body. I suggest the tool is not passive. The tool has a push, one might say an aesthetic push. As an extension of bodily powers, technology is continually pushing from its motivational origin for additional use. The more we enjoy using it, the more uses for it we will find. I can testify to this with regards to my long history of affection for various cars, and more recently for my stable of bicycles. I can imagine many bulldozer operators feel similarly about their machines. I know truckers feel this way. The aesthetic push of those big rigs as they roll down the highway is certainly convincing, if not altogether pleasing, to those of us in lesser craft. Computers are probably the best example of this phenomenon. Is it the case that before computers came on the scene, many things were going undone that really needed doing, and when they became available we all heaved big sighs of relief for a lightened work load? No, this is not the case. The fact is, the push of the technology and the enjoyment of exploiting its potential have dramatically enlarged the amount of the work that now needs to be done.

Assessing the push of a technology in order to decide whether or not to use it can be a tricky business. Since technologies are extensions of human abilities, it can sometimes help to be a bit animistic in our assessment of their biases. I was once party to a discussion at a Volkswagen garage in Eldoret, Kenya about what to do with a colleague's recently rolled vehicle. It was repairable, but the service manager called us into his office and quietly urged the owner not to repair it for his own use because it was obvious the car was out to get him. This was the second accident he had had with this car in six months. I would not go this far in my animation of technology, but something of this precautionary impulse is certainly preferable to the sleepwalking stance of complete neutrality.

It is not a matter of technology taking on a life of its own, or of tools being imbued with unaccountable powers, but rather of recognizing the information-energy-action feedback loop that constitutes the human-technology system. My suggestion is that every technology and each tool should be evaluated for its bias, and a decision made on utilization according to its ability to function with little or no ecosystem or societal damage. A conscious and discriminating refusal to use technologies that degrade ecosystem or societal integrity would be a cultural achievement of high order.

There is another level of bias I will just mention in passing – the bias of scale. In addition to the specific biases of specific technologies, there is a general bias attached to considerations of size. Large scale concentrations of people in cities and the scale of technology required to maintain these concentrations is clearly antagonistic to balanced ecosystem functioning. The relationship between technology and consumer society is not a chicken and egg question. The technology of mass production definitely came first and created the physical coordination and psychic structure of consumerism. Economist, Leopold Kohr, argues convincingly in his classic books, *The Breakdown of Nations* and *The Overdeveloped Nations,* that overgrown scale is at the root of virtually all economic, environmental, political, and social problems of our present time.

The second on my list of cultural flaws is the idea and deeply inculcated feeling of a continual flow of concepts, tools, machinery, and techniques from being "up-to-date" to being "out-of-date," from being "modern" to being "old-fashioned." To my mind, this is one of the most pernicious deceptions of consumer culture. This dynamic has a prestigious pedigree dating from the Renaissance and the Scientific and Industrial Revolutions. But instead of being confined to the specific details of knowledge and technique, where it is often appropriate, this ideology of progress became an article of faith in the religion of Modernity – the world turned into an ongoing fashion show. The psychology of fashion, in turn, has invaded technology and industry, causing designs, tools, and products to disappear not because they lacked utility, efficiency, or beauty, but because they were ruled unfashionable and out-of-date by the market economy in its drive for ever greater consumption and wealth accumulation.

For the better part of this century, the term "old-fashioned" has been an expression of derision. It is staggering to think of all the mental anguish induced by the fear of being out-of-date. It is stunning to think of the power accrued by the smoke and mirrors game of being fashionable. I cannot think of a single redeeming aspect of the psychology of fashion. I suppose one could say it feeds consumer behaviour, and consumer behaviour props up the market economy, and without this behaviour the market economy stops growing, and if the market economy stops growing it collapses. The conclusion of this logic is that we do not have a sustainable economy. Promoting the market-driven consumer economy is not a good way to plan for the future. In an important respect, the decade of the 1960s broke the tyranny of fashion. The label of being "old-fashioned" is now often a positive valuation. Old-fashioned food is good food. Nobody makes fun of the Amish anymore. Spiritual disciplines resurrected from the "old ways" now flourish. It is high time we put the whole idea of being "modern" to rest, and replace it with the quest to fit human settlements – technology and all – into the sustainable flourishing of Earth's various ecosystems.

With respect to technology, this means that we look at the whole history of human settlement and economic activity, and at all the tools and techniques of our heritage and employ them or not according to their contribution or lack of contribution to ecologically sound adaptation. Whether a tool or technique is up-to-date or old-fashioned should play no part in our consideration.

The third flaw is the notion that technological innovation is governed by a law of inevitability, that there are certain technologies, methods, and processes that humans are rightly bound to discover and utilize. Here, the prophets of progress reveal the character of their faith. There is even a sense of moral obligation in this faith that meshes with the thrust for wealth, power, and renown, all based on the assumption that Earth can and should be redesigned for human convenience, and that scientific-industrial technology is the door through which all cultures must enter this promised land.

The idea that our society would be better off if some technologies had never been developed is met with incredulity by the devotees of progress, and the suggestion that some existing technologies should be phased out is routinely met with the objection; "You can't turn back the clock;" meaning that once a technology is introduced, it can never be withdrawn. This is quite untrue, but continues to be repeated nonetheless. Various technologies and techniques have been effectively circumscribed and even banned outright.

A notable example of this cultural discrimination is detailed in Noel Perrin's *Giving Up the Gun*. This book tells the story of how a sophisticated firearms industry was progressively restricted and eventually banned in 16th century Japan because the use of guns in battle threatened to erode and destroy the elaborate and highly meaningful codes of honour and the skills of swordsmanship that were at the heart of the powerful Samurai culture. Or consider that the Roman Catholic Church long maintained an effective ban on the technique of usury until the cultural force of market capitalism overpowered its defense of the social economy. Islam still maintains the ban. In our time, the increasing frequency of bans on the production and use of toxic substances is further evidence that considerations of health and societal welfare can overrule the technological imperative. With the recent signing of the agreement to phase out intermediate range nuclear missiles, we have been treated to the long faces of nuclear arms proponents on television saying, in effect, "Don't get your hopes up, folks, nuclear weapons are here to stay." Their obvious apprehension about the future of their industry can be taken as a good sign.*

---

*On January 4th, 2007 The Wall Street Journal published a full-page statement calling for the elimination of all nuclear weapons. Former US Secretaries of State, Henry Kissinger and George Schultz, former US Secretary of Defense, William Perry, and former US Senator and Chairman of the Senate Armed Services Committee, Sam Nunn, had drafted and signed the statement. This is an extraordinary reversal of position on nuclear weapons technology by these formerly prominent US government officials.

One of the most intriguing examples of a technology stopped in its tracks comes from ancient China. Peter Marsh and Peter Collett tell the story in their book, *Driving Passion: The Psychology of the Car.*

Apparently, the first car was designed and built in China three thousand years ago. It is described as being a turbine-powered machine capable of high speeds. It had independent front steering and a single, direct-drive rear wheel. Accounts of this machine came to Europe by way of Persian translations of Chinese literature from the Chou Dynasty. Roger Bacon translated this literature for Pope Clement IV. A letter written in 1270 includes the specific reference to this first automobile, indicating it ran on its own power being neither pulled nor pushed by animals.

Although Roger Bacon was imprisoned for fourteen years by Pope Clement's successor, Jerome of Ascoli, the document survived and was known to Father Verbiest three hundred years later when he was appointed Royal Astronomer at the court of Chinese Emperor, Kang-Hi in 1620. Marsh and Collett conclude this story with a dramatic flourish.

> *According to historian Robert Christophe, the Astronomer was joking one day to the Emperor about the gullibility of Bacon and his story about the Chou dynasty car. 'Nothing absurd about that!' snapped Kang-Hi. 'We have the records of the matter in our Imperial Library.' And so they did.*

There is no record of what the rulers of the Chou Dynasty thought about this unique machine, but obviously they were not even willing to give it a place of amusement, as had been done with what we call "gunpowder." Marsh and Collett speculate that perhaps the noise and noxious fumes so offended the rulers they had the engineer executed on the spot. They probably saw it as a danger to life and limb and degrading to their social authority. Why would they want to travel about in such a contraption when they could move about in an elegant carriage held aloft by a dozen faithful servants, or ride a beautiful horse? In any event, the ancient automobile did not survive.

For several generations past it has been taken as an inevitably progressive development that the high-energy technology of European and American cultures would come to command the Earth and its inhabitants under a steadily modernizing jurisdiction. This dream, this faith in unfettered innovation, has now fallen on hard times as a variety of high-risk nightmare scenarios are also spinning out from the market-driven economy. I do not wish to ridicule the real achievements of our scientific-industrial culture, but the evidence of environmental damage and societal crisis is mounting so rapidly that it is no longer possible to imagine that human and planetary welfare will be well served by unlimited innovation.

The real task of responsible science is now the discipline of limitation. The goal of frontline engineering, as Buckminster Fuller so often repeated, should be to "do more with less." Twenty years ago, Paul Goodman proposed a new rule for the times, a rule designed to counter the immobilizing complexity of technological overdevelopment. He advised that a new precautionary watchword should be; "Innovate only to simplify." His discerning advice has gone largely unheeded and we are driving ever deeper into a condition of high-tech fragility.

For example, no one ever gave any thought as to whether chloroflurocarbons would damage the stratospheric ozone that protects the inhabitants of the planet from harmful solar radiation. This new family of synthetic chemicals was such a neat innovation, so cheap to manufacture, so easy to handle, so stable and apparently harmless, and with so many convenient applications that acceptance and widespread use was unquestioned. We now know that the decomposing action of these gases on the upper ozone layer is so dire that a movement toward a complete ban has begun. What should we learn from this? What other products and processes presently claimed to be harmless will prove to be environmental disasters? Genetic engineering is now a prime is candidate of concern in this regard.

As I stand at my writing desk pondering these thoughts, I can hear the rising wind soughing through the great white pine at the head of our farm lane. This wind, coming off the Atlantic Ocean, is battering the northeast coast of the continent from Boston to Newfoundland and is mounting toward the normal upper limit of a winter storm. There is now, however, a real question of what can be considered the normal upper limit. The vertically circular patterns of air movement around the Earth are limited in the height to which they can rise by a barrier of temperature differential between the troposphere and the stratosphere. The temperature of the stratosphere is maintained in part by the consistency of ozone distribution. With the depletion of ozone, the temperature differential at the juncture of troposphere and stratosphere is moderated, thus allowing the columns of air to develop higher and larger sweeps as they roll over the planetary surface. Increasingly violent storms are the expected, and now observed, consequence. All this for aerosol hair sprays, automobile air conditioners, and styrofoam cups, to name a few of the products utilizing chloroflurocarbons. Increasingly violent storms may be only a minor aspect of human induced climate change. Climatologists forecast that ozone depletion, combined with the greenhouse gas effect, will have a dramatic negative impact on the habitability of many now heavily populated regions. In addition to increasingly powerful storms, this forecast includes sea level rise and significant urban coastal zone inundation.

The idea of intentionally restricting technological innovation is anathema to the leaders of the industrial-consumer economy. Such a suggestion is met with the objection; "How could we have arrived at our present level of development had innovation been restricted?" This focuses the problem precisely. We need to look long and hard at what we call our "present level of development." Is it the inevitable outcome of a fate the human species is bound to play out? Or is it only one of a number of developmental scenarios that human settlement and economy might have followed, and might still follow? Given the high-risk, catastrophe prone situation of hyper-industrialism, should the present course of development be considered a deviant evolutionary flash, a spectacular dead end? The logic of development that is carrying the human world further and further into ecological maladaptation is strong evidence we are on a trajectory that will end badly. I am reluctant to be alarmist, but it seems to me alarm is not an inappropriate reaction, given the circumstances.* I am simply calling attention to the mistake of equating "human development" with the high-energy industrial-consumer economy.

---

*Since this was written another potentially dire consequence of high-tech fragility has become well documented. Coronal mass ejections (CME), otherwise know as solar flares, have the potential to knock out interconnected continental electricity transmissions systems. If a direct CME hit started a cascading failure of the North American grid, a catastrophe of unmanageable proportions would result. Thousands of transformers would be destroyed. Transformers are no longer manufactured on the North American continent. The current backorder time on transformers is 18 months to 3 years; and this is for the normal rate of replacement. Energy supplies, the food system, transportation, and communications would come to a standstill with no prospect of being brought back up within a timeframe that would forestall catastrophic economic and societal breakdown. This is the high-risk situation in which high-tech civilization now exists.

Technological Discrimination
and the Social Economy

Fortunately, there is another scenario of human development, another tradition of settlement and economy, another type of socio-economic organization, another kind of culture that may be regarded as a core strategy for ecologically sound adaptation. This kind of development appears in myriad permutations around the world, forming a highly variegated, yet deeply consistent, response to the quest for human security, dignity, and wellbeing. This core cultural tradition is known by various names: indigenous, vernacular, communitarian, subsistence, village, and tribal. The forms of settlement and economy that make up this cultural tradition are all centered in the human community's relationship with the Earth. This heritage is the foundation of human settlement, economy, and community. The quest for ecologically sound adaptation is now being built on a continuation, modification, and refinement of this tradition.

Much could be said in this connection about the judicious combination of old and new technologies, of traditional and emerging knowledge, and of the technical skills that can now be applied to the building of sustainable societies and economies. I would like here, however, to stress a slightly different point. I would like to open up the idea of having a tool kit that includes the knowledge of plants and animals, the skills of husbandry, household provisioning, art and craft work, shelter design and construction, a knack for games, story telling, poetry, music making, singing, meditation, dancing, modes of worship and celebration, methods of gift exchange, and mutual support. All these "soft tools" and activities of ecological and social integration are as important to human survival, and to human flourishing, as the "hard tools" needed to produce essential goods and services.

We need to re-establish the primacy of the social dimension. The good life does not depend so much on the correct arrangements of our technologies as on social arrangements that foster cooperation, mutual support and sharing. Although the relationship between social ecology and technology is not exactly sequential, there does seem to be a condition of primacy that obtains. The emphasis in indigenous Earth-based cultures is always on the social dimension. Right relationships are more important than technology. Even the best tools will function badly in a disordered society.

Social ecology is the key to environmental adaptation. Land-based, community-centered, self-provisioning, societies that enjoy a high degree of cooperative social and economic activity, do not contribute much, or at all, to the growth of the industrial-consumer economy. This strength of highly self-reliant societies is what the corporate leaders of the trans-national industrial-consumer economy call "backwardness." They stigmatize this strength of the social economy and seek to disable it in their quest for ever-larger markets for their products and services. This drive to universalize the market-driven industrial-consumer economy is the heart of the matter with respect to the mindset of technological inevitability.

Prior to the 18th century, economic activity was in no way separable from the structure of society. Economic activity was conducted within the governing patterns and norms of social life in such a way as to reinforce the integrity of societal functioning. At the end of the 18th century a new conception and practice of economic activity emerged in Western Europe. It had been developing slowly for over two hundred years, but only with the beginning of the factory system did it crystalize into a strikingly systematic strategy for the production of wealth. Those engaging in this new type of economic activity began to gauge their decisions and behaviour more and more in response to the governance of market calculations that maximize profits in the interests of wealth accumulation.

The rise of this market economy, as distinct from the social economy, shattered traditional settlement and livelihood patterns. Human energy became organized as a commodity to be bought and sold. Value became increasingly mediated by exchange in the market through the instruments of the monetary system. A new, one dimensional concept of human identity as an economic unit of production and consumption eclipsed the complex patterns of obligation, responsibility, and regard in which members of traditional, land-based, self-provisioning communities grounded their self-knowledge and identity.

The market economy, riding on a rapidly developing industrial technology, was hailed by its advocates as a new discovery in natural philosophy, a new science, a new natural law unfolding straight from the evolutionary process of the Universe. To resist its spreading hegemony was not only bad for profits and the accumulation of wealth, but was also seen as a defect in mental acuity and moral character. Thus, in the late 18th and early 19th centuries in England, Ned Ludd and his compatriots were vilified and crushed with a logic that has made his name a catchword for doltish backwardness to this day. Those who question any application of high-energy technology are now called Luddites and that is supposed to be the end of the matter. But like most forms of stigmatic labelling, this one is also based on error. Ned Ludd and his compatriots were not anti-technology; in fact, they were pro-technology. They were out to protect a particular technology and a specific organization of economic activity – the handloom and the cottage industry system. When they rebelled against the factory system and smashed the power looms in the Lancashire mills, it was the calculated strategy of independent entrepreneurs who owned their technology and controlled their working conditions, and did not want to loose their livelihood and be driven out of business. They were determined to protect a technology that had a strongly integrating role in a highly valued settlement and livelihood arrangement.

They, of course, lost the struggle and the factory system, with its high-energy technology and market logic, rolled the social economy, in this case, into the ditch of history. But the story of this contest does not end with this incident. The social economy did not disappear, and it has not disappeared to this present day. It was marginalized and went underground, but it has continued to serve many of the world's communities even though the market-driven industrial-consumer economy has been relentless in its effort to continually expand, and, in expanding, bring as much economic activity under its control as possible.

Viewed from the late 20th century, I think it is reasonable to say that the tables are turning with regard to the future of the high-energy industrial-consumer economy. There is growing evidence that the community-based, social economy is set to make a comeback. Unlimited hyper-industrialism is now running up against the ecological limits of the planet. Considerably more wreckage may accumulate before it becomes obvious that this kind of economic system is wildly incongruent with the way Earth's ecosystems actually work. What is clear, is that the myth of inevitability around this kind of economy and its technology is now being revealed as a tissue of unsupportable dreams. Perhaps, if we are lucky, we will live to see the day when to be a Luddite will mean to protect ecologically sound technologies and ways of life and livelihood. If so, the harness of technological inevitability may come to be regarded as a curious mental illness in the history of human intelligence.

The monolith of industrial-consumer technology that once appeared so solid, so progressive, so inevitable, is now riddled with fracture lines. And it is within this fracturing of technological inevitability that the movement of individual citizens, households, neighbourhoods, businesses, civic and cultural institutions, municipalities, and whole regions can pick up their tool kits and begin doing the spadework of ecologically sound readaptation. This is a path that holds security, dignity, and social wellbeing at the center of its focus.

The Evolution of
Environmental Education

Morris Mitchell and the Early Years of
Friends World College, 1965-1970

Based on a presentation made to Friends Association for Higher Education, June 15, 1991, Wilmington College, Wilmington, Ohio.

The desire to write an account of the early years of Friends World College has been with me a long time. When I received the call for papers issued by Friends Association for Higher Education for this conference, I thought, ah ha, the time has come. I submitted a proposal, it was accepted, and here I am. I am indeed grateful for the opportunity this occasion has afforded me to tell this story.

What I am presenting is in the nature of a memoir; an account written straight out of memory, drawing only on such documents as I have on file in my library from the time I was with the College. A number of persons with whom we shared those extraordinary years would also be in a position to tell this story. As far as I know, none of them has yet done so.

At the 20th anniversary reunion in 1985, I spoke with Richard Lannoy, a former colleague, about a writing and editing project documenting the early years of Friends World College. We talked about a two-volume work. The first volume we saw as a detailed narrative, with contributions by a number of participants. Volume two we saw as a selection from student journals, illustrating the kind of learning that takes place in this kind of educational program. Unfortunately, after the reunion Richard returned to England and I to Canada and no further work was done between us on the idea. Perhaps this paper will renew the idea and set a process in motion toward a more complete telling of the College's pioneering story.*

* * *

In 1964 Morris Mitchell was ready for retirement. He was nearly seventy years old and had been the president of the Putney Graduate School of Teacher Education for the past fifteen years. He had had a long and creative career as a teacher and educational innovator and was anticipating living and working full time on his rural property in Georgia. Dr. Mitchell's attitude toward the concept of retirement was the same as his attitude toward the idea of a vacation. He didn't hold with such notions. He said all that was needed was a creative change of pace.

As he was preparing to leave the green hills of Vermont for the piney woods of Georgia, Morris Mitchell was offered both a change of pace and a creative challenge he could not turn down. The change of pace was toward increased intensity and the challenge was to translate his seasoned concept of education and the learning process into a cross-cultural, world encompassing context.

*Work began in 2014 under the leadership of Susie Daniels to organize and research the archive of student journals with a view to initiating a publishing project that would document the extraordinary learning that was fostered and nurtured by the Friends World College experience. Susie Daniels, a student from the early years of FWC, is composing a network of former students who are interested in helping with this project. The project has the support of Global College of Long Island University where the archive is now held.

The challenge was also to his ability as a visionary humanitarian and as an inspiring leader of an administrative and academic team. He was offered the directorship of Friends World Institute.

In the late 1950's, members New York Yearly Meeting of the Religious Society of Friends (Quakers), led by Dr. George Nicklin, had a growing concern for a college level educational program that would be truly international in scope, bringing students from many regions of the world into a living and learning relationship; a program in which the social context of the college itself, in addition to the curriculum, would become a significant context of learning. A Committee on a Friends World College was established for launching the project. (If a Quaker had written Ecclesiastes it would surely say, "Of the making of books *and committees* there is no end.")

My earliest recollection of this project was reading material that had been sent to the Iowa City Friends Meeting in the early 1960's soliciting financial support. I remember being struck by the visionary quality of the proposal and thinking, "Here is an example of Quakers at their best!" Little did I realize that a few years later I would become immersed, along with my wife, Ellen, and our two young sons, in the struggles, satisfactions, and celebrations of the College's opening years.

By 1963 the Committee on a Friends World College had gathered enough dedicated volunteers and financial resources to begin making concrete plans toward the realization of its vision. The Committee had become increasingly successful in developing a wide-ranging support base. As with many Quaker projects, support from people who were not members of the Society of Friends became critically important. Among contributions received was a small estate property on Long Island donated by Henry Ittleson. This property, called Harrow Hill, provided the facilities for an administrative base and became the setting for a pilot project in the summer of 1963. Under the name of Friends World Institute, an international, cross cultural mix of students were assembled at Harrow Hill and, directed by Harold Taylor, became an experiment in world oriented education. (Harold Taylor published an account of this project in the November 14, 1964 issue of The Saturday Review under the title, "The Idea of A World University.")

Having taken this first experimental step, the Committee now took direct aim at its goal. This is where Morris Mitchell comes in. The Committee approached him with the opportunity to establish Friends World Institute on a full program basis. (In New York State the word "college" cannot be legally used until a program satisfies certain specific requirements of the State Board of Regents.) Morris Mitchell rose with alacrity to this challenge. He was later fond of saying that on his journey from Vermont to Georgia he was waylaid on Long Island. Actually he came to see the development of Friends World Institute and the acquisition of a college charter from the State of New York for a radically experimental educational program, under the auspices of Quakers, as a fitting capstone to his career. And, indeed it was.

Morris Mitchell, as an educator, was never off-duty. He had a disposition that utilized every circumstance in which he and his students found themselves as an opportunity for learning. Indeed, Morris Mitchell deliberately cultivated a pedagogic routine in which the range of learning opened to his students would be as broad and deep and practical as the multi-faceted panorama of real life. John Dewey was his mentor and he recommended the study and assimilation of Dewey's book, *Experience and Education*, the way an evangelist recommends the Gospels.

Morris Mitchell was deeply convinced, along with John Dewey, that real education, the best and most vital learning, was based on direct experience – first hand, intimate involvement in the circumstances of life and work. He saw this approach to education as a natural corollary to Quaker spirituality. His commitment to the Society of Friends was strongly rooted in a shared passion for justice, the vision of a world free from hunger and oppression, and both economic exploitation and war made unacceptable and obsolete by a rising tide of cooperative and mutually beneficial relationships between the peoples of the world; and for the realization of this vision, Morris Mitchell had a strategy. Working under all these problems, like a comprehensive antidote, he saw a process of learning based on experience which, slowly but surely, can move rational humanitarian cooperation into the forefront of world problem solving.

When the Committee on a Friends World College, with its own well developed vision and sense of mission, hired Morris Mitchell to direct Friends World Institute, two streams of commitment to human betterment, both uniquely Quaker and both uniquely world oriented, came together in catalytic fusion. The Committee had envisioned a college experimentally oriented from a cultural point of view. The hiring of Morris Mitchell introduced an experiential pedagogic technique that quite literally turned the programmatic element of the College inside out. He proposed that rather than bringing students and faculty from around the world to a North American campus, the College open centers in all the major cultural regions of the world; that indigenous faculty be hired; that students be admitted into the program in their home region and progressively move through periods of study in each of the other centers and, in the course of four years, come to have acquired a true world education; an education based not on studying about world cultures, but based on immersion in world cultures.

The Committee was captivated by the idea. With a single stroke of imagination this 70-year old educator had turned a liberal Quaker education project into a radical educational movement. This was Morris Mitchell's first contribution to the evolution of the College idea; but there was a second stroke to his pedagogic imagination, a stroke even bolder than the first. He proposed a curriculum based on a systematic study of what he called "world problems and their emerging solutions." By this he meant the type and scale of problems that are coming to adversely affect the stability, productivity and social development of human communities and the ecological integrity of all world regions. These various problems have particular expressions, but the growing interconnectedness of world cultures and economies gives even regional problems a global context. Some people, in those days, had difficulty understanding Morris on this point and were puzzled by his tenacious insistence that the real task of education was to honestly and ethically confront these problems and devote our intelligence and energy to their solutions. Others were galvanized into enthusiastic response by a vision that redeemed education from personal ambition, careerism, and nationalistic aggrandizement.

Morris Mitchell had been a professional educator for a long time and had come to some very definite conclusions about relevance and irrelevance in education. His sense of impending world crisis was so acute and his conviction that education must be turned toward preventing social, economic and ecologic breakdown so strong, that his point of view quickly became the ethos of the College project. Morris Mitchell did not devalue the traditional categories of knowledge. He was deeply committed to mastery in all the arts and sciences of human endeavour and welfare. He simply insisted they are learned best when students become engaged with real problems in the real world, when they become motivated by ethical commitment to human betterment and when they see the need for acquiring skills and mastering a discipline that equips them to be effective problem solvers. He encouraged students to see themselves as "agents of social change" – a phrase that would come back to haunt us all, as we shall see.

Morris Mitchell identified the critical world problems as including racism, poverty, environmental degradation, political and social oppression, economic injustice and war. He posited the emergence of countervailing spiritual, social, economic, political and technical forces that, in combination, can work toward the elimination of these world problems. He believed in the unfolding of these positive, creative social forces, based on the metaphor of a maturing humanity. He was not naive about the difficulty of what he proposed or about the timetable likely to be required, and he feared that nuclear war could totally subvert this creative movement. But, in his view, the rational, ethical response to our collective situation was to pitch in, full tilt, on the side of the creative social forces. This he urged students and faculty to do and this is the stance that shaped the founding of Friends World College.

Morris Mitchell identified the emerging, world level, creative social forces as including the following.

- World Government
- Universal Suffrage
- Racial Equality
- Social Planning
- Regional Development
- Producer and Consumer Cooperatives
- Democratic Socialism
- Intentional Community
- World Education

Morris saw this list as open ended and he challenged students to identify additional movements for inclusion. You will note this list is a mix of the highly abstract and the highly specific. This integration of grand vision with concrete commitments was characteristic of Morris Mitchell. He had a seemingly endless supply of stories with which to illustrate his points and that served to charmingly ground his lofty vision. You will also see that he did not shrink from including his own particular focus in the list of world level, creative social forces. World education came to be for Morris Mitchell a summing up of his life's work. He was a Southerner who had worked for racial equality long before it became a movement. He helped found community schools in the rural south where the first item on the curriculum for both students and teachers was to build a schoolhouse. The second item was to figure out what kind of self-help projects could be undertaken by the school that would benefit the whole community. Morris's schools became catalysts for upgrading both self-esteem and living standards. Learning to read, do math, understanding history, economics and basic science developed directly out of community building projects.

Morris Mitchell had worked on the Tennessee Valley Authority project and never lost his faith in comprehensive social and technical planning. He had been a teacher of students at all levels from grade school through graduate school. One time when he was without a job he went to Teacher's College, at Columbia University, seeking employment. Though he was eminently qualified they told him they had neither the financial resources nor any available classroom for additional faculty. Morris asked them if it would be all right for him to use an out of the way space in the corridor and do a little volunteer teaching. Permission was granted. Morris posted notices of his course offering and set up shop. At first a few curious students came and then many more. The course outgrew its space and was a huge success. As a result, Morris Mitchell was given a classroom and hired. As you can see, this was a man who truly knew how to do "environmental education". (I am here giving the term "environmental education" an expanded usage, to which I will return,)

For Morris Mitchell, World Education was more than just another creative concept. He saw it as an engine of creative social change, identifying, propagating, and even inventing the new concepts and movements with which to construct the future. The following quotations are taken from his 1967 book, *World Education: Revolutionary Concept.*

> *If one of these emerging concepts is more basic and important than the others, it could be this one of World Education. For through education that has made of itself a reverent search for universal truth appropriate to our age, mankind could creatively join with such impulses as these which shape destiny and hasten the progress that has been so needlessly tortuous. Then, with love, we could begin to mend the scars man has inflicted on Mother Earth, abandon war, advance knowledge, abolish poverty, provide for the sick, lengthen life, and prepare for the creative enjoyment of leisure. This is the direction of the emerging concept, the revolutionary concept of World Education. World Education must find a new focus for these critical times, which will integrate certain historical values we cherish with new theories of reality and knowledge.*
>
> *More specifically, World Education must bring into a single focus two great currents of human understanding; that ancient one which interprets reality by sense*

perception, and the new, sometimes contradictory, interpretation of reality as revealed by scientific investigation. If we tolerate the compartmentalization of the traditional and the new understanding of reality, science will remain amoral, its destructive potentialities a threat, and religion and education will continue to be ineffective.

That is the central challenge. With our new understandings and the powers of science to create and destroy, can we modernize our ancient preconceptions based on faulty sense perception? Can we embrace, before we destroy ourselves, the actuality of an existence of such incredible complexity and magnificence as to make childish the myths of our bibles and our tribal histories? Can we still nurture the impulses of respect, sympathy, and love that were inherent binding forces in tribal structure and yet deliberately outgrow the counterbalancing hostilities toward other tribes? Can we accept the reality that we are all of one family and all interdependent as, at once microscopic and macroscopic, we cling perilously to our incredibly complex globe?

We must accept a revolutionary change of attitude toward the nature and function of the educational process. For in content, too, we must outgrow the now universal, provincial pattern which employs education as a tool to transmit tribal beliefs, tribal attitudes, tribal structures, tribal skills, tribal habits, and tribal knowledge. Education must undertake a loftier-purpose, an aim of new qualities, new dimensions. It must become for now a tool of human survival, and that assured, must assume as its ultimate goal individual and social growth, based on reverence for life, as an end in itself. Then education on a world scale will be the social counterpart of the creative forces that shape our destinies. Then we shall have achieved Plato's dictum that education is "process not product." Indeed, man may find such education the means of so identifying with the progressive evolution of his environment as to share, through his inherent creative ability, in the primal processes of change. Education, in an almost new sense, must bring us into greater identity with the complex, systematic beauty of the universe, our world, ourselves. With new found ecological and anthropological perspective, man – creature of environment that he is – may approach the longed-for freedom of will by deliberately changing his environment in order to direct universal human betterment. This would call for the discovery, for each time period, of universally applicable concepts by which a creative cycle might come to replace the past, downward spiral of destructive exploitation leading to further destruction. Already there are inklings of this prospect. Let us call this new form World Education and seek to describe it.

Just prior to joining the faculty of Friends World Institute, I spent some time helping Morris Mitchell prepare his book, *World Education*. During this time I was also studying the works of Lewis Mumford. In reading Mumford's book, *The Conduct of Life*, I discovered a passage that electrified me. I took it to my next meeting with Morris and his response was equally enthusiastic. "That's it," he said. "That is really the potential of what we are doing." Mumford, writing during World War Two, was looking to the future and called for a new service/education program for youth. He writes:

*Once war armies are disbanded, peace armies, on a far
larger scale must be formed. Every young man and
woman, at the age of eighteen or thereabouts, should
serve perhaps six months in a public works corps. In his
own region he will get training and active service, doing
a thousand things that need to be done, from planting
forests and roadside strips, supervision of school children
in nurseries and playgrounds to the active companionship
with the aged, the blind, the crippled, from auxiliary work
in harvesting to fire-fighting.*

*Unlike military service, these forms of public work will be
carried out with the educational requirements uppermost;
... every effort should be made, for the sake of education, to
take the student out of his home environment for a period,
introducing him to other regions and other modes of life.
Those who show special interest and aptitude should be
given the opportunity to perform similar service in an
international corps in order to become active participants
in the working life and culture of other countries. In time,
these planetary student migrations will, let us hope, take
place on an immense scale ... with teachers to lead them.
The result of such transmigrations would be to enrich
every homeland with mature young men and women,
who knew the ways and farings of other men, who
would bring back treasures with them, songs and dances,
technical processes and civic customs, not least, ethical
precepts and religious insights, knowledge not taken at
third hand from books, but through direct contact and
living experience: thus, the young would bring back into
every village and city a touch of the universal society of
which they form an active part.*

*Such people would be ready for further study, further
travel, further research, for further tasks and adventures
... They would no longer live in their present parochial
world:...in time, their studies, their civic responsibilities,
and their vocational interests will be united in a new kind
of education;...The comradeship and understanding of
such a world fellowship of the young, based on common
experience and common purposes...would turn world
cooperation into a working reality; and in time create
a true world community. Such a course of education in
world citizenship...not by books and constitutions and
laws and technical devices alone...will create one world.*

You can see that what we are dealing with in this vision is a
greatly enlarged understanding of "environmental education."

* * *

During the early years of the College, there were two people on
whom Morris Mitchell particularly relied for administrative and
program support – Reny Hill and Arthur Meyer. Though it would be
uncharacteristic of the community ethos of Friends World College
to attribute its survival to a single person, I think there is no doubt
that Reny Hill would be unanimously declared the "key player" in
the equation. During those early and tumultuous years, she literally
held the College together and on course. No words are adequate
to describe her commitment and hard work; work always done in
such an easy going manner that it was a joy to consult with her
on development or program, the details of which she invariably
had a command. Reny Hill was listed as the Assistant Director
of Friends World Institute and later as Vice President of Friends
World College, but Morris Mitchell used to say that he, as Director

and then as President, was just a papier-mâché mask; pull it to one side, he said, and there would be Reny Hill.

Arthur Meyer, who earlier had done graduate study in education under Morris Mitchell, was the first Director of the North American Center of Friends World Institute. With unflagging energy and almost unbelievable patience and good will, Arthur Meyer piloted the early student groups through some amazing adventures and some stormy seas. After five years at that post, Arthur became Director of Admissions for the College and has only just retired (1991). He has been the longest serving staff in the College's history and became the continuing link with the inspiration of Morris Mitchell and the original New York Yearly Meeting Committee.

In the mid-1960s, ecologists were already sounding a warning that pollution was more than an inconvenience. Rachel Carson had rung her great bell of warning into an increasing silent sky. Murray Bookchin had already written his classic essay, "Ecology and Revolutionary Thought." A significant and growing number of young people knew in their bones that the American Dream was turning into – in the memorable phrase of Henry Miller – an "air conditioned nightmare." Not only were consumer values ripping up the ecosystem, they offered only a bizarrely superficial sense of identity and no moral or ethical guidance at all. The Civil Rights Movement was spreading from the South into the North and the war in Viet Nam was ominously and sickeningly enlarging. There was despair and rage in the streets. Ghetto uprisings turned into fiery riots in many US cities. Student demonstrations were bringing prestigious universities to a dead halt. This was the mid-60s; what a time to start a college!

As it turned out, it was probably the perfect time to start a college like Friends World. Morris Mitchell was fond of quoting

George Fox's injunction: "Ye have no time but this Present," (Fox was the founder of the Quaker movement in 17th century England.) And so, though many details of start up were yet unsettled, the decision was taken to open Friends World Institute in the fall of 1965. The site that became available was the abandoned officers' quarters of the old Mitchel Air Force Base, Westbury, Long Island. The stories from those early years are so numerous and so interesting it is tempting to digress. I will allow myself two, which, in fact, reinforce my theme of an expanded concept of environmental education.

The students and faculty were on a study trip in the southern states when civil rights worker James Meredith was shot. Ruby Magee, a faculty member and close friend of Meredith, hurried to him. The students resolved to follow and join the march of protest and solidarity being organized. Morris agreed to extend College support to this event and walked with the students, on his seventy-first birthday, the 18 miles to Canton, Mississippi. The day's march concluded with a rally that was brutally set upon by police releasing tear gas and indiscriminately clubbing participants. Several students and faculty were among the injured. As they regrouped Morris told the students, "This is a college for experience, not war" and he proposed they now return to Selma, Alabama and continue the study trip as previously planned. Not one student or faculty agreed. They were determined to see the march through and were prepared to take the consequences of their action. Morris commended them and declared the school temporarily closed so they could proceed on their own responsibility. The group continued with the march on Jackson. We have here a case of environmental education stretched to the limits of institutional accommodation, and beyond.

The second story comes from the end of those early years and looks north. Tom Findley joined the faculty of Friends World

College in the fall of 1968. He was a chemist who for some years had been the head of a research division of Swift and Company in Chicago, but who now was aiming at a life of service and simplicity. The value of his service to the College was immediately apparent. He brought a manner of calm deliberation and thoughtful rationality. His judgments were balanced and his advice clarifying. His approach to the simplification of life was direct and non-doctrinaire. When the car that had brought him to Long Island broke down soon after his arrival, it remained un-repaired and that was the end of automobile ownership for Tom Findley.

Tom Findley was an experienced canoeist and added environmental expeditions via this mode of transportation to the College's North American study-travel options. He had a keen interest in water quality and with his water test kit and expertise as a chemist, brought a research ethic to his canoe trips. In addition, Tom took full pedagogic advantage of the fact that traveling by canoe, like walking or cycling, puts one in direct contact and immediate rapport with the natural and cultural environment. Tom Findley's taste for learning, like the college, had a world context. He had been thinking globally for some time and had acquired an impressive collection of topographic maps which, when laid out, revealed the continental waterways which could be used to canoe around the world. Tom was low-key about this idea, but eager to discuss it and answer questions. Gradually, a number of students attached themselves to the first phase of this project – traveling from Long Island Sound into the Hudson River and then north by northwest to the Bering Strait.

This was not just an elaborate camping trip. Under Tom's guidance the opportunities for learning that this project offered were maximized. The problem solving method of learning was taken seriously and began with the building of canoes. A shipyard

facility on the North Shore of Long Island was made available
to the College. The project crew set up shop, designed and built
the needed forms and produced six expedition quality fiberglass
canoes. With a major learning component in design engineering
and fabrication behind them, the group launched the canoes from
the shipyard into Long Island Sound and began paddling toward
Manhattan and the Hudson River. I asked Tom what happens
when you reach the Bering Strait and the Soviet Union lay a
few miles beyond. Tom is an intensely practical person and he
simply said he didn't know if they could get permission to enter
the Soviet Union, but, if they had any chance at all, their mode of
transportation would probably be a point in their favour. That was
a distant problem. The work and learning that lay before them as
they moved through the cultural and ecologic regions of North
America – English, French, Cree and Inuit; urban, agricultural,
forest and tundra – was all that need concern them now.

The expedition moved through successive seasons and soon
moved beyond the scope of the College. Some students departed
to take up other avenues of learning or other ventures. Others
returned with Tom each spring to continue from the point they
had hauled out the previous fall. A core group carried on, settling
ever more deeply into the knowledge, skills and habits of direct
engagement with primary environmental process; the world of
photosynthesis, metabolism and mutual interdependence. Several
members of the expedition, including Tom Findley, were eventually
claimed by the land and culture of the North and have remained
more-or-less settled residents. Tom did make it to the Bering Sea
but instead of pushing on into other continental waterways, has
retired with his canoes and extensive journals to a northern Ontario
homestead. Solar energy collectors now power his computer but
his canoes are still powered by metabolism and imagination.

I have told these two stories because, though sharply contrasting, they both illustrate a dynamic of human association that has made Friends World College something more than an educational institution. It has been something like a small society, a small group culture in which shared experience creates bonding. It has been like a refiner's fire, producing elemental relationships, relationships that in some cases have endured and in many cases retain in memory an extraordinary mystique. I have thought about this a good deal over the years and have brought it to this point in my understanding; *relationships formed in the midst of vital learning resonate deeply in the soul and tend to endure in fact or in memory.*

At the 20th anniversary reunion, Richard Lannoy spoke of "a certain incandescence of spirit" he always finds in the presence of those associated with Friends World College. When I heard this expression, I knew exactly to what it referred; those especially bright moments of relationship that characterize the culture of Friends World. Those who lived through the stories recounted here will know what this means, as will many others whose stories from their days with Friends World are equally vital.

It should be clear by now, that in the experience of Friends World College, environmental education does not mean just studying about ecosystems or life cycles or the effect of a polluting industry. All that was included as sub-text, but the broader context and the approach that made Friends World daringly unique was its commitment to education in the environment as well as about the environment. For students who had rejected the narrow categories of conventional curriculums and the regimentation of bureaucratically administered education, Friends World was a breath of fresh air. For the faculty it was often a complex kind of dance. On the one hand we were free to connect our own expertise with events and actions that facilitated the kind of learning to which we were committed. On the other hand it was also necessary to be a competent advisor to students on areas of learning that developed from their interests and life experiences. And behind all this was the worldview of Morris Mitchell who saw the curriculum totally in terms of world issues, social forces, emerging solutions and problem solving. As this amalgam began to function as a college program, inevitable conflicts appeared and exactly what kind of environmental education Friends World was equipped to offer became an increasingly prominent issue. To this I will return, but first a closer look at the expanded understanding of environmental education.

Joining the faculty the first year and continuing until 1969, Richard Proskauer became a key influence in our definition and practice of environmental learning. Richard was a Harvard educated physicist and engineer and had been a member of the original Committee on a Friends World College. He had had a career in industry with Sperry-Rand that included the development of the oscillating gyroscopic compass that made it possible for submarines to navigate under the Arctic ice cap. His interests and values had changed, but his inventive and creative thinking had not. Richard Proskauer represented Science on our small faculty and for him that meant, most importantly, looking at what was happening to local, regional, and global ecosystems, and enabling students to appreciate the centrality of the environmental crisis to our cultural situation. So he began taking groups of students to a municipal incinerator in order to understand the magnitude of the consumer culture garbage problem. He paid visits to fossil fuel powered electric generating plants spewing a vast tonnage of toxic pollutants into the air and then coupled that with a trip to Levittown, Long Island to view the vast acreage of single family dwellings, all equipped with the same array of electricity consuming appliances. Richard was adept at calling attention to the elements of overlooked relationships and highlighting emerging realities.

Richard Proskauer, like Morris Mitchell, understood the importance of focusing on the emergent. He was fond of citing Descartes's philosophical error that the value of a proposition can be judged by its clarity. Richard's comment was that perfectly clear propositions are simply boring. It is only when a proposition is emerging into clarity that it has compelling interest and, hence, real value for learning. Richard made a habit of being one question ahead of the answer to anything. Complete understanding, he said, was fatal to learning. Things are either unfamiliar or familiar, but the minute we feel we have a complete understanding of something we have thrown up a barrier to further learning.

For Richard Proskauer, the best route to any particular goal was never a straight course. In a way he was the polar opposite of Morris Mitchell. Morris well understood the power of learning directly from experience in the environment, but he always moved from point to point in a direct and focused manner. Deviations annoyed him. He could never quite figure out what Richard was up to. To Morris's credit, however, he recognized pedagogic genius, even when it contrasted sharply with his own and Richard was not subject to the same scrutiny as the rest of the faculty. While he might have a particular field-study goal, Richard was always eager to use any eventuality that arose to the best pedagogic advantage. He was connoisseur of serendipity. He loved deviations and was convinced, that by allowing them, and even following them up, more could often be learned than by sticking to a predetermined plan.

For example, on a study trip to Vermont to learn about woodlot management, Richard's van load of students would arrive at our destination hours after the others with a wealth of improbable tales about a chance encounter with a store keeper who told them about an old mill where they could see apple cider being pressed and where they discovered the mill operator to be an articulate

Goldwater Republican etc., etc.. The other students had traveled in a straight mental line from Long Island to the Vermont woodlot. The students traveling with Richard had been out on a ramble and had already learned a good deal about economics, technology, politics and culture in Vermont. Richard did his best to infect us with his approach to environmental education, and though he may have sometimes thought us slow learners, I think he succeeded better than he realized. A few years later when conducting study trips in East Africa for the College, I would often think of Richard and allow openings in our itinerary that I might have otherwise closed off.

I have several times mentioned study-travel and I would like to indicate more precisely the role of this activity in the Friends World approach to environmental education during the early years. The introduction of this educational strategy grew from Morris Mitchell's conviction that students should have the opportunity for direct learning about the kinds of problems that plague certain peoples and places; but even more importantly, to come into direct contact with places, projects and people where social and economic problems were being addressed and solved.

Thus, for example, the southern study trip mentioned earlier included a visit with Myles Horton at the Highlander Folk School near Knoxville, Tennessee. It included visiting and learning about the reclamation and reforestation of previously strip mined lands and an extensive on site introduction to the history and development of the TVA by both the officials of the agency and by rural residents who could remember the life and hard times before this integrated regional development scheme brought in electricity, industry and jobs.

Morris was keen for students to understand cooperative economic structures and the importance of planned communities.

He included Columbia, Maryland and Reston, Virginia in the study-travel itinerary, both early examples of planned communities after Ebenezer Howard's garden city model. He would introduce the cooperative idea through visits to the impressive consumer coop supermarkets serving these communities. It was here that Morris began to encounter troubling student reactions. Some students said, in effect; "Hey, wait a minute. These are just bedroom communities full of affluent consumers and the coop supermarkets have all the same junk food and over packaged, plasticized products that any profit driven, capitalist store carries. And look at the TVA. It has become dominated by electricity production and has built coal fired generating plants that are fed by rapacious strip mining. And now TVA is going nuclear. Where are the creative, emerging solutions in all this mess? This is all part of the environmental problem."

This reaction saddened Morris. He wanted the students to see the core ideas, the concept, the original vision behind these social innovations and not be put off by what they had become. But students responded by pointing out that what they had become was exactly the crux of the matter. Cooperatives, planned communities, and regional development were all good, liberal, socially progressive ideas but, in the context they were being asked to study, something had obviously gone wrong; and it was in understanding what had gone wrong that the most interesting and relevant learning was to be found. Why was the industrial-consumer mode of adaptation having such a destructive effect on the environment?

Many students who came to Friends World College had already been to other colleges. Some were veteran activists and many of them were intuitive critics of consumer culture. Something was going wrong in our society and it was being felt at a deep level. Many students were on a quest for alternatives to the standard American way of life. They were primed for environmental learning.

They were inspired by Morris Mitchell's vision and charmed by his stories. They readily adopted his innovative immersion-in-the-environment style of learning, but they were coming up with their own conclusions.

Because Morris was so wedded to his core ideas of progressive social change and because students were reacting negatively to his examples, he, at first, came to the conclusion that faculty were insufficiently dynamic in putting across the college's vision of world education. He later came to the conclusion that most students were not sufficiently mature to appreciate the importance of world education's emerging concepts. Indeed, there was some truth in that view. It was often noted that the content of the program and the degree of self-discipline required was more suitable for graduate students than for undergraduates. Many of the students were right out of high school and were full participants in the curriculum of the youth culture of the late Sixties. These were lively, adventurous students and studious self-discipline was often not their strong point.

Despite Morris's disappointment with student readiness for his curriculum, the process of environmental education was really working. The students were simply taking in a different level of information. They were acutely attuned to the dissonance between ideals and reality and were drawing very different conclusions from what he expected. The environmental learning dynamic of Friends World College was beginning to chart its own course. It took several years, and more community meetings than most of us care to remember, to work through and accommodate the emerging student initiative for self-determined programs of study. Students were strongly attracted to environmental based learning, and eager to utilize the guidance and expertise of faculty, but they had interests and concerns that outran the pre-set College program.

For the first two years the learning program was based mainly on group activities with opportunity for only short-term individual study projects. In part, this was a fiscal consideration since program costs had been initially calculated on the discount rates available from airlines for booking the movement of student groups from one regional center to another. This arrangement soon proved unworkable as students began requesting to stay an extra semester in Kenya or go back to Europe rather than on to India. Environmental education was really taking hold and the learning and work-study priorities of an increasing number of students threatened to disrupt the orderly administration of the program. In hindsight it appears an entirely predictable problem; introduce students to the elixir of direct environmental learning and the directions and patterns of exploration that will inevitably emerge will require an appropriately flexible administrative response.

By the fall of 1967 the demands of students abroad, and the expectations of students arriving at the North American Center, were such that a medium level crisis was recognized by all. Morris agreed it was time for a little environmental learning on his part about the nature of students in the late Sixties. He understood that many students came with their own personal agendas that often included questions of identity, self-esteem, anger, and alienation. Added to all this, was the sickening expansion of the war in Viet Nam and the increasingly clear evidence that the American political establishment was quite prepared to violently suppress all demands for a significant change in policy. We were caught up in a social maelstrom, the full complexity and personal impact of which was hard to handle.

In my memory, a turning point came when, in one of the many community meetings devoted to the question of program structure and process, a student, Roger Mann, said to Morris; "Morris, you believe in economic democracy, why don't you believe in educational democracy?" For some of us who knew Morris well it seemed a cruel and unfair question. But in this case it reflected exactly the position Morris had assumed with regard to accommodating student initiatives for program modification. Morris was a calm and deliberate speaker and it was rare for him not to have a ready reply or comment. But in this situation, he just looked at Roger for what seemed like a long time and then made a half humorous diversionary remark. It didn't work. Roger's question was still in the air and became central to the subsequent unfolding of the College program.

Another aspect of Morris's own commitment came to work against his view of how the College should proceed. From the outset, in his writing about the College and in his talking with students and faculty, Morris used the language of community. He spoke of the whole College being a community of learners and actively promoted the Quaker method of considering issues and reaching decisions. Mutual respect and the inclusion of everyone, including the service staff, in decision-making gave the College a genuine sense of community process. When the conflict over the preset curriculum and the predetermined times of student movement came into sharp focus, the language of community, mutual respect, and consensus decision-making gave the students requests a framework of legitimacy that could not be denied. Documents of analysis and recommendation were drawn up. The problem solving techniques that students had been studying were now applied. Students from Europe and Africa sent impassioned requests for recognizing the validity of their self-determined programs. Students in Mexico and India were requesting changes in travel plans.

In the late fall of 1967 a general College meeting was called. Both the Board of Trustees and the New York Yearly Meeting Board of Overseers were requested to join all of us resident at the North American Center in an effort to understand what was happening to the College and to help decide what could be done to accommodate the increasing complexity of demands. One thing was clear, there was no lack of commitment. Everybody involved really cared. Students who had dropped out in frustration offered their perspective and even came back to campus to help out in the on going deliberations.

Three significant developments flowed from the general College meeting: 1) a new member of the Board of Trustees, Sidney Harman, emerged as a mediating influence; 2) a Central Coordinating Committee (CCC) was appointed with representation from all levels of the College community; the CCC was mandated to carry on the discussion about restructuring the program and make recommendations to that effect; 3) a "world conference" was scheduled for summer 1968, bringing together students and faculty representatives from all regional centers for a general evaluation and revisioning of the College programs.

Sidney Harman played a key role in the work of the Central Coordinating Committee. Our chief accomplishment was to work out the details of an independent study component for the College program and establish the Independent Program Committee. The Independent Program Committee established a system of proposal review, counselling, monitoring and evaluation that satisfied all concerned. A workable path had been found. Morris was apprehensive that if we once allowed independent study programs the College would fly apart and the unique orientation of world education, as he saw it, would be lost. No one wanted to see that happen. The CCC and the World Conference of 1968 both strongly confirmed Morris's vision of world education.

The change was simply – or perhaps one should say "complexly" – to enlarge the scope of environmental learning according to student interests and expand the time available for study in any given region. As it eventually turned out, most students came to develop deep attachments and on going interests in a particular region. Recognizing that this pattern was conducive to a better quality of learning, the requirements for graduation were modified from spending a semester in all six regional programs, to becoming deeply engaged with at least two cultural regions other than one's own.

The other change that flowed from the introduction of the Independent Study Program option was a surge of interest in culture as such and in music, dance, drama, poetry, arts and the crafts of culture. Many students were deeply interested in the religions and philosophies of other cultures. Again, in hindsight it seems obvious that an educational program that puts on its boots, rolls up its sleeves and walks right out into the great world environment will be stimulated by more than just the socio-economic realities of the planet.

In 1969, Morris Mitchell retired as president of Friends World College but continued, as Provost, to be active in the administration of the College. Sidney Harman became the new president.*

* Sidney Harman was the founder and CEO of the Harman Kardon Corporation, an innovator and manufacturer of high fidelity sound systems. He was also a man deeply committed to social justice. When Prince Edward County, Virginia closed its public school system rather than comply with the Supreme Court desegregation order, Sidney Harman flew his plane from Long Island several times a week to help teach in the schools that the African American community had put together for their children. Sidney was drawn to Friends World College, in part, because the learning environment included the governance culture of the Quaker tradition. He recognized that the Quaker practice of consensus decision-making had profound implications for human social development. Sidney Harman later pioneered the introduction of the "worker circle" management techniques in his US manufacturing plants. During the Carter administration, he was appointed to the position of Under Secretary of Labor. He also founded the Harman Family Foundation which is devoted to supporting performing arts and art education programs in the culturally under served areas of East Coast inner city regions.

Following on the successful work of the Independent Program Committee, he introduced further structural changes in this direction. Again, part of the rationale was fiscal, but this time from a different view. Group programs were becoming increasingly expensive. Emphasizing independent study programs made it possible to shift expenses that had originally been paid by the College, like travel and room and board, to the students.

Through the early 1970s this program direction became established as the pattern of the College and has continued to serve the varied interests of students. A common orientation is still part of each regional center's responsibility and group seminars are regularly provided. But a student now traveling through Friends World College is predominantly engaged in designing and carrying out his or her own learning program. Programs may include time spent auditing classes in economics at a university in India, working with abandoned children in Central America, working with a wildlife ecology research team in Kenya, helping to build a school in South Africa, studying the desalination of sea water in the Middle East, living and working with the nomadic peoples of northern Scandinavia, teaching English in China, and studying Japanese language and drama in Kyoto. The list goes on and on in fascinating variety and the stories of student adventures and their subsequent career paths are equally diverse and equally fascinating.

*   *   *

I should not leave you with the impression that the early years of Friends World College were all a glorious struggle. There were disasters stemming from a lack of cultural sensitivity. When Morris Mitchell encouraged students to think of themselves as agents of social change, he neglected to say, but only in your home culture.

Young men with shoulder length hair and young women in jeans promoting radical social values was not a recipe for good cross-cultural experience in many parts of the world. Some students of that era were on a pendulum swing away from being conventional in appearance and behaviour. When Morris Mitchell told students to "treat the world as your campus" it meant one thing in his mind, but often something different in student response. North American and European youth culture of the Sixties did not translate well in other cultural regions and some students did not succeed in making the adaptations required for the kind of learning that Morris and the College had clearly in mind.

An aspect of this situation was, of course, drug use. Morris could not fathom why students who were interested in understanding world problems and in becoming agents of creative social change would be interested in drug experiences. But this was the late Sixties; the North American Center was 20 miles from the East Village in Manhattan. Students were traveling to Mexico, London, Amsterdam, Africa, India and Nepal. The world of youth was awash with exotic substances. One observer tagged Friends World as "a traveling psychedelicatessen". That was unfair to the College as a whole, but it was characteristic of a segment of students at this time.

The fact that Friends World advertised itself as a place for experiential learning put it in a curious position with regard to drug use. The program attracted some adventurous individuals who stretched the idea of experiential learning and of being an agent of social change to cover the use of drugs. The use of psychoactive substances was not within the experiential learning purview of the College's educational horizon, but it was hard to completely discount the significant learning that could emerge from this kind of investigation.

Unfortunately, students who failed to accommodate themselves to regions that took a strict view on drug possession occasionally found themselves in serious trouble. Students suffered emotional breakdown in faraway places and had to return home. Students were deported. Administrative ineptness and financial misappropriation at regional centers had to be dealt with. Whole programs had to move. Faculty problems and manipulative behavior by individuals with influence over College programs tested the community's problem solving methods and Quaker conflict resolution skills. In retrospect, it seems quite amazing that through it all the core vision of world education withstood the turmoil of the times. The value of the learning that was being facilitated was no doubt the key factor that kept the College afloat and on course.

This brings me to a chronic weakness of Friends World College. It never succeeded in attracting and incorporating more than a token number of non-North American students. It was simply too expensive and the scholarship money too slight. The original vision of the founding Committee, and continued by Morris Mitchell, of a multicultural student body mutually sensitizing, stimulating, and enriching the learning experience, never came to pass. Professionals from the regional culture have almost always staffed regional centers, and a small number of students from cultural regions other than North America have always been in the program, but the College has remained, mainly, an opportunity for young North Americans from relatively affluent settings. Because this element of cross-cultural learning was often absent from student interaction, intensive orientations to cross-cultural experience and behavior became an added focus of the North American Center program.

During the early years of Friends World College, when the structure and process were being developed and modified, I was in my early 30's. I understood and supported the kinds of

changes that progressively broadened the scope of this new kind
of environmentally-based world education. I had long discussions
with Morris Mitchell about the importance, from a pedagogic point
of view, of students, with the help of faculty advisors, designing
their own learning programs. I was the first Coordinator of the
Independent Study Program. I still believe the direction the College
took was the right one, perhaps the only one possible, considering
the circumstances.

The College has worked well for many students at a personal
and vocational level. But has it worked well as a sustained
catalyst for creative social change? Or has this emphasis become
muted, a memory of the social consciousness of the Sixties? Has
Friends World adapted to the ideology of individualism and
mainstream career building? In part, this seems to be true, but
the cultural mainstream is no longer monolithic. It has bifurcated
and a powerful confluence of ecological, social justice, feminist,
human rights, community organizing, human service, grass roots
democracy, sustainable economics, renewable energy, and local
cultural movements now define an alternative mainstream. It is
not yet dominant but it is seeded in every region of the world in
some form. Many students entering Friends World College became
educated to this confluence of movements for social betterment
and ecological integrity, and found their niche in its unfolding. It
is not exactly what Morris Mitchell had in mind, but it is definitely
in the same tradition. If he were still living, I am sure he would
recognize its continuity with his vision.

Friends World College, like the Society of Friends that founded
it, has had an influence on higher education quite out of proportion
to its size. Friends World College stands as one of the seminal
institutions in an educational revolution. It helped open up a
panoramic concept and practice of learning that has generated

similarly innovative programs across the face of education. More and more colleges and universities are now recognizing the value of international, cross-cultural, experiential education and incorporating this option in their academic programs.

But more than this, Friends World helped alter basic assumptions about relevance and social commitment in education. Morris Mitchell's vision, while rooted in a classic, progressive, liberal worldview, became translated and updated through Friends World College into a ecologically mature understanding of the human-Earth relationship and the dilemma of human adaptation. As Morris insisted, education that does not place itself in the service of advancing both social justice and a mutually enhancing human-Earth relationship is failing to respond to the central challenge of social and ecological integrity, which, in plain language, is now a matter a decent human survival.

There is also a darker side in all this reminiscence. I now realize in a new way that Morris Mitchell was right in his emphasis on understanding the structure of economic activity and social organization. As we all know by now, or should know, human betterment in the long run depends entirely on the preservation of ecosystem integrity. And ecosystem integrity is exactly what the worldwide, high-energy, capital-driven market economy is destroying. The capital-driven, command economies have done even worse. Economics is the key.

I have suggested that Friends World College pioneered a new definition of environmental education, a definition that includes learning from a wide range of experiences in the cultural and natural worlds. For example, some of the learnings of students I happen to know about range from woodlot management to organic gardening to municipal composting systems; from refugee resettlement to literacy work to intergenerational housing design; from sumi-e painting to video production to landscape architecture; from bicycle repair to solar photovoltaics to biogas cookers; from organizing a health information collective to peace tax lobbying to non-violent direct action on ecosystem protection; all this, and much more, accomplished by direct engagement with process and people. But behind and around all this great diversity of opportunity for learning, hangs the question of the economy, the way we adapt to and utilize Earth's ecosystems, and the fact that in the last twenty-five years the destructive impact of economic activity on the integrity of the Ecosphere has vastly intensified.

Nothing any of us has done has appreciably altered this momentum of destruction. All our environmental education of whatever definition or practice has, thus far, been to no avail. The great hope of Morris Mitchell, that education, effectively employed, could become an instrument of human survival and betterment, is far from fulfillment. Perhaps a caveat is in order; at least the arms race of the Cold War is over and survival on that score seems advanced. Degradation of ecological integrity remains an equally ominous sword of Damocles over our heads – or should I say, in our hands.

I am not constitutionally a pessimist and it does not please me to strike this note at the end of an otherwise hopeful and upbeat report. But I think we cannot honestly avoid acknowledging the desperateness of our ecological and, by extension, our economic and social situation. Neither am I a radical in the conventional left-wing sense. But I have, nevertheless, come to the conclusion that our economic system must change, that the capital-driven market economy must be replaced because its innate expansionist dynamic has, apparently, no countervailing mechanism of limitation that will prevent it from driving the planetary ecosystems into collapse.

There is, of course, a control mechanism on human economic activity within the ecosphere. That is what "collapse" means – ecological limitation. It would be nice, and sign of intelligence, if we could manage to put in our own well designed limitations somewhat earlier. The activity of "marketing" is not, in itself, the problem. Markets worked well in human history long before they were seized by capital accumulation and technological aggrandizement. The market process must mature out of its simplistic motivation – the production and accumulation of money, power, and convenience. It must take on a more challenging and complex task – the creation of social value, secure livelihoods, ecosystem integrity and environmental resilience. We need an ecologically determined social economy.

As I have compressed decades of study, environmental education, hands-on work, and business experience into the previous few lines, I had a strong sense of Morris Mitchell's presence. They are not exactly his words, but I think his spirit would be satisfied that we, who shared a few intense years with him, have not abandoned the cause.

In summing up, it can be said that Friends World College was often a life changing experience for students. Having intense contact with a diversity of human cultures affords a kind of learning that nothing else can accomplish. I remember a quiet conversation with a student who had returned to the North American Center to complete the last semester of the four-year program. He told me he was surprised to realize he no longer saw the world from a North American point of view. The effect Morris Mitchell knew was latent in experientially based, world education was working. The Friends World College experience, at its best, was creating a sense of world citizenship. And that, to my mind, is the highest kind of environmental education.

Postscript: 2014

Friends World College continued in operation as an independent institution until 1991 when it became the Friends World Program of Long Island University. It has continued to operate as a division of LIU with pretty much the same experiential, world education design that was established during its early years. I have followed the reports of its operation as an LIU program over the ensuing decades and have been continually pleased to see how durable and rewarding the program remains.

In particular, I have paid attention to the reports of students on their work and on the affects this kind of educational experience has had on them. If the reports of students from the last few decades were undated, I would be unable to distinguish them from those of the students who pioneered the program in its early years. It comes as a great satisfaction to realize that the work done in those early years to set up this kind of educational program, and convince the New York State Board of Regents that what we were doing at Friends World was worthy of being recognized as a legitimate form of higher education, has not only been sustained, but has secured an increasingly valued place at Long Island University. This speaks not only to the design of the program, but to the vision and quality of commitment of the Friends World Program staff at LIU. The program has recently been renamed Global College of LIU but retains clear reference to its Friends World College origins. With its new Director, Jeffrey Belnap, Global College seems to have its sails well set for continuing the model of world education that Morris Mitchell brought to this Quaker initiative.

Addendum

The following quotation is taken from the closing paragraphs of an evaluation report on Friends World College prepared in 1969 by Judson Jerome (Antioch College) for the New York State Board of Regents. (See Bibliography)

> *I have not yet begun to discuss the characteristics of the college which make it one of the most exciting educational institutions in the nation today. The democracy of its governance is a model—as there seems to be a true and complete partnership with students in all decision-making. The vision and philosophy of Morris Mitchell—as well as his delightful presence—are resources I would gladly trade for many a richer college's endowment. Operational evidence of the words of the program is its ability to hold such highly qualified and dedicated staff as well as to attract such bright and able students.*

In the Ruins of a
Faith-Haunted World

Based on an essay published in the Telegraph Journal, Saint John, New Brunswick, April 7, 1997

Seems like I was born a long way from home and I've been trying to get back there ever since.

Bob Dylan from "No Direction Home"

So are some souls like stars / And their words, works and songs / Like strong quick flashes of light.

"Johnny Cash on Bob Dylan" on "Nashville Skyline"

When I heard Bob Dylan was coming to New Brunswick, a panorama of memories began unrolling in my mind, a panorama of both sweeping perspective and luminous detail, a panorama that paralleled the cultural reach and unforgettable images of his landmark music.

Dylan is one of those artists born with a finger on the pulse of his time. He is an artist who feels the social and ecological disasters of the era in his bones but who, nevertheless, remains a witness to faith. He is unsparing in his coverage of greed, duplicity, and violence but, at the same time, he also creates songs that illuminate a generous upwelling of human solidarity flowing in hopeful measure within the social and ecological disintegration of our down-swept times.

Starting long before the cultural earthquake of the late 1960s, the struggle to create a sustaining faith in the face of disaster had become the work of poets and seers throughout the modernizing world. The voice of this tradition took special rise in the work of William Blake who understood that the twinning of industrial technology and commercial greed posed an ominous threat to the order of the soul and the integrity of Earth.

Since Blake's time, many artists and moral philosophers have heroically resisted the objectifying and disintegrative drive of reductionist science and the trivialization of the human-Earth relationship that has attended the invasion of the market economy into every area of human consciousness and decision-making. They have valiantly endeavoured to keep the order of the soul alive, to keep the dream of human solidarity and a vision of Earth's integrity in good working order.

The road has been a hard one. With the shock of two world wars, the gut-punch of the Great Depression, the horrors of the Nazi holocaust and Hiroshima hanging heavily in recent memory, with the normalization of nuclear terror and the mindless consumptive behaviour of a money-driven culture staring us all in the face, Bob Dylan stepped into this great countervailing tradition and took up guitar, harmonica, and voice in defense of the human spirit and the long suffering Earth.

In the cauldron of this struggle, Bob Dylan has given voice to the faith behind faith. He is a witness to that movement of spirit which, in spite of personal loss, failure, and pain, in spite of a culture in absurd self-destruction and denial, and in spite of a mute implacable Cosmos, still rises invincibly in the soul and gives itself, as best it can, overflowing, into the world.

There is a certain temperament of soul that rises in witness for the life of the spirit, rises in lucent expression of human potential, and on the ways of creativity, integrity, and communion. Those who come into the world with this window in the soul flung open often become artists. It may be in poetry and story telling, it may be in song and dance, it may be in colour and design, it may be in sculpted forms, it may be in architecture and construction, it may be in gardening and landscape art, it may be in food preparation and service, it may be in tool making, it may be in human caring and nurturing relationships, it may be in meditations on the Cosmos and the human condition, it may be prayer and worship, but, whatever the path of expression, the work is always recognizable for its aura of integrity and its celebration of communion.

The problem, however, is that so much of what has happened in the modernizing world is highly destructive of integrity, destructive of the *integral* relationships in human community, and in Earth's larger biotic domain. The experience of communion – of social and ecological solidarity – has also withered and become trivialized within the context of industrial-commercial domination. With the virtually total monetization of society and its relationships, the profit-driven bottom line more and more swings the axe and the chips of fragmentation and alienation, lying where they fall, become stifling mulch on the seeds of communion.

As a result of this dilemma, of this progressive blight on the human spirit, artists, like Dylan, have responded with a variety of expressions, expressions that often range from quizzical and sardonic to angry and prophetic. But the mockery, anger, and protest, while necessary, are not the main thing with Dylan. If you look carefully at the lyrics, it is plain to see they are often driven by a vision of something better that might be, something that might be better in personal relationships, in social and political behaviour, and in the way we make use of and care for Earth.

For a poet like Bob Dylan – a poet with a gift for ballad, with a talent for startling juxtapositions of images, and a genius for extraordinary metaphoric compression – the cruelties, vanities, absurdities, and looming catastrophes of our inequitable and unsustainable civilization are grist for the songwriting mill. While these downbeat circumstances and events just naturally spill into expression in his music, there is, behind it all, a faith that never gives up on the guidance of integrity and the call of communion.

There is a memorable line from the ancient Greek poet, Archilochus, which runs as follows: "The fox knows many things, but the hedgehog knows one big thing." Taken metaphorically – as was done by Isaiah Berlin in his essay on Tolstoy, *The Hedgehog and the Fox* – this aphorism neatly sums up a distinct difference in temperament that divides creative and searching minds in the way they see the world, and in the way they approach their work.

Occasionally, there comes a poet who is double-gifted in these angles of vision, and, instead of producing work that comes down on one side or the other of this divide, confounds and delights us by transcending these partialities of temperament and expression. Bob Dylan is an artist of this transcendence. From the dark foreboding moods of his cryptic allegories and poetic prophecies to the tender songs of love and loss, from the half-talking blues built on a laundry list of life's absurdities to the pointed and didactic statements and advice on faith, Dylan certainly has a primal hedgehog quality.

Sometimes he is a hedgehog with a sledgehammer, smashing the images of culture into prisms of vision through which we catch a glimpse of a better place to be. Sometimes he is nurturing, sometimes playful. Often, he is just plain tricky and leaves us with the impression of having heard something profound, but, at the same time, elusive as to "meaning." The "meaning" often just sits out there, like a smiling hedgehog, inscrutable and yet, somehow, transparent, bearing witness to the dance and power of poetry.

At the same time, the man is a fox. He covers so much ground. He makes tracks into the unknown like a shaman and then walks backwards and goes off in a different direction over rocks in the streambed of consciousness where the sunlight of song and the shadows of mystery play forward into ripples of beauty. He is an artist who picks up on the smallest quirks of life and turns them into fireworks. He tweaks the nose of the philosopher and shakes the hand of the preacher. He behaves like a rabbi with his own religion, and then stops, turns, and gives Christianity a "shot of love" and his blessing whether it wants it or not.

The man is mercurial. He takes the name of a famous dead poet and Robert Zimmerman disappears. He is a down-home folksinger turned hard-driving rocker turned tender-minded broken-hearted bluesman, ending up as the creator of a unique musical signature that is always recognizable no matter the genre in which it is presented.

Following in the footsteps of Woody Guthrie and Pete Seeger with the "talkin' blues," he was a "rapper" long before "rap." He breaks his neck in a motorcycle crash, disappears from view for a disturbingly long time, and then comes back with new and stunning songs easily equal to his best work of the 60s. Then he cuts a winning album of songs for children. He never talks to his audience and almost never gives interviews, but we never forget the sound of his voice and the bounce and weave of his lyrics. He keeps his distance, but is a constant presence.

In Dylan, the hedgehog and the fox abide, the wisdom of the seer and the songs of a wayfaring stranger coalesce into a body of work that is nothing less than a "scripture" of the late 20th Century; the story of our agony, the tragedy of our ignorance, and the call of justice, which, in the end, in "the still of the night," "under a shooting star," cause us to think of integrity and communion – the solidarity of peoples and Earth.

Having said all that, I come back to Dylan in New Brunswick, and am confronted with the prospect of whether to scramble for tickets to the show. I have decided against it. I am glad to know he will be here in this corner of the continent, but there is no chance that a live concert at this late date can add anything substantial to my memories of the 60s.

I turn instead to a dusty collection of vinyl records and some recently acquired tapes to reignite my sense of this extraordinary troubadour. As I flip through the albums standing on the bottom shelf of the stereo cabinet, looking for a particular favourite – *John Wesley Harding* – I have a momentary shock; it is nowhere to be found. Then, I remember; years ago my youngest son convinced me that most of my records from the 60s should be combined with his collection. This made sense. Pass it on. Farewell *John Wesley Harding*.

So, for the moment, all I have at hand are *Nashville Skyline, Slow Train Coming, Down in the Groove*, and the more recent albums, *Oh Mercy* and *Under a Red Sky*, as well as *The Bootleg Tapes*. But that is enough. *The Bootleg Tapes* gathers material from a very early Dylan, going back to the time when he lived and worked under the mythic spell of Woody Guthrie. *Oh Mercy* and *Under a Red Sky* contain some of his most haunting expressions of tricky wisdom and tested faith, and some of his most grounded evocations of living as whole and clear as possible in a badly broken and tangled up world.

To understand Bob Dylan it is necessary to hear Woody Guthrie, and I mean *hear*, not just listen. It is necessary to feel the pulse of hard-working, poor-living people and take the true measure of the high and mighty – the folks Pete Seeger calls "the high up muckity mucks." You have to feel yourself pulled through the vortex of all human labour and accomplishment with "The Great Historical Bum." You have to feel the despair of "I Ain't Got No Home in this World Anymore," and the grit and the grime and the broken land and rambling spirits of the *Dust Bowl Ballads*. You have to feel a twinge of satisfaction at the story of "Pretty Boy Floyd the Outlaw," and understand why those "Banks of Marble" keep people in poverty. And you need to feel a "Pastures of Plenty," a "ribbon of highway," and a "dusty boot heels wandering" kind of love for the Earth.

All this, and much more, flows directly from Woody Guthrie to Bob Dylan; and no matter how far he travels, how eccentric his orbit through the world of superstar music, and no matter how far his own success has removed him from the realm in which Woody Guthrie lived and worked, there remains in Dylan's music the indelible mark and the extended aura of his great mentor.

Dylan never played with Woody Guthrie, but he played *for* him. In a rare interview given to the BBC years ago, he tells of first hearing Woody Guthrie's records and later playing for him.

> *He had a sound,...a particular sound. And he had something to say that needed to be said.*

> *I had a lot of time to make up. I mean I had to really find out who this guy was...I started learning his songs. I mean, there was a time when I did nothing but his songs.*

I was completely taken over by him. By his spirit, or whatever. You could listen to his songs and actually learn how to live, or how to feel. He was like a guide...

When I finally met him, he wasn't functioning very well, but I was there more as a servant – I mean. I went there to sing him his songs. [Brooklyn State Hospital, where Woody Guthrie was in the latter stage of Huntington's disease] *That's all I went to do, and that's all I did. I never really talked too much to him. He couldn't talk anyway. ...He always liked the songs and he would ask for certain ones. I knew them all! I was like a Woody Guthrie jukebox.*[1]

Years later, on the album, *Slow Train Coming*, when Dylan sings, "You gotta serve somebody," it's not just an expression of his new found interest in the Christian faith, it's also an ethos that comes right out of the working class struggle and union organizing days immortalized in the songs of Woody Guthrie – "Which side are you on boys, which side are you on?" As is evident in the above interview, Dylan came early to a strong sense of reciprocity and service.

Bob Dylan's overt "Christian period" was a conundrum for many folks who were learning from him the way he learned from Woody Guthrie. Given the tenor of the times, I was even tempted to wonder if it was a marketing move. These were the days when long haired "Jesus freaks" were turning in Beatles' records for sacrificial burning. But Dylan's attraction to the Christian story and its ethos was nothing new.

In 1967, a student at the college where I was teaching gave me her copy of *John Wesley Harding* as she was leaving for a year's work-study program in Africa. I had not yet heard it and she said to me by way of introduction, "This is a very Christian album." This assessment, coming from a Jewish person, about a singer/songwriter also of Jewish background, was, I thought, most curious. But it was on the mark. The Christian element, however, is very odd, and not at all traditional. But there is something in the dark amalgam of brokenness and compassion, something in the sense of apocalypse rising from this album that evokes a creative appropriation and reworking of certain elements of the Christian ethos.

The question of faith – the struggle to "keep on keepin' on" – is ever present in Dylan's music. The tension of this struggle, the drama of the search, and the restless roving poetry of his metaphoric genius makes even his lesser songs more interesting than most of the rest of popular music. I have no idea whether a specific framework of Christian faith has remained significant for Dylan, but as his later music has emerged it is sprinkled with allusions to the Bible and biblical culture, including the Christian tradition.

His music is dense with images of brokenness ("Everything Is Broken") and redemption ("God Knows," "Where the Teardrops Fall"). He has a keen sense of Murphy's Law, if things can go wrong, they will ("Cat's In the Well"). He holds out no more expectation of happiness for those who are seriously awake to the doings of the world than can, perhaps, be achieved in the temporary and melancholy tenderness of lovers and friends ("Born In Time," "Shooting Star").

Bob Dylan has an unmistakable reading on the social and ecological devolution of modern culture, a kind of distinct sense of a slow motion apocalypse ("Under a Red Sky," "Ring Them Bells"). His music continues to sound ominous warnings. He is no less a prophet now than in the days of "64th Street" when he felt the changes "blowing in the wind." In "Ring Them Bells" he manages to compress into a few lines a profound recognition of the ecological, social, and spiritual disaster that is accompanying the technological and economic modernization of Earth and its cultures.

> *Ring them bells Saint Peter where the four winds blow.*
> *Ring them bells with an iron hand so the people will know.*
> *Oh it's rush hour now on the wheel and the plough,*
> *And the sun is going down on the sacred cow.*

I don't know if lines like these just pop into Dylan's head and then assume their meaning on reflection, or if he knows exactly what he is doing when, for example, he writes; "Oh it's rush hour now on the wheel and the plough." This is a stunning compression of the whole epoch of high-energy modernization. The wheel and the plough, ancient, primary tools of human culture, now powered by high-energy fossil fuels, have entered the "rush hour" mode. The result? The development of a motor vehicle addiction that is destroying the physical environment and the fabric of social and economic life of both urban and rural communities, plus poisoning the atmosphere to the point of human health damage and deleterious climate change. In addition, the "rush hour" has led to the industrialization and commercialization of food production in a way that has destroyed the self-renewing capacity of cultivated soils, and the self-reliance of ecosystem-based cultures around the world.

And then with a metaphoric sweep of equally profound import, he adds; "And the sun is going down on the sacred cow." This reference is clearly to the religious culture of India, but it stands for all the cases in which the sacred connections with Earth are being obliterated by the "rush hour" of high-energy, capital-driven economic development.

An equally intriguing feature of this stanza is how it starts with a Christian reference, invoking Saint Peter to "ring them bells," and then moves on to a traditional Aboriginal American cultural reference, "where the four winds blow", and then ends with a reference to traditional South Asian culture. The cultural sweep of this poetry, driven as it is by the prophetic voice, sounds a universal warning about the unprecedented changes being unleashed upon the world.

I have no idea if Dylan engages in this kind of reflection on this combination of words, concepts, and cultural references. He may not. It doesn't matter. They have been given to him, and once given they take on a life of their own. He may not have "meant," in a didactic way, the associations I hear in these lines. But words, concepts, and cultural references come with a context and when joined, even if only for the music of juxtaposition, can conjure up what may be unforeseen "meanings." This is the magic of poetry. The muse delivers a basket of stars and – presto – a new galaxy is born!

With release of the album *Slow Train Coming*, Dylan began speaking with the overt accents of Christianity. For a time it appeared that the freewheeling genius of Dylan was being sacrificed to, or at least proscribed by, the personal salvation mindset of Christian theology. However, certain songs from this period that put the question of Christian commitment right up front also display an awareness of social and temperamental diversity that crosses over into a non-sectarian context. For example, "You Gotta Serve Somebody" issues a universally valid call to a decision on moral commitment and a life of service regardless of how you interpret the theological language in the refrain – "it may be the Devil or it may the Lord, but you gotta serve somebody."

You don't have to be a convert to Christian theology to understand the pertinence of this injunction. It really is true, no matter what we believe, and, as Dylan says, no matter what our name or who we think we are, there is a profound sense in which our lives are inevitably engaged in some kind of service. We don't really have a choice in this matter. The dimension of service is implicit in being born; it is the essence of ecological and social reality. All social relationships and economic interchange have a reciprocity component. But, as Dylan insists, we do have a choice over the way we set up and direct our engagement with service. If we don't make good choices about the kind of service we will render for the good of the world, but remain cocooned in a personal and cultural narcissistic consumerism, we will end up serving ourselves into ecological and social loneliness, disorder, and breakdown. Dylan puts the question right up front. It cuts to the quick and across any belief system we may have. He may have been tempted by a theology of personal salvation, but the heritage of cultural critique and social justice that the music of Woody Guthrie implanted in his youthful consciousness remained the drumbeat of his artistic voice.

In due course, Dylan returned to a more open and universal language and to a renewed social critique. In his later songs he savages the culture of corrupt and mendacious politics ("Political World"). He is, by turns, aghast and bemused at the pass to which the capital-driven, consumer society has come ("Unbelievable," "TV Talking Song," "Everything is Broken"). He pillories the self-indulgent jet set ("Handy Dandy") and the world of high finance capitalism ("10,000 Men"). One deeply mysterious song from this period, "Man in the Long Black Coat", seems like a lament for a friend lost to a religious cult, although it might also be heard as an encounter with death.

In Dylan's later work there seems to be a strengthening of the deep moral stance that came into folk music with the songs of Wood Guthrie and Pete Seeger. Dylan has been on a lot of strange trips into various and contrasting aspects of the American cultural milieu, but there is something in him that continually circles back to the moral core of the musical tradition that picked him up, gave him standing, and which he has come to serve as a defining artist.

In the world of cultural expression there are those who speak for the moral traditions, the philosophers, the theologians, the social activists, and those who present a range of aesthetic experience that nourish and round out our souls. Rarely do we get these two realms, the moral and the aesthetic, fused into an expression that transcends the convention and becomes, as it were, a voice from a third place.

Again, William Blake is a prime point of reference for the mastery of this integration, this melding of lyric genius and moral intuition into a vision of wisdom and guidance. This vision is anchored in the harmonies of the soul, harmonies that are a potential birthright, but of which the young are often robbed by enculturation into a mechanistic, competitive, cost accounting, and money-driven society. With this kind of enculturation comes the wounded heart often in pursuit of wealth, and the unsatisfied mind lusting after dominance or falling into obedience.

We have a rich tradition of aesthetic/spiritual/moral culture that has long countervailed against this "single vision of Newton's sleep," as Blake put it, and against the hypnotic mindset of economic self-interest as the be-all and end-all of human life and work. In the main, this countervailing culture has been marginal to the force of industrialization and commercialization within modern societies until the late 1960s; then something happened.

Many volumes have been written about what happened in the 60s. A long building confluence of circumstances and events helped rattle the windows and blow a few wheels off the train of so-called progressive civilization. The signal achievement of the era was to alert a sizable number of folks to the fact that our route to the promised land of consumer bliss was leading to a quagmire of social fragmentation, continuing racist discrimination, ecological destruction, and economic rapaciousness. In no small part, the re-emergence of an alternative aesthetic/spiritual/moral culture at that time has enabled us to see the disaster we are making and the catastrophe toward which we are heading in our drive to monetize the value of Earth's commonwealth, including most human relationships.

Thirty years down the road now, and it's not at all clear that this re-emergence can be considered successful. A good case can be made for the almost complete co-opting of the countervailing culture by the marketing savvy of business as usual. In a situation where access to the means of life is entirely dependent on access to money, those who control the monetary system will determine not only the course of socioeconomic development, but also the aesthetic/spiritual/moral context in which that development takes place.

What does it mean, for example, that the Bank of Montreal is now using Dylan's song, "The Times They Are A-Changing," to help get a leg up on the electronic leap the banking industry is making into cyber-space service? The changes that song prophesied were moral and spiritual, not digital and fibre-optic. What does it mean that Dylan, apparently, released that song for the Bank of Montreal's use? Is it a disheartening example of the way the moral/spiritual force of aesthetic experience can be expropriated by money and converted to another display in the petting zoo of the capital-driven marketplace? Sure seems like it to me.

I can imagine a hip advertising wag making the pitch on the bank's behalf. And I can imagine it seeming to Dylan like probably not a bad thing, considering that we all need financial service, and it being a Canadian bank at that, all burnished up with the moral patina of the "true north." Who knows what happened? (See "Second Postscript.")

What we do know, is that some folks will now remember "The Times They Are A-Changing" as a kind of anthem for the new age of computer banking, and all the mind salving, imagination hijacking wizardry of the silicon-chip boys who promote a "revolution" of cascading options for our "never to be satisfied human nature." But it isn't really that glorious; it isn't really about a future of limitless possibilities at all. It's about money, now and in the near future. It's about who profits from what. It's about who controls the narratives of change and about continuing to expand consumer culture.

The "changes" of which Dylan sang were changes of the heart, of the soul, of visionary experience, of walking away from the world of never enough and then working with friends on a world of enough for all. They were changes that challenged "the masters of war" and plumbed the heartache of how we sometimes hurt the ones we love. They were changes that cut the Gordian knot of the competitive mind-set, and spread the mantle of cooperation like a soft linen cloak over the highlands of ambition.

They were changes that sang consciousness into transcending "the sky cut flat." They were changes that rallied the imagination, the hunger for beauty, and the spirit of communion into a search for a better way to be, a better place to be, a homecoming of the spirit, a homemaking of the body. They were changes that called for right relationships with all persons and the commonwealth of life. They were changes that dreamed the dream the American "new world" dream missed because it had its eyes on lumber, sugar, cotton, beaver skins, buffalo robes, wheat, corn, and minerals galore, all in the glow of gold and silver and greenback cash spurring the growth of riverboats, railroads, iron and steel, an explosion of manufacturing, gushers of oil, a flood of motor vehicles, a chemical bonanza, and a wonderland of endless innovation of more and more consumer products.

In the music of Dylan, and in a growing cadre of artists at that time, the dream was rescued and became the "dream of Earth," the dream of an Earth renewed and of a civilization that was passing from the age of industrial extraction, rampant consumption, social inequity, racism, and war, to a time of ecological harmony, economic sharing, social peace, and reciprocity in the great commonwealth of life.

It may now, in the re-telling, seem like too much. It may seem like a dream as extravagant and utopian as is the dream of unlimited economic growth that is now driving us to ruin. But there is a difference, a telling difference that makes the vision of a conserver society, ecologically adapted to the biological carrying capacity of its land base, a much better fit for the long run than the truly utopian fantasy of a consumer society ploughing its way ever deeper into ecological deficit.

Extraordinary vision is not required to see that this latter path will lead to a crash. The 60s blew a few wheels off the Consumption Unlimited Train, that runs on the Entrenched Inequity Line. But the "masters of war," now turned "master of debt," have not only refurbished the train and rebuilt the track, they have now rolled out the tarmac in vast amounts in order to insure that as many persons as possible will take the automobile trip to consumer-land on their own, so to speak, and never look back, and never really look ahead either.

The belief is now commonly held that the 1960s cultural revolution more or less failed, that it was an extended adolescent storm of little lasting import. This is incorrect. While it is true that media hype and the powerful co-opting ability of commercial marketing turned the challenge for fundamental change into mostly flash and fashion, it is also true that a significant residue remained and has continued to spread rhizome-like through subsequent decades.

There is a shift in values and a change in attitudes flowing from that time that has reoriented a significant and growing part of our society. The consciousness that emerged and informed the 60s has deep roots and living branches. These are the roots and branches of the aesthetic/spiritual/moral tradition. They have not disappeared. They continue to challenge the technology obsessed, objectifying and commercializing force of the capital-driven market economy.

The value shifts forged in that period set the stage for the emergence of ecological consciousness. We now understand that socioeconomic equity and ecological integrity are two faces of the same issue. We also understand that fundamental change with regard to equity and the restoration and maintenance of ecological integrity are imperative, and that if we do not effect these changes in creative and positive ways, increasingly chaotic and disintegrating changes will likely continue toward a bad end.

Despite this growing awareness in our society, the market economy and those who control the money system seem to have an intractable block against the penetration of ecological consciousness and the holistic understanding it engenders. The aesthetic/spiritual/moral tradition, which fuelled the 60s, and which is the countervailing force to this ruinous tunnel vision, is still at work, and when conditions are right will, no doubt, emerge once again into forceful channels of change. How many turns of the wheel it will take to achieve an equitable, conserver society is hard to guess, but this dream, never the less, is the only future for which it is truly worth working.

It is precisely this sense of the future, combined with stunning vignettes and summations of the violence, confusion, waste, and boredom of the "air-conditioned nightmare" that Dylan puts into song after song, songs that drive deep into the psyche and leave you feeling like an oracle has spoken. Had his songs been only spiritual in a hippy-dippy psychedelic way, or had they been only aesthetic in a mind-candy kind of way, they would not have helped shift the magnetic pole of the music and cultural world as they did during that brief illuminated era. The fact that Dylan's intuition is rooted in solidarity, which is to say grooved into the gift of faith, gives his muse a scope of endowment that fuses the aesthetic/spiritual/moral voice into a clarion call.

Where does this voice come from? Could it really be coming from a little guy named Robert Zimmerman who wandered from Minnesota into "hard times in New York town," learned everything from Woody Guthrie, and then, while remaining largely incognito in a personal sense, writes, plays, and sings his way into becoming a mentor of a subsequent generation of artists? Just think how often you now hear a gravelly voiced folksong artist or a down-home blues singer that reminds you of Dylan. Many of them are nearly as good, and many of them have the same social critique and moral stance.

Where is that voice – that voice in a collective sense – coming from? Well, it certainly comes from Woody Guthrie and Pete Seeger. But there is, it seems to me, more to it than that. If I were to locate its source in a way that did honour to all those who here remain unnamed, and to all those who, though they did their part, will, as far as history is concerned, remain forever nameless, I would say it is, in Woody Guthrie's imperishable expression, the voice of the "Great Historical Bum." Just listen:

> *I'm just a lonesome traveler, the Great Historical Bum,*
> *Highly educated, from history I have come.*
> *I built the Rock of Ages, 'twas in the year of one.*
> *And that's about the biggest thing that man has ever done.*

This song moves on through the human works of ancient and modern history and winds up with the moral vision of human solidarity that permeates folk music, and which Dylan, along with many others, has carried into the progressive and holistic spiritual ethos of our time.

Aside from the use of the male pronoun, which marks the song's era, it is a stirring memorial to the blood, sweat, and tears of those who essentially built the human world, built all the past versions of it on which our own now stands. This is a tradition of faith that transcends creed, a faith that comes before thought and persists past argument, a faith that looks squarely at the worst, but endures, and, in enduring, holds out for the best, a world at peace. And, as we now know, peace needs justice; it needs the end of poverty and must include ecological peace, the end of war on the environment. This is where the voice comes from, "the voice that is great within us."

Dylan's 1989 album, *Oh Mercy*, occupies a special place in this picture. Not only does it recapitulate and update his critical and prophetic vision ("Political World," "Everything Is Broken," "Ring Them Bells"), but it also includes a close investigation of personal morality ("What Good Am I?"). It rolls through a dissection, root and branch, of a snare that chokes our ability to live in a well-balanced and socially harmonious way ("Disease of Conceit"). And, for good measure, it provides an excruciatingly elusive examination of the problem of spiritual guidance ("What Was It You Wanted?").

"What Was It You Wanted?" is like a drifty Zen Master's dialogue with a guru-seeking novice. Oh that perennial quest for a spiritual master of some kind, always looking in the wrong place, the wrong way; looking for that mystical face, that luminous word, that hand that will lift you up from your weakness and confusion. Given Dylan's music and the image of the persona that stands behind it in the shadows, he has probably had his fill of hangers-on, of persons seeking the "torn hem of his garment," or even just a slight tip of the hat and a rare grin.

The song, "What Was It You Wanted?," seems to be making a gesture of assistance to all those who look to Dylan the Guide. In a playful, absentminded, self-depreciating way he sets up the seeker for an interview, and then repeatedly interrupts the focus in a manner worthy of Kafka. It is a perversely elusive song that circles back on itself and ends with the Guide getting so drifty that the questions of identity and dialogue go into a kind of collapse. It is a masterpiece of spiritual sleight of hand. It is like a Zen Master who, instead of whacking the student with a stick on the shoulder, throws a handful of fog in her face. Like much of Dylan's best work, the song ends and you are not sure what has happened or what it means; but it leaves the distinct impression of something gracious and elusively helpful at work.

Oh Mercy ends with a small gem of song, "Shooting Star", that takes us back to the heartache of friendship and loss, the kind of song that made *Nashville Skyline* such a classic. But even here, even in this context, Dylan rolls out lines that challenge us to think about what is really happening, what we are on the edge of and where it will all end.

Listen to the engines,
listen to the bells
as the last firetruck from hell
goes rolling by;
all good people are prayin'.
It's the last temptation,
the last account;
the last time you might hear
the sermon on the mount;
last radio playing.
Seen a shootin' star tonight, slip away.

This is not a major song but it strikes me as, perhaps, a good example of the place to which Dylan has come, deep into a sense of last things. In this fragment of a simple lyrical song he has placed the following: A cosmic reference, four specific Christian references, heavy-duty technology, electronic media, and, of all the incongruous concepts, "the last firetruck from hell." Firetrucks from hell? Where would they be going? Are they delivering fire? The whole fragment is saturated with a sense of crisis, a sense of urgency, but then he rounds off his sense of last things with a glance at the Cosmos, and it all slips away. If this is the work of a man thinking long thoughts in middle age, what will he come up with when he sees the journey approaching its end; probably more of the same. His muse seems inexhaustible.

So many brilliant artists of the music scene have died young. Dylan has survived, as have a few others I continue to follow and listen to with care for the same reasons I listen to him – that echo of faith in the face of disaster. I listen to Leonard Cohen, Bruce Cockburn, and Bruce Springsteen, poets and song makers in whose work I also hear the voice of the Great Historical Bum, and all the agony, toil, beauty, love, and devotion that inform the best telling of the human experience.

I hear Bruce Cockburn sing about "this cold commodity culture / where you lay your money down / its hard to even notice / that all this earth is hallowed ground" ("The Gift"). I hear him sing about "the gift" that is always passed on and I know he is illuminating integrity and celebrating the communion of solidarity. I hear him sing about the "shadow on the step / where the body was before / shipwrecked at the stable door," and, although I don't know quite what it means, I know it unrolls an odd, inverted allusion to the Christian faith, and poses the conundrum of why our civilization has turned out so badly. No one takes on questions like these without being immersed in a faith-haunted world.

I hear Leonard Cohen sing "The Sisters of Mercy," and the best of human compassion rises up before me in a suggestive Christian form. I am stunned when in the song, "Suzanne," I hear him sing:

> *Jesus was a sailor when he walked upon the water*
> *He spent a long time watching from his lonely wooden tower*
> *And when he knew for certain only drowning men could see him*
> *He said all men will be sailors then until the sea shall free them*

Hearing this from an artist who, like Dylan, has the great heritage of Judaism behind him, I think, perhaps, whether intended or not, he is engaged in rescuing Jesus, the Jewish mystic and moral teacher, from Christianity, and bringing this figure of high spiritual and ethical drama into the more universal significance he deserves. He probably does know what he is doing because he ends that stanza on Jesus with the line, "he sank beneath your wisdom like a stone."

This kind of work, this reconfiguration of powerful mythic images, is not undertaken without deep personal involvement in the brokenness of the human condition, and is not accomplished without the gift of a faith behind faith. As Cohen says in a recent song; "There is a crack in everything / that's how the light gets in." ("Anthem")

In the song, "My Father's House," I hear Bruce Springsteen sing about his homecoming being turned away because "no one by that name / lives here anymore." The song ends with this:

> *My father's house shines hard and bright.*
> *It stands like a beacon calling me in the night.*
> *Calling and calling so cold and alone,*
> *Shining across this dark highway where our sins lie un-atoned.*

This may sound like the end of faith, but, no, it's the end of a spiritual ethos that no longer serves in a world where good and evil are daily ground into an amalgam of culture, technology, and mixed motivation of which conventional theology can make no sense at all. Springsteen knows this dilemma well. He has made it his stock in trade. But, remarkably, the song that follows the lament of "My Father's House" is called "Reason to Believe." Here, he presents a sequence of characters in misery and loss of various kinds, but ends each vignette with the lines, "at the end of every hard earned day / people find some reason to believe." The last verse ends with the question, "Lord what does it mean that at the end of every hard earned day people find some reason to believe?"

Good question; perhaps, *the* question. The human species is incredibly resilient in body and mind. The Great Historical Bum has scraped through catastrophes before, even catastrophes, like presently, of his own making (in this case the male pronoun is accurate). One thing in all this is clear; faith is not a matter of personal effort. Faith is a hard road if you try to walk it alone. Faith is a collective gift. Some folks seem better at it than others. We hang together to balance out our weaknesses and strengths.

Solidarity is the soil of faith. We get through hard times because we know that solidarity and survival do not depend on just me or just you. Solidarity in survival draws on all the cooperation, all the sharing, all the teaching of skills, all the nurturing, all the respect and love of Earth, all the celebration of beauty, all the homecoming to community that is accomplished, and all the songs that are sung the world around. This is the gift of our humanity at its best.

When Dylan found Woody Guthrie in Brooklyn State Hospital, he went there as a "servant" to sing him his own songs. This is the gift of solidarity. This is the gift that is given, yet ever returned to the giver and given out again and again. Dylan later explained it like this:

> *Woody Guthrie was who he was because he came along in the time he came along in. For me he was like a link in the chain. Like I am for other people, and like we all are for somebody.*[2]

Some folks are much given to speculation on where the gift comes from; this is called theology. Others are more concerned with exercising and implementing the gift; this is called service. The gift, and its translation into service, is surely the signature of faith, a signature that Bob Dylan has writ large across the ruins of our faith-haunted world.

Postscript: 2013

Since 1997, Dylan has recorded eight additional albums including *Time Out Of Mind*, *Love and Theft*, *Modern Times*, and *Tempest*, all of which include work that stands with his best. Numerous songs from these albums could be cited to extend and amplify the analysis and appreciation I have unfolded in this essay. As a postscript, I wish, however, to focus on *Tempest*, released in 2012.

I earlier raised the question of what kind of songs Dylan might create in old age. With *Tempest*, we now know. No stranger to loss, tragedy, and death from the beginning, the songs gathered on this album strike me as now rising from an old man's gaze down the few remaining and uncertain years.

In the lead song, "Don't You Hear That Duquesne Whistle Blowing," Dylan pens a set of soulful and even whimsical lyrics about that last train ride; "Don't you hear that Duquesne whistle blowing / blowing like it's gonna sweep my world away." Each repetition of the refrain varies the theme a bit, but then becomes explicit; "Don't you hear that Duquesne whistle blowing' / blowing like it's gonna kill me dead." And then ending with; "Listen to that Duquesne whistle blowing / blowing like she's blowing right on time." This sounds like acceptance to me.

Song after song on this album resonates with a sense of ending, sometimes personal, sometimes cultural. The saddest and most moving of all is "Roll on John," Dylan's tribute and belated advice to John Lennon and a meditation on death all rolled up together. It's as if after all these years, Dylan recognizes that John Lennon's soulful song, "Hey Jude," was addressed to him and it's time to reply.

But it is the title song, "Tempest," that brings this sense of an ending to something like a cosmic focus. This song, ostensibly about the sinking of the Titanic, is more a sad and final salute to a cultural milieu, or even a civilization, that has unwittingly sailed its way into catastrophe. This song, 45 verses and 14 minutes long, is so wide-ranging in its historical and cultural references, and so well crafted in its metaphorical flair and narrative voice, that it may well come to be Dylan's signal effort to encompass the past, present, and future of a failing civilization.

The odd thing about "Tempest," however, is the neutral to sympathetic voice employed in recounting the disintegration and fateful ending of the great voyage. A kind of sad sweetness permeates the tale as character after character and incident after incident of the slow motion disaster is sketched out and passed on. One character, however, recurs throughout the story, "the watchman." And true to Dylan's typical flair for paradox, each time he reappears he is introduced with the line; "The watchman he lay dreaming." Dreaming? Shouldn't the "watchman" be on watch? Shouldn't he be warning of what is to come? But it is already too late for the "watchman." Perhaps he tried, but now the catastrophe is like a bad dream come true.

Pretty obviously, the "watchman" is telling the story. Dylan has spent his life with his artistic antenna tuned into this story. He has done his best as a "watchman" and reported faithfully on what has come to him. He has told a warning story over and over in myriad ways. And still the great ship is going down. "The watchman he lay dreaming / The damage had been done / He dreamed the Titanic was sinking / And he tried to tell someone."

The Titanic did not sink in a tempest. It sank in a calm and starlit sea. Yet, Dylan calls the song and the album, "Tempest." There is calmness in this song, a steady cadence of narrative falling toward an ending. In contrast, the modern human condition rises more and more to a tempest like disturbance, and the "watchman," in his closing hours, can only repeat the dream he has seen; the dream which, for Dylan, seems still to include a kind of faith behind faith even though the ship is going down.

Despite his prophetic songs, Dylan has always insisted he is not a "prophet." In this first album from his seventh decade, he seems willing to at least be known as a "watchman." He is still watching and working so perhaps more reports are yet to come.

Second Postscript 2014

Does the 2014 Super Bowl television advertisement Bob Dylan did with the Chrysler car company give the lie to my assessment of his place in what I have called the great aesthetic/spiritual/moral tradition?

When I heard about this ad after the fact, and then viewed it on the Internet, I suffered a rapid rewind through my laudatory construction of Dylan's counter-culture status. I had already encountered this conundrum in the Bank of Montreal radio ad previously described. But this Chrysler ad, with its overtones of chauvinistic patriotism, was something different. Not only had he now lent his persona to the adulation of car culture during the spectacle of an American consumerism ritual, but, I discovered, he had previously appeared in an ad for Cadillac, and, of all things, in an ad for Victoria's Secret.

How could the guy who wrote and sang all those songs laying out a merciless critique of economic inequity and pillorying the wasteland of capitalist culture in the tradition of Woody Guthrie end up doing ads for Cadillac, Victoria's Secret, and Chrysler? Is this a case of selling out? Is this a case of forfeiting integrity for big bucks in old age? Or is it a case of my assessment of Dylan mapping inaccurately over the cultural landscape in which he lives and works? Is the overlay of my own deeply ingrained vision of right relationship and ecological guidance distorting the mercurial reality of the man himself? I suspect it may be a bit of both. But we will never know, because, if he remains true to form, he may never give us the satisfaction of talking about his motivation.

If I am troubled by this advertising business, and what seems to me a rank inconsistency of values, I am also bemused by the way it adds to the enigmatic layering of his persona. If we want consistency from Dylan, this is it, he is consistently enigmatic. And "persona" is the right word. There is a reason why he adopted the name of a famous dead poet, does not talk to his audiences in performance, and rarely gives interviews. There is a mask, there is a performance persona through which the songs are launched and this enigmatic element is part of his cachet and enduring allure. Forays into advertising certainly tweak the persona and extend the enigma.

The fact that Dylan has twice lent his persona to car ads raises a doubt about his comprehension of the ecological deficit and climate crisis to which the growth of consumer culture has now brought our society. It is entirely possible that although he grew up in and contributed to the social and economic critique of his times, the full implications of ecological economics has not dawned on him. He may well think that more jobs producing more cars in America is a good thing.

There is a precedent for this in the worldview of his mentor, Woody Guthrie. In the late 1930's Woody Guthrie signed up and was paid to write songs about the great progress that would come from the damming of the Columbia River in the American Northwest. The song, "Roll on Columbia Roll On," extolling the economic growth that would result from the electric power generated by Grand Coulee Dam, can still bring a lump to the throat and tears to the eyes of those of us who remember the shadow of the

Great Depression. Although those days are long gone, and our crisis is now one of over-development and un-economic growth foreshadowing ecological collapse, most people still think that more people buying more things creating more jobs and more economic growth is the only way to organize a prosperous society. Building and selling more cars may seem like a good deal to Bob Dylan, and giving that wheel a little shove may seem like a good thing for American workers.

Clearly we make a mistake when we try to pin up an image of the "true" Dylan. In fact, in the few times he has deigned to speak of such things he has consistently refused to be pigeonholed, refused the prophetic mantle, and insisted he is just a storyteller, a balladeer. Fair enough. If he wants to be a car salesman and purveyor of women's undies on the side, "who am I to judge," to quote Pope Francis' recent comment about homosexuality.

One thing we can say for sure, "the times they are [still] a changing." And another thing for sure is that Dylan's songs, and his performance of them, will always be an iconic path through the ruins of our faith-haunted world regardless of what their creator decides to do with the persona he has created. We don't think less of Dylan Thomas' poetic gift for his having fallen down drunk and dying in the street outside the White Horse Tavern in New York. If the other "Dylan" now takes what seems like a dive into endorsing the flameout of consumer culture, his poetic and musical archive remains a witness and lends strength to the "great work" of cultural and economic transformation on which the human future now hangs.

"There'll Come a Day"

*The key to the future is finding the optimistic stories and
let them be known. Participation – that's what's gonna
save the human race.*

Pete Seeger

We had parked our car in the lot near the train station in
Beacon, New York and were walking over to the Farmer's Market
set up in the wharf area of the town's Hudson River landing
when my son, Eric, said, "There's Pete Seeger. Why don't you go
introduce yourself and talk to him." I am not a person who acts
easily on impulse, but before I could make a decision Pete Seeger
was coming down the sidewalk toward our family group, which
included Nathan, our four-year old grandson. He stopped in front
of us, bent down to look directly at Nathan, and said, "Hello there
young fella." And then added, "Why in forty years you're gonna
be running the world."

That was it! All my reserve melted away. I spoke up and engaged
Pete Seeger in conversation. I told him that the first time I had
seen him in concert was in Iowa City in 1959 and that he had
performed two songs that changed my life. He said, "Oh, really?
What songs were they?" I replied, "If I Had a Hammer" and "Oh Had
I a Golden Thread."

I can imagine Pete Seeger has had this kind of conversation with any number of people any number of times, but his attention to my story was as if he was hearing such a thing for the first time. He thanked me and said he was glad to hear about the effect these songs had had on me.

Eric, who lives in Beacon and knew Pete Seeger had an electric powered half-ton, then asked him about his truck. With that, he took us over to the truck, popped the hood, and proceeded to explain how he had made the conversion to an all-electric vehicle. He said the truck was not very fast on the highway, but was fine for going back and forth to town, and, with a seven-speed transmission, "the gearing is so low I can pull stumps out of the ground with it."

The memories of my life are braided with the recorded voice of Pete Seeger. This late, direct encounter and conversation, so easy, so natural, so exemplary of the man, has added a capstone of memory to the guidance that flows from his life and work.

Over the past fifty-five years I have often thought about that Pete Seeger concert at the State University of Iowa and the way those particular songs put solid ground under the path of faith that was coming into view for me at that time. I had already concluded there was something deficient in any religious faith that staked its claim on exclusion and partiality, or insisted that the only route to authentic spiritual life was to be found in its theological constructions. So even though the abstract elements of theology were fading from view, I had the good fortune of a Mennonite heritage and of its ethos of service and community on which to rely for ethical grounding.

When I heard Pete Seeger sing "If I Had a Hammer" and "Oh Had I a Golden Thread" something came to me for which I did not at the time have a name, but which I knew without a doubt was a guiding expression of the way I was drawn to live. There was a joyous sense of presence in this occasion; a sense that the path was clear and that guidance would faithfully emerge. I later learned that "solidarity" is the word for what had become vivid to me in the presence of Peter Seeger's music. From that word, which is not so much a concept as it is a state of being, flows a whole orientation for living. Solidarity picks up the ethos of service and the ethic of right relationship; it starts with community and extends to Earth's whole commonwealth of life.

"If I Had a Hammer" is a stirring anthem of action and solidarity. Each verse ends with a call for "love between my brothers and my sisters all over this land." "Oh Had I a Golden Thread" is also a song of solidarity and compassion. On that night long ago, Pete Seeger made evident to me, through the beauty of this song, a spirit of compassion from which trustworthy guidance also flows.

> *Oh, had I a golden Thread*
> *And needle so fine*
> *I'd weave a magic strand*
> *Of rainbow design*
>
> *In it I'd weave the bravery*
> *Of women giving birth*
> *In it I would weave the innocence*
> *Of children over all the earth*
>
> *Show my brothers and sisters*
> *My rainbow design*
> *Bind up this sorry world*
> *With hand and heart and mind*

The Psalmists says; "My cup runneth over." That was certainly the case for me when I emerged from that concert and into the continuing ambience of Pete Seeger's musical service to the world. I began to collect his recordings and have never stopped. Solidarity and compassion, frequent humour and gentle needling, no trace at all of a performance persona, not an ounce of self-righteousness, a buoyant hard working devotion to lifting the human spirit, a scourge to scoundrels, an obvious love of children, a story teller par excellence, not adverse to a bit of tom-foolery, and an unbreakable faith in the capacity of people to lift themselves together to a better way; this is the sound track of a way of life devoted to justice, peace, and the integrity of Creation.

Over many years, Pete Seeger skilfully traversed the overlapping terrain of justice and peace. In the movement for bringing about a better human world there have been those who emphasized the pre-eminence of working for peace and the use of non-violent means. Others have emphasized the need to seek and establish justice in place of injustice, arguing that authentic peace is possible only when justice prevails. Strong coercion and the use of aggressive force in the pursuit of justice are sometimes regarded as justified in this latter view. Gandhi and Mandela personify the difference.

Pete Seeger was never reluctant to insist that justice is the foundation of a better human world. Flickers of militancy regularly play around the edges of his songs, especially those in support of the Union movement. At the same time he is firm in his rejection of violence, war, and militarism. A plea for international understanding and cooperation in addressing the ills of poverty and oppression around the world are a central theme in his music. His commitment to the Civil Rights Movement and the fight against racism never abated. It's still right there in his last album in the song, "Take It From Dr. King." He neatly summed up his skillful handling of the justice/peace tension when he lettered this statement around the head of his banjo: "This Machine Surrounds Hate and Forces It to Surrender."

In 1964, Peter Seeger demonstrated a small example of his philosophy at a concert in Syracuse, New York. It was, perhaps, such a minor event that it may be nowhere recorded. It has, however, loomed large in my memory over all these years, and, to my mind, perfectly illustrates the spirit of good will and generosity that was always so much a part of his message to the world.

In 1964 the folk music revival was well under way. Pete Seeger was booked for a concert in the middle of the winter in a large auditorium in downtown Syracuse, New York. This was also the time when the John Birch Society was organizing to save the American Republic from left leaning influences and hoping to install Barry Goldwater in the White House. The John Birch Society activists in Syracuse were not about to let Pete Seeger invade their city with his subversive music without a show of opposition. They rallied the troops and set up a protesting picket line outside the entrance to the auditorium.

The night was cold. The protesters gathered, set up their picket line, and waved their accusatory signs. They hoped their action would turn people away. The crowd ignored them. At some point, someone told Pete Seeger what was going on. His response was to order enough hot coffee to warm up all the shivering protesters and invite them inside.

* * *

Leaping over the years and all the other songs of Pete Seeger's repertoire that could be called up into a cavalcade of witness and testimony, I come to the last album in which he gives himself, at over 90 years of age, to a project of song writing and singing with a fourth grade class in his hometown of Beacon, New York. The result is *Solartopia*, an album that features the Rivertown Kids and a collection of songs that express an unbridled enthusiasm for the brighter day to come when all this foolishness of nuclear power, big oil addiction, wasteful consumption, polluted rivers, racism, and conflict over power and the control of resources are things of the past, and we have all gotten down to work creating the kind of cooperative, prosperous, self-reliant villages, towns, cities, and countryside we know are possible if we just pull together, embrace solar energy, and do the right thing for the children.

The last lines above came to me in the lilting cadence of Pete Seeger's voice. How many times have we heard him call out his faith in people and in the future we can build together? He has repeated this kind of message for decades, and now in his last album his shaky voice rings out with the added optimism of solar energy's real and burgeoning potential. This last musical offensive, furled out to meet and reinforce the hopes and dreams of a new wave of youth, a new generation of savvy kids, is a humble and fitting farewell from Pete Seeger.

At the end of his life he makes his best effort to join up, once again, with the children. It's all about the children; it's all about the future. He tells us we should "listen to the children; they have something to say." He tells the children, and all of us, "it's gonna be a long haul." But then, with head held high and chin thrust out in his characteristic way, and with his fingers still bringing that old banjo to life, he tells us with utter conviction "there'll come a day" when dreams converge and

Let the light shine out upon the land,
Let the love flow out on every hand,
And the way will break on the
Darkness of the storm.
There'll come a day. There'll come a day.

With that faith behind faith bequeathed to us in the undying strains of Peter Seeger's passion for music and devotion to bringing out the best in people, how can we go into the future except with an answering passion and devotion, no matter how dark and uncertain the times may seem to be.

March 2014

Tracking Down Ecological Guidance

Assembled in 2014 from writing and talks of the last four decades.

Starting Down the Trail

Among the persistent interests of my childhood was the search for arrowheads. My brother and I regularly walked the freshly ploughed fields near our home in northeast Ohio watching for that tell-tale shape offering clear evidence of the deep human past. Harlan, five years my senior, was well versed in woodland skills and historical lore. We had a keen awareness of the original people who had lived here before us between the Cuyahoga and Chagrin Rivers, inland from the south shore of Lake Erie.

Harlan was adept at spotting arrowheads; I was not. I seemed to lack the visual concentration needed for success in this quest. Watching the clouds was more my natural inclination. Then one day walking home from school, I took a shortcut through a neighbour's cornfield; there on the open ground between the edge of the woods and the first row of corn was an arrowhead. I was overjoyed! My first!

I can still remember the feeling of picking it up. I wiped it off, polished it against my pants, and then realized it was peculiar. Instead of being the lustrous gray flint of typical arrowheads, it was a variegated combination of milky-rose and reddish-brown, about half the size of regular arrowheads and of a rough, irregular cut. But no mistake – it was definitely an arrowhead.

That evening after milking, and while we finished up our barn chores, I told Harlan I had something to show him. I put the arrowhead in his hand. He looked at it very carefully, turned it over and rubbed his finger along the cutting edge. He studied it some more and then said something that lodged in my mind and has never let me go. "It was probably made by a young Indian boy who was still practicing at making arrowheads."

The image of that boy, probably about my age, rose up before me. I thought about him when I woke up the next morning. I thought about him in school. I thought about him on Sunday in church and I knew from that time on, knew of a certainty, there was something incomplete about my religious heritage. That arrowhead was incontrovertible evidence of a truth not accounted for in any theology I had yet heard.

That aboriginal boy flaking out his rough arrowhead, and the whole cultural world to which he belonged, was a truth that stood outside the whole of Christendom. From that experience, my woods wandering feet were set on a particular path of inquiry. I did not reject my Christian-Anabaptist-Mennonite heritage, but I knew in my bones there was a larger tradition, a broader story of human culture that had to be taken into account, and with which I felt a deep affinity.

Gaining Focus

Years later, at the State University of Iowa, I became interested in the emerging science of ethology – the study of animal behaviour – and the adaptation of species to various and particular environments. It seemed to me it would be useful to look at human cultures and environmental adaptation in a similar way. One evening, during a conversation with a professor at the bookstore where I was employed, I mentioned my interest in the study of animal behaviour with a view to shedding light on human behaviour. I got a sharp negative reaction. I was told that human beings are creatures of reason and culture and animals are creatures of instinct and conditioning, and there is no common measure between them. Period!

This professor was a learned and, supposedly, wise man, but I knew what he had said was incorrect. I had grown up in close association with various kinds of animals, both domestic and wild, and I knew that learning and behaviours that could be called cultural were clearly evident in many species. I was already well enough acquainted with the study of animal behaviour to know there was a professionally credible basis for my interest. I was working my way toward areas of study we now call historical ecology, social ecology, and sociobiology.

By this time it was clear to me that the story of my own culture was embedded in the wider story of human culture in general, and that the human story was embedded in the larger story of the primate and mammalian world, which, in turn, along with all other forms of life, was embedded in the whole land community – the biosphere. And I understood that the biosphere was part of the still more comprehensive story of Earth's evolutionary unfolding. I let the remarks of my professor pass uncontested and continued with my studies.

A few years later, in the library of the College of Forestry at Syracuse University, I read Clark Wissler's pioneering monograph,

The Relation of Nature to Man in Aboriginal America.[1] This study put a new light on my path. It helped focus the lens of adaptation through which I was more and more seeing and understanding the human-Earth relationship. Shortly thereafter, I discovered the work of the American geographer, Carl Ortwin Sauer. I became immersed in his collection of classic studies, *Land and Life.*[2] Encountering this master of historical geography and human ecology turned the light on my path into a sunrise, illuminating the whole of human history in relation to the environments of Earth in just the way I had been sensing was needed for a fully rounded ecological understanding.

This essay details some of the findings that have come to me as I have worked to develop an ecological worldview and track down the guidance it provides in relation to the human crisis of our time, a crisis manifesting in both the human spirit and the human-Earth relationship.

The Ecology of Faith

While the study of adaptation usually concentrates on resources, population, technology, and economic behaviour, it also encompasses culture in general and religion in particular. There is an ecology of faith at the core of cultural adaptation.

Religious faiths are fundamentally strategies of adaptation. They evolve and devolve. Some work better than others. Some gain in efficacy and others fade at different points in their trajectories. But they all exist and function in an ecological context. This context can be thought of as a kind of faith behind faith, a kind of primal grounding that underwrites the human enterprise.

In religious discourse, faith is often taken to mean trust in the truth and efficacy of a particular story about how things have come to be the way they are, how things are going to work out, and what it all means. In these terms, there are a variety of particular faith stories. People often inherit one of these stories or, at some point, make a choice about which story makes sense to them. This is not, however, what comes to me when I reach for a fully rounded sense of faith. What interests me with regard to the ecology of faith is primarily the energy, the relationships, the sense of reality, and the growth of identity that makes it possible to have a faith of any kind.

It has long seemed to me that there is a kind of faith behind faith, a primal energizing, organizing, and motivating sense of being in the world that backgrounds and continuously underwrites all particular configurations of faith. It is an upwelling sense of positive response to life that makes it possible for us to creatively negotiate each day despite the vagaries of experience, and even the shifting persuasions of belief that may emerge on our path.

This dimension of faith is like a solar energy cell for the soul. It is like photosynthesis for the psyche. It is a gathering from the whole context of Creation that suffuses the entire expression of life, and is articulated in every living form. If we look with full attention, we can see this dimension of creative energy in all the forms and processes of Earth.

One of the most profound thinkers in the dialogue of religion and science has been the great French Catholic priest and palaeontologist, Pierre Teilhard de Chardin. In the later years of his life he became especially concerned about this primal dimension of faith. He said what concerned him most about the spiritual condition of modern societies, and alarmed him about the human future, was "a dying down of the zest for life."[3]

In the terms I am using, his concern was about the loss of the faith behind faith, the loss of that primal connection in which we are energized and animated by an *unquenchable urge to flourish*. When we consider this flourishing and look upstream, we can see it flowing from the mystery and totality of our incredible planetary home. When we look downstream we can see it flowing into the mystery of Earth's astounding biodiversity.

This surrounding mystery is the origin of our sense of the Divine. Something is going on, we are in the middle of it, but it is way beyond our ken. What we know most closely is an uplifting "zest for life," which, in its most fully rounded expression, includes the unfolding of gratitude and compassion. Meister Eckhart, the great Christian mystic of the late 13th and early 14th centuries, had a succinct way of expressing this dimension of our human situation. He wrote: "The eye with which I see God is the same eye with which God sees me." And again; "If the only prayer you ever say in your entire life is 'thank you' it will be enough."[4]

The Ecological World View and the Faith of Ecology

A fundamental reorientation is taking place around the question of collective human security and wellbeing. Issues of justice, peace, ecological integrity, and even a continuing faith in the human enterprise are all converging on the reality of the human-Earth relationship and its expression in economic adaptation. The human future will be reasonably secure or disastrously disrupted depending on the way economic life is arranged and carried on. The relationships that are generating resources wars, social triage, entrenched inequities, and ecological disruption are all focused in economic adaptation. Ameliorating these conditions and altering the human trajectory toward greater equity, security, and wellbeing requires rebuilding economic activity within the biotic integrity of Earth's ecosystems. This is the faith of ecology.

This is the broadest possible concern that can be placed before the conscience of all human communities. We might ask why this concern should be of particular interest for faith communities since it must be addressed at all social, economic, political, educational, and professional levels? The answer is simply that religious authenticity depends precisely on bringing the energy of love and the work of community to the broadest possible concern for the human future. This is ecology of faith.

To understand the ecological worldview and the faith of ecology we need to ask what are the main areas of information, knowledge, and experience that must be brought into focus? For the purpose of this discussion, I will identify and briefly describe four tracks. Each track is referenced to a person whose work has contributed in a significant and accessible way to the creation of the ecological worldview. Although the figures referenced are well known to many students of ecology and culture, it will be useful to present their contributions in a way that links their work into a composite understanding. Each of these figures has been adept at coining phrases that catch and communicate the organizing concept of their work. In the scientific track we have James Lovelock with "The Gaia Hypothesis." In the cultural history track we have Thomas Berry with "The New Story." In the ecology and economic adaptation track we have Barry Commoner with "The Closing Circle." In the human-Earth relationship track we have Aldo Leopold with "The Land Ethic."

The Gaia Hypothesis. In considering James Lovelock's work, a clear distinction must be made between his formulation of the Gaia hypothesis and the subsequent adoption and promotion of the concept by others. The scientific work and scientific reasoning so ably recounted and illustrated in his book, *Gaia: A New Look at Life on Earth*,[5] has stood the test of almost three and half decades. It is this scientific work that is the focus of this discussion.

Through his experimental work on the interaction of chemical elements and compounds in Earth history and in the development of life, James Lovelock recognized a feedback and regulatory process. The history of this process helps provide an explanatory context for the persistence and flourishing of life within the environments of the planet. The evidence with which he was working led to a surprising and compelling conclusion; the evolution of the chemical composition of the atmosphere, and its increasing suitability for the flourishing of biotic process, could only be explained, in scientific terms, through the regulatory contribution of the whole biotic complex itself – the biosphere. The evidence indicated that once having gotten started, life, as a collective phenomenon, became a direct contributing agent to the maintenance of Earth's atmosphere within a certain range of chemical composition – the very range required for the further development of life. And it is only through this continuing regulation of the atmosphere by planetary life, that planetary life continues to exist and is able to flourish with a high level of diversity.

The Gaia hypothesis provides ecological intuition with a comprehensive scientific context. People who were predisposed toward seeing Earth as a holistic process, responded with delight. Some elders from within Aboriginal cultural traditions responded with amusement and a kind of patience tolerance. They said, in effect; "That's good medicine you have there. Too bad it took you so long to come up with it. Welcome to the Circle of Creation." Certain people who had always regarded Earth's environment as a stockpile of raw materials for human manipulation and consumption, became alarmed that their industrial ventures and the quest for endless economic growth and wealth accumulation could now be held to account against the history and science of biotic integrity.

Lovelock's scientific work provides a comprehensive context for the study of ecological relationships. It sets all life communities, including the human, squarely within the history of Earth process, and shows them to be entirely beholden for survival to the continuing integrity of Gaia – life process at the planetary level.

The New Story. Thomas Berry, a Catholic priest, trained in theology and the history of culture, came to regard himself as a "geologian." After a long life in the scholarship of religion and culture, Berry developed an understanding of the human story that brings the human-Earth relationship into focus. He sees the human-Earth relationship as central to the unfolding of culture, and all the facets of guidance, adaptation and behaviour that culture encompasses.

Berry observes that modern Western cultures are in a state of confusion with regard to guidance and adaptation, and are destructively floundering with regard to the human-Earth relationship. The story of human origin, cultural development, and moral orientation that has been built up out of the Judaic-Christian and Greco-Roman contexts has become seriously dysfunctional. Individuals and subculture groups may still organize their lives and behaviour according to some version of this "old story," but in its larger public and cultural dimensions it is failing to provide adequate guidance.

Among the most notable examples of this failure is the contemporary state of the human-Earth relationship. Berry notes this cultural failure as an autistic-like blindsiding of the organic circumstances of our lives and of Earth's biotic processes in general. The Western narrative has not engaged the human-Earth relationship in a way that offers adequate guidance. Instead, it has spawned a dominion story that now provides the only comprehensive guidance taken seriously at a public level in modern societies. This is the narrative of technological domination, maximum resource exploitation, unfettered capital accumulation, and unlimited economic growth. This story is promoted, and largely accepted, as the only reasonable scenario for the human-Earth relationship.

Thomas Berry describes an alternative. He sees a "new story" and a new sense of guidance in a composite narrative of scientific cosmology, evolutionary biology, global cultural history, and ecological knowledge. He combines the story of Earth as it has emerged from cosmic process, the story of life as it has emerged from Earth process, and the story of the human as it has emerged within Earth's biosphere. He sees ecological understanding emerging from both scientific work and an increased awareness of the beauty and diversity of Creation. He introduces this "new story" in his book, *The Dream of Earth*.[6] In *The Universe Story*[7], written with mathematical cosmologist, Brian Swimme, he presents the whole sweep of cosmic unfolding, Earth history, and human emergence. In *The Great Work: Our Way Into the Future*[8], he details how the new guidance we need emerges from ecological understanding and leads to a "mutually enhancing human-Earth relationship."

The concept of a "mutually enhancing human-Earth relationship" is one of Tom Berry's ecological guidance masterstrokes. It is a transforming conceptual advance over the conventional dualism that sees humans on one side and "nature" on the other. As Berry reminds us, the context is always the biosphere and biospheric relationships. The human-Earth relationship is our primary reality. "Mutually enhancing human-Earth relationship" expresses precisely the dynamic to which ecologically sound adaptation aspires. Berry is also responsible for introducing the concept "Earth process" into contemporary discourse. This is a functionally helpful replacement for the concept of "nature," which is made up of a confusing array of quasi-theological cultural constructions. The process of the planet, in all its diverse complexity, is what we are dealing with, not some metaphysical unity called "nature." Berry's clarifying concepts have been of cardinal importance to the development of the ecological worldview.

While Lovelock speaks mainly to the scientific track, Berry incorporates the scientific into the story of culture and re-presents the human as a constituent part of Earth's revelatory emergence and unfolding. Berry's work honours the scientific-cultural dimension and the religious-cultural dimension in the same discourse, and has become a principle guide for the cultural track feeding into the ecological worldview.

The Closing Circle. In the mid 1960s Brian Hocking, a well known Canadian biologist of the time, published a book with an arresting title, *Biology or Oblivion: Lessons from the Ultimate Science.*[9] He argued that the trajectory of our society's industrial-commercial adaptation is in serious conflict with the way the organic world actually works, and if we persist in this conflict, we are bound to crash our civilization. The book was issued by a small publisher, received little attention, and rapidly disappeared from view.

Less than a decade later, Barry Commoner, also a biologist, published a book that picked up on Hocking's theme. *The Closing Circle: Nature, Man, and Technology*[10] was issued by a mainstream publisher, received major attention, and became a prime text of the emerging environmental movement. As a professional researcher and educator on the physiochemical basis of biological process, Commoner is especially qualified to address the fundamental conflict between biospheric integrity and the technology of our economic system. He points out that behind the form and functioning of Earth's biotic environment there is, so to speak, two to three billion years of "research and development."

As a way of understanding the intervention of modern technology into this context, he offers a striking analogy. If you open the back of a fine Swiss watch and poke a sharp pencil into its works, there is an infinitesimal chance you will improve the functioning of the timepiece. The probability is much greater, of course, that the watch will be damaged. The watch is the result of a long tradition of highly skilled craftwork, and is not likely to be improved by such intervention. From the standpoint of biological systems, the modern capital-driven economy is wielding its technology in a similar way, with predictably disruptive and damaging consequences.

Barry Commoner was among the first to apply biological systems analysis to the dilemma modern economics has created within the human-Earth relationship. This dilemma is clearly illustrated by the fact that in order to maintain the capital-driven economy under present conditions, it is necessary to increasingly damage the functional integrity of Earth's ecosystems, and the biosphere as a whole. From the standpoint of science, this situation is devolutionary; from the standpoint of enlightened humanism, it is absurd; from the standpoint of religion, it is blasphemous.

Commoner's analysis of this dilemma is based on the "four laws of ecology:"

- Everything is connected to everything else.
- Everything must go somewhere.
- Nature [Earth process] knows best.
- There is no such thing as a free lunch.

At first glance, these statements may appear simplistic, but they are solidly rooted in biological knowledge and in the thermodynamics of energy and matter. Taken together, they describe the ecological worldview and offer guidance for an ecologically based economic system.

In a second book, *The Poverty of Power: Energy and the Economic Crisis*,[11] Commoner develops a schematic formula that is both profound and memorable. Human settlements and social order depend on the operation of three great, interrelated systems:

- the planetary ecosystem,
- the human production system,
- the monetary exchange system.

Ecologically speaking, the interrelationship of these systems goes like this:

- the planetary ecosystem is the source of all materials and energy processes that support human life;
- the production system is the network of agricultural, industrial, and service activities that convert Earth's resources and relationships into the wealth that sustains human settlements and social life;
- the monetary system represents the value of this wealth in ways that facilitate its exchange; it governs how this wealth is distributed and what is done with it.

In an ecologically sound arrangement of these three systems, the governing influence would flow from the ecosystem, to the production system, and then to the monetary system. The continuing integrity of the ecosystem would determine the design and operation of the production system. The stability and good service of the production system would determine the design and functioning of the monetary system.

Our contemporary economic reality, however, has the relationship of these three primary systems exactly the wrong way round. The monetary system drives the production system into unlimited, consumption-based economic growth. The production system, in order to meet this demand of the monetary system, generally operates without regard for the health and integrity of the ecosystem. The governing influence is flowing the wrong way, and the environmental crisis is the result. These comparative relationships can be diagrammed as follows:

Governing Influence	->	->	Outcome
Monetary System ->	Production System ->	Ecosystem ->	Ecological Breakdown
Ecosystem ->	Production System ->	Monetary System ->	Ecological Health

Barry Commoner's formula clearly illustrates the science-based approach to an ecological sound economy, and the policy issues that must be addressed to achieve an ecologically sound way of life.

The Land Ethic. And lastly, consideration must turn to the founding figure of modern ecological consciousness, Aldo Leopold. Leopold was a conservation biologist whose work encompassed field research, university teaching, public policy, and philosophical reflection that holds up the ecologically embedded basis of ethical development. He had the ability to frame his thoughts and insights in plain, memorable language. His best-known book, *A Sand County Almanac,*[12] published in 1949, collects his sketches from the field and his reflections on humanity's relationship with the land community. One would never suppose from such a modest title that this book would become one of the prime sources of ecological consciousness in our time. Leopold's skill was twofold; he articulated a philosophy of ecology in a language of such quiet beauty that we get not only the conceptual understanding, but also the experience of the spirit in which he lived and worked.

In *A Sand County Almanac* he argued that the recognition of the "land community" is the preeminent discovery of modern science. This may seem a curious claim when such an array of dramatic discoveries, especially since his time, could be named to this honour. But if we think carefully about this, I believe we will see he is correct, and will continue to be correct for as long into the future as we care to imagine. The scientific recognition of the "land community," and its ecological integrity, is the fundamental context of human adaptation and wellbeing. The same cannot be said for any other context of scientific discovery.

Leopold suggested the next major step in the evolution of human moral sensibility would be the development of "the land ethic." He offered this formulation: "A thing is right when it tends to preserve the integrity, stability and beauty of the biotic community. It is wrong when it tends otherwise." Many volumes have since been written on the philosophy of ecology, but it is this simple statement, with its emphasis on the aesthetic factor in moral awakening, that has become the touchstone of the ecological worldview.

In brief, **James Lovelock** describes the emergence of life as an expression of Earth-process that is characterized by a homeostatic regulatory function within biotic development itself, which maintains the chemistry of Earth's environment in the very condition required to enable the flourishing of life to continue. Understanding this ecological relationship inducts us into the great responsibility of being co-workers in the maintenance of the commonwealth of life.

Thomas Berry describes the cultural context of this relationship, and details the range of activities that flow from the exercise of this responsibility. He calls these activities "the Great Work." **Barry Commoner** describes the process and relationships that compose the organic world. He explains why the capital-driven market economy is deconstructing ecosystem integrity and cannot be sustained. He describes the ecological orientation toward economic adaptation. **Aldo Leopold** describes the enhancement of the human-Earth relationship based on the emergence of "the land ethic." The land ethic, according to Leopold, comes into full effect when scientific knowledge and aesthetic experience of Earth and its life communities rise into reverence, respect, and love.

This is the point at which science, culture, economics, and the human-Earth relationship converge into the ecological worldview, and the ecological worldview becomes the expression of authentic, revelatory experience – the ecology of faith and the faith of ecology. This experience, in its most fully rounded expression, unfolds with a sense of presence that calls us to wake up within the greater life of beauty, service, and love. If we can collectively, and globally, take up this ethic and become responsible citizens of the Earth community, a mutually enhancing human-Earth relationship may yet be achieved.

Faith Behind Faith:
Steps to an Ecology of Practice

Within the panorama of human cultures and behind the particularities of each culture's story of faith, there is another story, another level of deep faith, a background context of energy and relationship that animates human experience and nourishes creativity. I have a sense of this faith behind faith as a fluorescence of the spirit, as an incandescence of the soul. It is the energy and creative orientation of this deep background faith that is the funding source of culture, and that enables us, within our cultures, to create our particular stories of faith.

This faith behind faith is a gift, not a mental construction or theological exercise; it is a gift given not only at the human level, but into Earth-process as a whole, and most notably, into Earth's biotic process, manifesting in every form of life as an *unquenchable urge to flourish*. It is as simple as that. It is also the great mystery. On the human side, it underwrites the scripts of culture in which various images, metaphors, story lines, and systems of symbolic representation and meaning become expressions and amplifiers of faith.

The faith behind faith is not looking for allegiance; it is looking for expression. It is not the song, but the signal; the pulsing energy that animates. It is both before and after words. It is the most illusive, yet the most intimate breath of things that draws us up into the warp of life and out into the weave of the world. It gives us a way of working for the good of all, even if we must go through the worst of times.

Whatever collective, public policy choices on the human future are made, and then worked out over the next several decades, it seems likely that most of us currently alive, and certainly our descendants, are in for a journey of readaptation that will test the resilience of faith. As to what specific, practical steps can be taken to build up the resilience of the faith behind faith, here are four suggestions.

The Metabolic Step. The metabolic factor in the maintenance of faith is rarely considered, but it can be critical. The cells of brain tissue are nourished in exactly the same way as muscle tissue. Everyone understands that muscle tissue cannot function normally if it is inadequately nourished. The brain, likewise, cannot function efficiently if the cells of its tissue are lacking the full compliment of critically essential nutrients. The brain is the seat of consciousness in general and thought processes in particular, factors that are central to the operation of faith in our lives. Yet, almost no attention is given to brain nutrition by the scholars of faith. The same observation can be made with regard to the endocrine system – the seat of emotional response and balance. Emotional response, emotional balance, or lack thereof, are important factors in the functioning of faith.

The neurological and endocrine systems, in particular, are the context in which the experience of faith emerges, and through which we develop and extend our spiritual life. This is not a startling insight. Our metabolic situation is the only house we have. Nutritional shortfall and metabolic inefficiency directly impacts our ability to function in all ways, including the spiritual. The emergence of a sustaining, primal faith – the faith behind faith, is, in part, a matter of nutritional intake and metabolic efficiency. The fact that neurological and endocrine processes are subject to considerable variation due to genetic and environmental factors, makes attention to nutrition and metabolic efficiency a frontline step in the ecology of faith. Appropriate nutrition underwrites the zest for life and supports the faith behind faith.*

The Metaphysical Step. The thorniest metaphysical problem in the whole of human experience, the problem that gnaws deep into the marrow of faith and raises the temptation of fatalism, is the question of evil. Much theological ink has been poured over this problem, but it is not a theological solution that is required. On the contrary, as George Fox, the founder of the Religious Society of Friends (Quakers), discovered, an experiential solution is needed to release the paralyzing hold of this problem. In Fox's case it was experiencing a vision of the "ocean of light" overflowing the "ocean of darkness" that accomplished his release.[13]

Within the structure of human perception and mental functioning there is an unremitting dualism that continually foils our great desire for unity. We know without doubt the goodness of many things, but, at the same time, evil has a pattern of recurrence that keeps us on the metaphysical rack. The structure of human knowledge and the processes of moral reasoning are constituted in such a way that a comparative element is always at work in the way we come to know and understand things. But we can take a further step and observe that this comparative dynamic has a characteristic substructure; in the dance of opposites, the positive

*Friedrich Nietzsche, the renown German philosopher, became aware of the importance of the "metabolic step" near the end of his life and wrote the following lament: "I am interested in quite a different way in a question upon which the 'salvation of mankind' depends far more than it does upon any kind of quaint curiosity of the theologians: the question of nutriment. One can for convenience sake formulate it thus: 'how to nourish yourself so as to attain your maximum strength?'...My experiences here are as bad as they could possibly be; I am astonished that I heard this question so late...Until my very maturest years I did in fact eat badly...With the aid of Leipzig cookery, for example, which accompanied my earliest study of Schopenhauer (1865), I very earnestly denied my 'will to live.'... German cookery in general – what does it not have on its conscience!" *Ecce Homo*, translated by R. J. Hollingdale, 1979. New York: Penguin Books always sets the stage and leads the performance. As bad as things may seem to be, evil can only emerge and take shape against a background of goodness.

So even in our darkest moments, even when we are confronted by what seems to be the absence of goodness we have this insight to rely on; absence can only be known in relation to the experience of presence. A sense of absence cannot even begin to emerge without the reality of presence. Likewise, evil can only be known within the larger reality of goodness.

This realization does not magically remove the experience of anguish or exempt us from any moral task with respect to evil, and it may not be helpful at all for some folks, but it is the experiential moment of understanding to which many struggling souls have come. If not a complete resolution, this perspective is at least a resting place for the metaphysical problem of evil – a resting place that allows the faith behind faith to catch a better stride for the journey.

The Social Step. As important as it is to get the metabolic step on track and the metaphysical step into perspective, they are mainly background to the full emergence of primal faith in the social context of our lives. Human associations are the richest and strongest support for the emergence and maintenance of faith. The special place of communities, whether religious or not, is of particular importance. Participating in community-based associations is the terra firma of the faith behind faith. This is the step and the context that is most self evident and familiar to us.

There is, however, another dimension of the social that is also important but which is often overlooked. The entire biospheric realm is, in every detail, an intensely social phenomenon. Energies, relationships, reactions, and responses are flowing back and forth, up and down, and crosswise everywhere throughout the weave of the world. From the microbial composition of soils to the great flocks of migratory birds, from the ocean cruising pods of whales to forest tree succession, from the companionship enjoyed between animals and humans to the honey bee scout communicating through dance-like movements to the rest of the hive's workers where the best nectar harvest of the day can be found, a vast tapestry of social relationships compose the biosphere; all this, and everything in between, reveals relationship as the primary context and expression of life.

There is no end and no "outside" to the sociality of Earth. Human social order is embedded in and completely dependent on the larger domain of relationships that make up Creation as a whole. The extent to which we are knowledgeable about these relationships, and take human embeddedness in this larger social realm into account, the greater will be our adaptational integrity and resilient functioning within Earth's commonwealth of life. The more the scope of these relationships are realized in the practical details of our lives, the more our communities will become places of ecological and social coherence, and thus foster and nourish a fully rounded and flourishing faith behind faith.

The Ecological Identity Step. In her important book, *The Ecology of Imagination in Childhood*,[14] Edith Cobb focuses on the significance of experience in the natural world for cognitive and creative development. Her research reveals a common pattern in the development of emotion and imagination in children. It goes like this; at some point before the age of 10 or 12 an experience, or perhaps a series of experiences, with some aspect of the natural world gives rise to a sense of beauty and mystery, wonder and awe.

Such experiences may occur in the close presence of animals, or when under certain trees in a special place in the woods, or when watching the moon rise and turn a dark lake to silver. Such experiences can come just watching a humming bird at a feeder, or spotting a red tail hawk in a city park, or watching the endless rolling of the ocean. Gazing into the night sky bright with stars, or out over landscapes, either well known and comforting, or new and mysteriously beautiful, can provide deeply formative experiences. All these experiences, and many others of a similar sort, call up a sense of communion and open a window in the soul. When the heart and mind go out and enter a part of the larger natural world, and when that part of the larger world, in turn, enters one's life and becomes, in effect, a part of one's identity, a deep natural connection settles in the soul.

This kind of experience can become a lifelong source of intuitive understanding. It can provide a deep and ongoing sense of affinity. It can serve as an aesthetic reference point, an ethical compass, and a guide to compassionate moral action. Such experiences open a path of development into ecological consciousness and ecological identity; they comprise a relationship with the primal; they give rise to the faith behind faith.

Although these experiences seem to occur most readily in childhood, they are by no means confined to that period, they can also be cultivated in adulthood. The extent to which adults are now seeking out these experiences may be judged by the fact that researchers in developmental psychology are now studying what they have named "ecological conversion." The ecological identity step transports the imagination into the consciousness of communion and helps strengthen the faith behind faith.

These four areas of attention do not complete the steps to an ecology of faith, but they are something of the matrix from which the faith behind faith develops and is sustained. In this context, it may also be asked what has happened to the theological particularities of belief that are conventionally associated with religious faith? The answer is, nothing in particular has happened to them. Depending on our cultural circumstances, they may remain of the same significance, or they may evolve into new configurations. The point of this exploration is not to replace the particularities of one faith with another, but to recognize and suggest ways of nourishing the faith behind faith. The steps outlined here constitute a practice that can be usefully allied with various cultures of faith. They can help avoid the dead end temptation of fatalism and, hopefully, better equip us with ecological guidance to weather the great difficulties that are likely to come.

What Does Creation Have in Mind?

We are in great need of ecological guidance. Teachers of indigenous wisdom tell us to remember our "original instructions," our intuitive understanding of our place in Earth's commonwealth of life, and how to live with integrity in our home place. Ecological science now provides substantial confirmation that indigenous wisdom is on the right track. What *does* Creation have in mind? Faith behind faith comes back again and again to this question, the question of how to live in a mutually beneficial relationship with the integrity of Creation, the question of "right relationship."[15]

It is not unreasonable to wake up in the morning and wonder how long our modern civilization can go on like this. How long can the capital-driven, industrial-consumer economy continue its unremitting growth? Can it go on forever? If not, what happens when it stops? Or what happens, if before it stops, the quest for maximizing wealth destroys the natural health and balanced functioning of Earth's ecosystems on which human communities ultimately depend? If we take the integrity of Creation, the integrity of Earth's ecosystems, as the fundamental context of the commonwealth of life, it is not hard to see that our current industrial-consumer economy is steadily degrading the planet's ability to support life, and, if carried to its logical conclusion, will end in ecological, economic, and societal collapse. Exponential growth on a finite planet simply won't work.[16]

From the standpoint of science, this is a devolutionary situation – the unraveling of Earth's biotic complexity. From the standpoint of an enlightened humanism, it is absurd. From the standpoint of religion it is blasphemous. From the standpoint of the faith behind faith it is the "dying down of the zest for life." How have we gotten into this situation and how can we get out of it? How can we bring the ecological guidance that is now available to us into full effect?

Modern life is based on the assumption that the environment is part of the economy. This assumption is an error. The human economy is actually part of the environment, a wholly owned subsidiary of Earth's larger biotic and geochemical functioning. This recognition is a profound upheaval in our culture's understanding of the human-Earth relationship. For those who think in theistic terms, it means a significant theological reassessment of humanity's place in the larger context of Earth process. For those who think in scientific terms, but are still wedded to the notion of human dominion, the same reassessment of the human-Earth relationship is required. The Earth sciences in general and ecological science in particular, require a worldview in which the human-Earth relationship is understood to be a continually emerging and unfolding process of adaptation and reciprocity. This understanding of relationship goes to the core of human identity within Creation. It makes ecologically coherent adaptation a matter of spiritual significance and religious responsibility. It places economic and social life under the guidance of the integrity of Creation and brings the ethic of right relationship into clear focus.

When we ask the question, "what does Creation have in mind?" we are mostly asking what kind of economic adaptation is favoured with ecological resilience and sustainability. It may be difficult for mathematically trained economists to approach this question, but that just illustrates the difference between mathematics and ethics, and tells us why we need to bring the ethical perspective into the study and practice of economics, a perspective that will help economics be the kind of science it really is, a *social* science.

The question, "what does Creation have in mind?" can be phrased in a variety of ways. Earth system scientists can ask, "What does the biosphere have in mind?" Ecologists can ask, "What does this ecosystem have in mind?" Educators can ask, "What does this school, this learning programme, have in mind?" City planners can ask, "What does this urban region have in mind?" Folks who live on flood plains *should* ask, "What does this river have in mind?" Foresters and woodlot owners can ask, "What does this woodland environment have in mind?" Farmers can ask, "What does this land, this climate, this market have in mind?" This question of right relationship can be applied to all vocations, employments, and habitations, and through the whole range of activities that constitute the adaptation of human communities to their various ecosystems.

Now if this seems like too much of a stretch, allow me to explain why I think this is really what is going on, or should be going on, as we try to figure out if the human project can be put on a more Earth friendly footing. Although the question can be framed in many ways and at different levels, it is always keyed to the human-Earth relationship. From the mystic and theologian trying to read the mind of God in Creation, to the city planner and home gardener trying to figure out what should go where, the question is basically the same; what kind of relationship and what kind of adaptation is appropriate for life's flourishing and the common good, for the continuing integrity of Creation? What is potential in this situation? What are the emergent properties, encompassing tendencies, and creative processes that are available to us as we move into, settle on, and work with any particular environment, either natural or cultural, or, as is usually the case, a combination of both. The context is always the human-Earth relationship, and the question is always how to make the relationship mutually enhancing.

I have been challenged on this line of reasoning by those who argue that nothing has anything in mind with regard to the way Earth works, that the entire cosmological context, including the human-Earth relationship, is wholly experimental. Some of these folks insist, as an article of "faith," that randomness rules, and that we are simply free to make of it whatever we will. To which, I sympathetically reply; but of course, Isn't that just the problem? Human economic behaviour is free to trash the environment, to destroy ecological and social integrity, but that in no way alters the context or question of resilient and sustainable adaptation. It only puts us on notice for wising up and staying alert to the realities of how the biotic processes of Earth's ecosystems actually work.

What does Creation have in mind? The full force of this question came to me over thirty years ago when I was in the middle of developing and managing a farm operation in as ecologically coherent a manner as possible. During this time, I sketched out the following meditation.

By great good fortune we live in place where, on clear nights, we can go out and gaze at the galaxy – the Milky Way – flowing like the River of God across the sky. From horizon to horizon this great wheel of light flows with the turning Earth and shifts its angle with the seasons. Tonight, its course has an east-west bearing and the other stars fall away to the north and south like the slow rolling wake of a great cosmic ship.

Part of being a farmer in this particular place on Earth has included, for me, this midnight conversation with the Cosmos. Resting from the manure hauling of the day past, and thinking of the potato digging of the day to come, I take this lonely but comfortable time to once again ponder on what it all means: all this expenditure of energy, all this human cunning, all this seedtime and harvest, all this buying and selling. How does it all work? How do we keep it all going?

Down in the valley of the Saint John River I hear the steady drone of heavy trucks and speeding cars. For the moment, I hear it all from a distance, but so often I am in the middle of this energy-sucking caravan; restless souls and endless commodities flowing to and fro over the Earth. Around the hill to the south, large tracts of forestland are being clear-cut for newsprint, advertising, packaging material, and to keep the growth-driven, high-consumption economy rolling. Is this what Creation really has in mind for human communities and their relationship to the land?

When I gaze into the night sky and feel the great wheel of life turning, I am struck by the fact that most of what we experience as positive and progressive in our high-energy civilization, Earth's biosphere experiences as negative and retrogressive, as the breaking up and closing down of life support relationships. Surely this cannot be what Creation has in mind! To accept this ravaging of life as somehow normal or necessary is to disable the compass of faith. As surely as the River of God flows across the heavens and throughout the cosmic deep, we know it flows in nurturing and creative presence throughout life on Earth as well. We are of this Earth, the biosphere is our home, and if we better harmonize our economic activity with the way Earth's ecosystems actually work we can get ourselves on a better footing with the great flourishing of life that Creation has so clearly, so consistently, and so beautifully in mind.

Our "original instructions" come to us through the way of the heart, and the way of the heart leads unerringly to a sense of home. A sense of home is the origin of our sense of the sacred. Here we find our "original instructions" and the guidance we need begins to unfold. Only when we have a strong sense of solidarity with the whole commonwealth of life, and a strong sense of Earth as the home place of life's commonwealth, will we live and work for the common good with the love we naturally have for home. Our economic adaptation will then be devoted to creating a mutually enhancing human-Earth relationship, which, after all, is what tracking down ecological guidance is all about and what the faith behind faith is for.

Epilogue: Down to Earth With an Eye on the Future

The preceding essays are primarily concerned with intellectual, emotional, spiritual, and cultural survival. While I have spent most of my life on the front lines of business enterprise and community economic development, the concerns of these essays have been at the centre of my vocation as well. This Epilogue deals with the down to Earth issues of energy, economics, finance, eco-justice, and public policy, thus rounding out my perspective on the task before us. A version of this essay was first published in *Beyond the Growth Dilemma: Toward an Ecologically Integrated Economy*, Edited by Ed Dreby and Judy Lumb (2012)[1]

As the movements for social justice and ecological integrity have come together, the realization has dawned that there will be no sustainable progress in eliminating poverty and reducing inequality if the degradation of Earth's ecosystems continues on the trajectory that has been set by the capital-driven industrial-consumer economy.

Economic growth that alleviates poverty and public policy that reduces vast inequality cannot effectively address these social ills if, at the same time, it is systematically undermining the functional integrity of the ecosystems on which the entire scenario of human settlement and livelihood depends. On the one hand, the way our society and its economy are organized require constant economic growth, but, on the other, constant economic growth is now undermining the integrity of the ecological conditions that are required for human societies and economies to function effectively and equitably, or at all.

This growth dilemma was clearly recognized and fully articulated in the 1960s and early 1970s by a number of prescient biologists and economists. Had government and industry taken ameliorative and precautionary action at that time, local, regional, and global economies might now be operating at a high level of steady-state resilience. However, aside from regulations to control pollution, nothing effective was done to frame economic behaviour within a sustainable ecosystem and energy context. We are now in a situation in which the dilemma is acute and certain consequences seem likely to unfold that are beyond effective management or mitigation.[2]

For a whole complex of reasons the economy to which we have become accustomed is badly stumbling, and, in some cases, simply failing. In the midst of incredible wealth, adequate access to the means of life is a growing crisis for an increasing number of people. At the same time, the basic ecological relationships of Earth's entire life system are being disrupted, damaged, and increasingly destroyed by the operations of the growth economy and the efforts to keep it going as long as possible.

Many economic and social analysts are trying to work out what is happening. The end of low cost oil is certainly a factor.* The collision of the growth economy with the reality of Earth's ecosystem, and the increasing costs of dealing with this incoherency, is often noted. Population increase is obviously significant. Militarism and continual episodes of war consume resources and damage environments at enormous cost. A monetary system that creates "phantom wealth" by perpetuating unrepayable debt, and

---

*Since this was written, oil prices have temporarily crashed due to a worldwide decrease in the rate at which oil consumption is growing, and a surplus of supply in the market. After the current imbalance in supply and demand is past, oil prices are bound to resume increasing, as conventional sources are further depleted and more costly, hard to access sources are ramped up to fill in.

repeatedly produces cycles of boom and bust, is also clearly at the center of our economic and social distress. We are deeply troubled by a loss of faith in the narrative of progress and prosperity, and doubly so because we can now see that what has been promoted as the hallmark of human achievement – the economic growth of industry and commerce – has brought us to this impasse.

The economic growth we have been enjoying now appears, more and more, to have been based on a short sighted and faulty reading of our ecological situation. The consequences of this error are now coming into play, and can be seen at a fundamental level in the energy analysis of biophysical economics. We are now being forced to take a realistic view of our economic and ecological situation. Fundamental issues of adaptation and survival are on the table.

The Energy Base of the Economy

Behind the impasse of economic growth lies the relationship of energy and the economy. This impasse is addressed from the ecological side by the discipline of   biophysical economics, which goes to the heart of the matter with regard to the energy basis of economic activity and human adaptation. Historically, economies expanded according to the availability of a dominant energy source, and then contracted when that source became depleted to the point that energy return on energy invested no longer yielded a net benefit to society. Charles A. S. Hall, a leading energy science researcher, points out that the situation of our industrial-commercial economy in relation to oil is following the same trajectory that other economic eras have followed in relation to their energy sources.[3]

We are in big trouble with the economy because civic, political and business leaders have not paid careful attention to the energy factor that is the foundation of economic activity. The historical facts of our energy situation are clear. Since the early days of the 20th century the development of modern societies have been based on a huge injection of hydrocarbon energy. This sudden and unusual injection of energy must realistically be understood as a temporary subsidy. There is no way it can go on forever, or even for very long, historically speaking.

At the beginning of the hydrocarbon era, large deposits of oil and natural gas were easily accessible. The energy return on energy invested (EROEI) for early oil wells was often 100 to 1. This means 100 barrels of oil could be extracted using the energy of only 1 barrel of oil. This ratio steadily dropped as the deposits of easily accessible oil were depleted. In recent years the ratio has plummeted. Increasing amounts of energy are required to produce new oil as it becomes harder and harder to extract from deeper, less accessible, and lower quality deposits. The EROEI ratio is now down to approximately 18 to 1 worldwide. The ratio for North America is down to 15 to 1. Alberta tar sands extraction is down to 5 to 1, and perhaps much lower; some calculations put it at 1 to 1.

This rapidly declining ratio of energy return on energy invested is a fundamental reality of our energy situation. Energy science analysts and biophysical economists now calculate that 5 to 1 is about as low as the ratio can go before oil extraction is no longer a profitable investment. At 3 to 1 they calculate the oil industry will come to a stand still. Energy corporations will no longer be able to earn a profit and investment will stop. Investment will likely taper off even earlier as investors see the EROEI ratio steadily drop. This is simply the logic of our economic system.[4,5,6,7] There is no work-around for this future energy scenario. There is simply nothing in the energy picture that can replace the oil subsidy on which modern industrial-commercial economies have been built up and now run. As this oil subsidy is depleted and becomes economically inaccessible, the energy basis of our society will inevitably contract. By building up an economy that is now dependent on this limited oil subsidy, we have created a trap from which there is no obvious escape.

Charles Hall advises that this trap is not one from which we will escape by means of technology, or by adjusting the economy away from material and energy throughput toward services and culture. Nor will the current temporary surge in natural gas and unconventional oil extraction do anything more than slightly delay the inevitable contraction. The discontinuity between the current structure and functioning of the industrial-commercial system and its depleting energy base will become so vast, and so fast moving, that no patching together of technical fixes will be able to forestall the decline of economies that have been built on low cost oil.

The Compounding Role of Climate Change

The oil depletion protocol has generally been thought of as switching to renewable energy sources in time to keep the industrial-commercial economy functioning without major disruption. It has been assumed that we can keep using oil as long as it lasts, and the more we continue to find, the longer we have to make the switch. However, it now appears that a very large part of the fossil fuels that are still in the ground must be left in the ground if Earth's climate is to stabilize in a temperature range that allows human settlements to continue within their present tropical and mid-latitude geographic zones.[8] Private and state owned energy companies have fossil fuels on the their books that will release 2,795 gigatons of carbon dioxide into the atmosphere if they are extracted and burned. Current calculations estimate that no more that 565 gigatons of carbon dioxide can be released over the next 50 years without breaching a 2 degree Celsius temperature increase – the increase within which climate scientists consider that some semblance of human civilization can survive.[9]

On November 12, 2012 the International Energy Agency released its annual flagship publication, *World Energy Outlook*, in which it states, "No more than one-third of proven reserves of fossil fuels can be consumed prior to 2050 if the world is to achieve the two degree Celsius goal." Two degrees Celsius is the scientifically based, internationally recognized limit for average global warming in order to prevent catastrophic climate change.[10]

On November 19th 2012 the World Bank released a new report, *Turn Down the Heat: Why a 4 Degree Warmer World Must Be Avoided*, in which it states;

> *Humankind's emissions of greenhouse gases are breaking new records every year. Hence we're on a path towards 4 degree global warming probably as soon as by the end of this century. This would mean a world of risks beyond the experience of our civilization – including heat waves, especially in the tropics, a sea-level rise affecting hundreds of millions of people, and regional yield failures impacting global food security.*
>
> *If we venture far beyond the 2 degree guardrail, towards 4 degrees, we risk crossing tipping points in the Earth system. ...The only way to avoid this is to break with the fossil-fuel-age patterns of production and consumption. ...Lack of action on climate change threatens to make the*

*world our children inherit a completely different world
than we are living in today...we need to assume the
moral responsibility to take action on behalf of future
generations...*[11]

The Collapse of Complex Societies

The work of Joseph Tainter adds another dimension to the
growth dilemma. Tainter, a foremost researcher in social and
economic history, shows that the collapse of complex societies
throughout history exhibit a pattern of remarkable consistency.[13]

Complex societies fail when the level of resources devoted to
maintaining their complexity is so great that almost no margin
remains for dealing with unexpected trauma, shock, or stress. At
that point, even a seemingly minor challenge, poorly addressed,
may become a trigger of collapse.

Some societal collapses in history have been sudden and some
protracted. The common factor is growth in complexity that requires
a high percentage of social, economic, and environmental resources
just for maintenance, leaving little or no margin for adapting to new
circumstances. High cost complexity reduces resilience and ramps
up the level of risk a society is required to live with. Historically, the
consistent consequence of increasing societal complexity has been
collapse. Although Tainter is a cautious scholar, he observers that
the increasing complexity of our modern industrial-commercial
society is following the same trajectory of escalating risk that has
led previous societies into collapse.

Ulrich Beck, a leading German sociologist, argues that the
contemporary situation of complex "super-industrialism," has

created the "risk society," and, on a global level, the "the world risk society."[14,15] Beck observes that human adaptation has moved from being concerned primarily with natural hazards to now dealing continuously with manufactured hazards, hazards that appear as the result of the pursuit of economic growth and the decision making associated with this quest. With the advent of chemical, hydrocarbon, nuclear, genetic, and nanotechnologies, the ecological and social context of manufactured risk has become total. According to Beck, the risks introduced by these technologies are beyond accountability.* The hazards of these technologies are potentially catastrophic to the degree that the collapse of industrial civilization is a logically foreseeable outcome. When we add the analysis of energy return on energy invested (EROEI) to the risk scenarios of our complex society, the extreme dilemma of the growth economy is not hard to see.[16]

Five Reversals

For those of us living through the flush times from the late 1940s through the 1990s, the reversal of economic growth and the subsidence or collapse of industrial society is almost unthinkable. But the unthinkable now seems highly probable and perhaps unavoidable. In order to get a handle on what is happening to our economy and society, it is important to consider a series of economic reversals with which we are now confronted.

---

*This essay was written before the Gulf of Mexico deep-water oil well blowout and the Fukushima nuclear power plant explosion and meltdown. These technological failures are exactly what Ulrich Beck is pointing to when he speaks of "total risk." Not only are the consequences of such failures beyond any measure of risk calculation, they are beyond any possibility of damage compensation. And to make matters worse, they occurred in environments of complexity that had no technology capable of dealing with the failures. Only drilling a secondary well to take off the pressure stopped the Gulf oil well blowout. In the case of Fukushima, no technology exists to deal with cleaning up the melted reactor cores, and experts in the field say there is no current engineering that can envision what this technology might be. They never thought this would happen.

1) Fossil fuel use must be phased out and most remaining deposits left in the ground. The fossil fuel industries, of course, reject this scenario out of hand, but, judging by their advertising and public relations efforts, seem to realize that the evidence is building toward this conclusion. With regard to fossil fuels, we are in a showdown between the precautionary principle of sound scientific evidence as applied to the long-run common good of the whole commonwealth of life, and the high-risk principle of maximizing wealth accumulation and convenience in the short-run for a select few of the human species.[17,18,19]

2) We can no longer expect that each successive generation will have a more affluent standard of living than the previous one. This reversal is a shock, a wake-up call. It unhinges public faith in the industrial-consumer economy. It hits young people like a betrayal. If the economy can no longer deliver a steadily improving standard of living, then what is the economy for? If it cannot even provide access to the means of life for an increasing number of citizens, then what kind of economy do we have? The evidence of a broken and failing economic system is mounting. Conventional economic thinking has not been able to offer a believable formula for repair or for reconstructing a better economic future that makes sense in our ecological context.

3) The conventional economic model has failed. The standard economic model shows a circular flow involving goods, services, labour, and money. Despite booms and busts and acts of God, this model has long been accepted as accurately representing the self-perpetuating activity of economic life in human communities. The fundamental flaw in this model has now become obvious at the intersection of economics and ecology; it fails to account for the stocks of ecosystem capital, including energy, that feed the economy, nor does it account for the costs of the pollution the economy creates. The failure to account for the depletion of ecological capital and the cost of pollution, is creating a cumulative crisis of degradation and toxification that is increasingly disabling Earth's life support capacities

4) The current monetary system is destroying democratic society. The monetary and financial systems are now systematically moving wealth from the middle and working classes to corporate and political elites, from the poor to the wealthy, and from borrower to lender.[20] The for-profit, debt-money system requires governments to increasingly impoverish public services, and load unrepayable debt on taxpayers. With deregulation and corrupting financial innovations, the monetary system is now revealed as a tool of wealth accumulation for the already wealthy,[21] rather than a public service that enables the equitable development of all citizens and all communities within society.

5) The contraction of consumption and the rejection of debt. The 2007-2010 financial and economic collapses brought on a renewal of interest in frugality. As businesses and households were economically squeezed, they tended to take precautionary action; they wisely reduced consumption, increased savings, and decreased or refused debt. This reversal is a clear signal that the financial management of the debt-based consumer economy is not working for many people. But this reversal, while prudent at the household and business level, is the enemy of the growth economy. This reversal of consumer behaviour stalls economic growth. Less consumption and less debt are good for households and businesses but bad for the growth economy. More consumption and more debt are good for the growth economy but bad for households and businesses. Frugality and debt rejection exacerbates economic recession. This new frugality seems likely to continue and even increase as households and businesses find new security in reduced expenditure, debt elimination, and increased savings.

What Can Be Done?

The conventional formula for recovering prosperity is to ramp up the growth of the consumer economy, but we know that our consumer economy is already overshooting the bioproductive and bioassimilative limits of Earth's ecosystems, and that further growth will accelerate the destruction of Earth's life-support capacity. We generally acknowledge that reducing debt and cutting back on consumption is a good thing, but if consumption is reduced and debts are paid off, the economy stalls. Re-floating the debt-based monetary system is a conventional response, but this will keep the boom and bust cycle churning out financial and social insecurity.

Meanwhile, the structural violence of poverty grinds on while, at the same time, vast amounts of both cash and capital wealth continue to accumulate in a small number of hands. Basic economic growth is needed to end poverty in many geographic and cultural zones, but unless zones of wealth and affluence begin a compassionate retreat in material and energy consumption, the growth needed to end poverty will add to the ecological overshoot already bending Earth's ecosystems toward collapse. This consideration of ecojustice now stands at the intersection of economics and ecology. Unlike Charles Dickens, who could say in *The Tale of Two Cities*, "It was the best of times, and the worst of times," it looks like the best of times for economic growth are over, and a big adjustment on the edge of survival is beginning.

There is an upside to this downward trending impasse. The clearer it becomes that the current growth economy is heading for ecological and societal breakdown, the sooner the opportunity to redefine what the economy is for and how it should be governed will come into view. If we are to work through the change that is coming with the end of the oil era, rather than be derailed into disaster, our strategy must be to move from an economy of never-ending growth to a steady-state economy, an economy of "enough."[22] Returning to the five reversals outlined above, we can begin to plot a response that could make these trends important steps toward a steady-state economy that works for the common good of both people and planet.

1)**Unburnable fossil fuels:** The prospect of leaving large amounts of coal and hydrocarbons in the ground is, perhaps, the most difficult thought many us can imagine. To complicate matters further, it is not likely that renewable energy technology can be scaled up within the market system to compensate for the dramatic reduction in the use of fossil fuels required by a timely response to climate change risk. This means that capitalism is unlikely to facilitate the transition to renewable energy within a safe timeframe. This dilemma, at first, looks like a disaster, but it may be an important opportunity for the transition to an economy of enough. Why should renewable energy technology be expected to keep up the output of the current fossil fuel regime as it goes into decline and is phased out? Energy use should, in fact, decline in order to bring the material throughput of human consumption back from its ecological overshoot position. A quite reasonable way of life can be organized and enjoyed around a much lower use of energy.[23]

We already have the renewable energy technology we need; it can be widely and flexibly deployed, and the economic activity around its manufacture, installation, and maintenance will provide a significant level of jobs and income.[24,25] For the full benefit of renewable energy to be rolled out in a way that supports the rapid transition to an ecologically integrated economy, it will probably have to be done in a public interest economic framework, very much like that deployed and widely accepted during the Second

World War. This means politics must get serious about public policy that pulls together for the common good of the whole society.

2)**Living standards:** Living standards in a subsiding economy can be addressed by recognizing that the link between market based jobs and income has been broken for many people and households, and is unlikely to be restored. This means that access to the means of life should be placed within a framework of basic income, stakeholder grants, and public interest employment. Although the material standard of living in the future may be less affluent, an economy of enough need not be impoverishing if the vocations and employment that make for a satisfying, secure, and dignified way of life are supported by a nonprofit, public trust monetary system (See #4). Developing this scenario depends on a package of policies and legislation that emerge from a political process genuinely focused on the public interest.

3)**Ecologically integrated economy:** Although the circular flow model of the economy may still be taught in economics classes, the reality of natural capital throughput and pollution costs are now an acknowledged part of the economic picture. Full cost accounting for the use of material and energy sources and for the effects of pollution is now fundamental to rational, real world economics.[26,27] Getting this discipline firmly in place is the first step in the change over to an ecologically integrated economy.

A second critical step is identified by Jane Jacobs in her prescient book, *Cities and the Wealth of Nations.*[28] She shows that regions in general, and city regions in particular, have historically gained in prosperity and vibrancy through strategic patterns of *import replacement*. Import replacement is the key to building a prosperous, resilient economy under any circumstances, but it will be especially significant with the subsidence of the global growth economy and the change over to economies of enough at the regional and local level.

Urban region agriculture is a good example of import replacement that can ensure a continued measure of prosperity even as the global supply lines of industrialized food production fall victim to the oil economy contraction. This contraction will also open up a renaissance of opportunity for local and regional manufacturing, processing, and repair businesses.[29] If this redevelopment of local and regional economies proceeds on the basis of resource stock maintenance, energy conservation, renewable energy, and materials recycling, the subsidence of the industrial-commercial era could balance out into a steady-state conserver economy of fair prosperity. Public policy and smart legislation should support the revitalization of local food systems and the redevelopment of local manufacturing and repair businesses.

4)Monetary system reform: A collective reconsideration of what the monetary system is for arises from the question of what the economy is for. If general agreement can be reached that a good economy should provide equitable access to the means of life for all people, and preserve and enhance the resources on which human settlement and cultural life depend, then the way the monetary system works becomes a matter of critical importance.[30]

Most modern governments have allowed the operation of their national currency system to be controlled by for-profit financial corporations. But why should a sovereign government, which has the essential authority to create and regulate the national currency, default on this responsibility in favour of the private banking industry? Why should a national government have to borrow the national currency from private banks? Why should a government have to pay millions in interest on borrowed money? None of this is necessary; it is simply a historically determined convention. The monetary system could just as well be set up as a nonprofit, public service institution that insures adequate circulation of legal tender to all citizens, and funds public interest expenditures on a debt-free basis.[31,32] Monetary system reform of this sort is an essential step in the change over to an ecologically integrated economy.

5)**Conservation and relocalization:** Reducing consumption, getting out of debt, and increasing the means of local provisioning will increase security as the economy subsides to an appropriate level within the biophysical limits of Earth's ecosystems. Our sense of prosperity, security, and dignity will flow from solid social attachment, vibrant community commerce, and a rich flourishing of local and regional culture. If a national, nonprofit, public service monetary system can be put in place, and a range of local currencies emerge in many communities,[33] a platform can be developed on which a variety of other precautionary and conserver policies and practices can be implemented and supported. A subsiding economy may then be able to settle around an ecologically sound steady-state, in which a reasonable and equitable level of prosperity can be maintained.[34] All this will take a rebirth of broad support for public interest politics and governance for the common good.

If all this came to pass, and the presence, beauty, and integrity of the living Earth became our guide to economic adaptation, we may yet achieve the wisdom to become the creators of a resilient survival.

References

Preface

1. Thompson, William Irwin, 1978. *Darkness and Scattered Light: Four Talks on the Future.* Garden City NY: Anchor Press, Doubleday.

2. Higgins, Polly, 2010. *Eradicating Ecocide: Laws and Governance to Prevent the Destruction of Our Planet.* London: Shepheard-Walwyn.

3. The situation at Fukushima is a prime example of this point. See references. www.washingtonsblog.com/2012/10/fixing-fukushima-is-beyond-current-technology.html www.aljazeera.com/indepth/features/2011/06/20116166482830 2638.html www.washingtonsblog.com/2012/04/the-largest-short-term-threat-to-humanity-the-fuel-pools-of-fukushima.html The Deepwater Horizon explosion and the Macondo well blowout in the Gulf of Mexico is another prime example. See: Tainter, Joseph and Tadeusz Patzek, 2012. *Drilling Down: The Gulf Oil Debacle and Our Energy Dilemma.* New York: Springer Media.

4. Jackson, Tim, 2011. *Prosperity Without Growth: Economics for a Finite Planet.* London: Earthscan.

5. Gilding, Paul, 2011. *The Great Disruption: Why the Climate Crisis Will Bring on the End of Shopping and the Birth of a New World.* New York: Bloomsbury Press.

6. Hawken, Paul, 2007. *Blessed Unrest: How the Largest Movement in the World Came into Being and Why No One Saw It Coming.* New York: Viking.

7. Rifkin, Jeremy, 2011. *The Third Industrial Revolution: How Lateral Power is Transforming Energy, the Economy, and the World.* New York: Palgrave Macmillan.

8. Heinberg, Richard, 2011. *The End of Growth: Adapting to Our New Economic Reality.* Gabriola Island BC: New Society Publishers.

9. Barnes, Peter, 2001. *Who Owns the Sky? Our Common Assets and the Future of Capitalism.* Washington: Island Press.

10. Ciscel, David, Barbara Day Keith Helmuth, Sandra Lewis, and Judy Lumb, 2011. *How on Earth Do We Live Now? Natural Capital, Deep Ecology, and the Commons.* Calker Caye, Belize: Quaker Institute for the Future.

Angel of History, the Storm of Progress, and the Order of the Soul

1. Rogers, Raymond, 1994. *Nature and the Crisis of Modernity: A Critique of Contemporary Discourse on Managing the Earth.* Montreal: Black Rose Books.

2. Caldwell, Lynton Keith, 1999. "Is Humanity Destined to Self-Destruct?" *Perspectives: Occasional Paper of the Dean's Office, School of Public and Environmental Affairs*, Bloomington IN: Indiana University.

3. Benjamin, Walter, 1968. *Illuminations: Essays and Reflections*. New York: Schocken Books.

4. Boulding, Kenneth, 1956. *The Image: Knowledge in Life and Society*. Ann Arbor MI: University of Michigan Press.

5. Berry, Thomas, 1988. *The Dream of Earth*. San Francisco: Sierra Club Books.

6. Northcott, Michael, 2004. *An Angel Directs the Storm: Apocalyptic Religion & American Empire*. London: I.B. Tauris.

7. *Bible* (King James Version), I Kings, chapter 18.

8. Kaufman, Gordon, 1972. "The Concept of Nature: A Problem for Theology." Cambridge MA: Harvard Theological Review No. 6.

9. Kaufman, Gordon, 2000. "Ecological Consciousness and the Symbol, 'God.' *Christianity and the 21st Century*;" edited by Deborah A. Brown. New York: Crossroads Publishing Company.

10. Bulliet, Richard W., 2004. *The Case for Islamo-Christian Civilization*. New York: Columbia University Press.

11. Rainwater, Lee and Timothy M. Smeeding, 2003. *Poor Kids in a Rich Country: America's Children in a Comparative Perspective*. New York: Russell Sage Foundation.

12. Schwartz-Nobel, Loretta, 2002. *Growing Up Empty: How Federal Policies Are Starving America's Children*. New York: HarperCollins.

13. Currie, Elliot, 2005. *The Road to Whatever: Middle-Class Culture and the Crisis of Adolescence*. New York: Metropolitan Books.

14. Jamison, Kay Redfield, 1999. *Night Falls Fast: Understanding Suicide*, New York, Random House.

15. Diamond, Jared, 2005. *Collapse: How Societies Choose to Fail or Succeed*. New York: Viking.

16. Turnbull, Colin, 1972. *Mountain People*. New York: Simon & Schuster.

17. Wood, Ellen Meiksins, 2002. *The Origin of Capitalism: A Longer View*. London: Verso.

18. Daly, Herman and Joshua Farley, 2004. *Ecological Economics: Principles and Applications*, Washington, Island Press.

19. Christian, David, 2004. *Maps of Time: An Introduction to Big History*. Berkeley CA: University of California Press.

20. McNeill, J.R., 2000. *Something New Under the Sun: An Environmental History of the Twentieth-Century World*. New York: W.W. Norton.

21. de Vries, Bert, and Goudsblom, Johan, eds., 2002. *Mappae Mundi: Humans and their Habitats in a Long-Term Socio-Ecological Perspective*. Amsterdam: Amsterdam University Press.

22. Harvey, Graham, 2006. *Animism: Respecting the Living World*. New York: Columbia University Press.

23. Brody, Hugh, 2000. *The Other Side of Eden: Hunters, Farmers and the Shaping of the World*. New York: North Point Press.

24. Nabokov, Peter, 2002. *A Forest of Time: American Indian Ways of History*. New York: Cambridge University Press.

25. Bottero, Jean, 2000. *The Birth of God: The Bible and the Historian*. University Park PA: Pennsylvania State University Press.

26. Dubuisson, Daniel, 2003. *The Western Construction of Religion: Myths, Knowledge, and Ideology*. Baltimore: Johns Hopkins University Press.

27. Turner, Nancy J., 2005. *The Earth's Blanket: Traditional Teachings for Sustainable Living*. Seattle: University of Washington Press.

28. Hyams, Edward, 1976. *Soil and Civilization*. New York: Harper & Row.

29. Weisman, Alan, 1998. *Gaviotas: A Village to Reinvent the World*. White River Junction VT: Chelsea Green Publishers.

30. Walker, Liz, 2005. *Eco-Village at Ithaca: Pioneering a Sustainable Culture.* Gabriola Island BC: New Society Publishers.

31. Berry, Thomas, 1999. *The Great Work: Our Way Into the Future.* New York: Bell Tower, Random House.

32. Bookchin, Murray, 1989. *Remaking Society.* Montreal: Black Rose Books.

33. Brown, Peter, Geoff Gaver, Keith Helmuth, Robert Howell, Steve Szeghi, 2009. *Right Relationship: Building a Whole Earth Economy.* San Francisco: Berrett-Koehler.

34. Ciscel, David, Barbara Day, Keith Helmuth, Sandra Lewis, Judy Lumb, 2011. *How on Earth Do We Live Now? Natural Capital, Deep Ecology, and the Commons.* Caye Caulker, Belize: Quaker Institute for the Future.

35. Dreby, Ed and Judy Lumb, editors, 2012. *Beyond the Growth Dilemma: Towards and Ecologically Integrated Economy.* Caye Caulker, Belize: Quaker Institute for the Future.

First Light & Last Things

1. Camus, Albert, 1955. *The Myth of Sisyphus and other Essays.* New York: Alfred A. Knopf.

2. Austin, Mary, 1974. *The Land of Little Rain.* Albuquerque NM: University of New Mexico Press.

3. ...the mighty Sierra, miles in height, reposing like a
    smooth cumulus cloud in the sunny sky, and so gloriously
    colored, and so luminous, it seems to be not clothed in
    light, but wholly composed of it, like the wall of some
    celestial city. Along the top, and extending a good way
    down, you see a pale, pearl-gray belt of snow; and below
    it a belt of blue and dark purple, marking the extension
    of forests; and along the base of the range a broad belt of
    rose-purple and yellow, where lie the miner's gold-fields
    and the foot-hill gardens. All these colored belts blending
    smoothly to make a wall of light ineffably fine, and as
    beautiful as a rainbow, yet firm as adamant. When I first
    enjoyed this superb view, one glowing April day, from
    the summit of Pacheco Pass, ...the luminous wall of the
    mountains shone in all its glory. Then it seemed to me
    the Sierra should be called not the Nevada or Snowy
    Range, but the Range of Light. And after ten years spent
    in the heart of it, rejoicing and wondering, bathing in its
    glorious floods of light, seeing the sunbursts of morning
    among the icy peaks, the noonday radiance of the trees
    and rocks and snow, the flush of the alpenglow, and a
    thousand dashing waterfalls with marvelous abundance
    of irised spray, it still seems to me above all others the
    Range of Light, the most divinely beautiful of all the
    mountain-chains I have ever seen. Muir, John, 1961. *The
    Mountains of California*. Garden City NY: Anchor Books,
    Doubleday and Company and American Museum of
    Natural History.

4. Maloof, Joan, 2005. *Teaching the Trees: Lessons from the
    Forest*. Athens GA: University of Georgia Press.

5. Nickerson, Mike. Sustainability Project / 7th Generation Initiative. www.sustainwellbeing.net/index.html

6. Smyth, Angela, 1990. *SAD: Winter Depression, Who Gets It, What Causes It, How to Cure It.* London: Unwin Hyman Limited.

7. Terman, M., 1988. "On the Question of Mechanism in Phototherapy for Seasonal Affective Disorder." Journal of Biological Rhythms, vol. 3, no. 2, pp. 155-172.

8. Terman, M., Terman, J., 1990. "New Light on Winter Depression." Clinical Advances in the Treatment of Psychiatric Disorders, vol. 4:1, pp. 1-11.

9. Liberman, Jacob, 1991. *Light – Medicine of the Future.* Santa Fe NM: Bear & Company Publishing.

10. Krimsky, Sheldon, 2000. *Hormonal Chaos: The Scientific and Social Origins of the Environmental Endocrine Hypothesis.* Baltimore MD: Johns Hopkins University Press.

11. Kroeber, Theodora, 1961. *Ishi In Two Worlds.* Berkeley CA: University of California Press.

12. Kroeber, Theodora, 1964. *Ishi, Last of His Tribe.* Berkeley CA: Parnassus Press.

Additional Suggested Reading

• Albert, Michael, 2006. *Realizing Hope: Life Beyond Capitalism.* London & New York: Zed Books.

- Anderson, M. Kat, 2005. *Tending the Wild: Native American Knowledge and the Management of California's Natural Resources.* Berkeley CA: University of California Press.

- Berry, Thomas, 2006. "Loneliness and Presence." *Evening Thoughts: Reflecting on Earth as Sacred Community.* San Francisco: Sierra Club Books.

- Brinton, Howard, 1973. "Evolution and the Inward Light." *The Religious Philosophy of Quakerism.* Wallingford PA. Pendle Hill Publications.

- Freeman, James, 1992. *Ishi's Journey from the Center to the Edge of the World.* Happy Camp CA: Naturegraph Publishers.

- Gumbrecht, Hans Ulrich, 2004. *Production of Presence: What Meaning Cannot Convey.* Stanford CA: Stanford University Press.

- Kroeber, Karl and Clifton Kroeber, editors, 2003. *Ishi in Three Centuries*, Lincoln NB: University of Nebraska Press.

- Harper, Ralph, 1991. *On Presence: Variations and Reflections.* Philadelphia: Trinity Press.

- Isenberg, Andrew, 2005. *Mining California: An Ecological History.* New York: Hill and Wang.

- Lear, Jonathan, 2006. *Radical Hope: Ethics in the Age of Cultural Devastation.* Cambridge MA: Harvard University Press.

- Lewis, Corey Lee, 2005. *Reading the Trail: Exploring the Literature and Natural History of the California Crest*. Reno NV: University of Nevada Press.

- Lovelock, James, 2006. *The Revenge of Gaia: Earth's Climate Crisis and the Fate of Humanity*. New York: Basic Books.

- Mathews, Freya, 2005. *Reinhabiting Reality: Towards a Recovery of Culture*. Albany NY: State University of New York Press.

- Merton, Thomas, 1976. *Ishi Means Man*. Greensboro NC: Unicorn Press.

- Merton, Thomas, 2006. "Ishi: A Meditation." Reprinted in *Passion for Peace: Reflections on War and Nonviolence*. New York: Crossroads Publishing Company.

- Muir, John, 1911,1998. *My First Summer in the Sierra*. Boston: Houghton Mifflin.

- Nadeau, Robert L., 2006. *The Environmental Endgame: Mainstream Economics, Ecological Disaster, and Human Survival*. New Brunswick NJ: Rutgers University Press.

- Nicholsen, Shierry Weber, 2002. *The Love of Nature and the End of the World: The Unspoken Dimensions of Environmental Concern*. Cambridge MA: MIT Press.

- Rifkin, Jeremy, 2009. *The Empathic Civilization: The Race to Global Consciousness in a World in Crisis*. New York: Tarcher/Penguin.

- Snyder, Gary, 1990. *The Practice of the Wild*. San Francisco: North Point Press.

- Solnit, Rebecca, 2006. *Hope in the Dark: Untold Histories, Wild Possibilities*. New York: Nation Books.

- Solnit, Rebecca, 2009. *A Paradise Made in Hell: The Extraordinary Communities that Arise in Disaster*. New York: Viking.

- Steiner, George, 1989. *Real Presences*. Chicago: University of Chicago Press.

- Walker, Brian and David Salt, 2006. *Resilience Thinking: Sustaining Ecosystem and People in a Changing World*. Washington DC: Island Press.

Indigenous Wisdom and Ecological Guidance

1. Hau de no sau nee (Six Nations Iroquois), 1978. *A Basic Call to Consciousness*. Rooseveltown NY: Akwesasne Notes Mohawk Nation.

2. www.goodreads.com/author/quotes/345131.Chief_Joseph

3. Harding, Walter, 1965. *The Days of Henry Thoreau: A Biography*. New York: Alfred A. Knopf.

4. Morgan, Lewis Henry, first published 1851, 1962. *League of the Iroquois*. New York: Corinth Books.

5. Morgan, Lewis Henry, first published 1881, 1965. *Houses and House-Life of the American Aborigines*. Chicago: University of Chicago Press.

6. Pearce, Roy Harvey, 1953, 1964 revised. *The Savages of America: A Study of the Indian and the Idea of Civilization*. Baltimore: Johns Hopkins University Press. Republished in 1988 as *Savagism and Civilization: A Study of the Indian and the American Mind*. Berkeley CA: University of California Press.

7. Waters, Frank, 1963. Book of the Hopi. New York, Viking Press.

8. Waters, Frank, 1950. *Masked Gods: Navaho and Pueblo Ceremonialism*. Denver: Sage Books, Alan Swallow.

9. Waters, Frank, 1942. *The Man Who Killed the Deer*. Denver: Sage Books, Alan Swallow.

10. Waters, Frank, 1998. *Of Time and Change: A Memoir*. Denver: MacMurray & Beck.

Additional Books by Frank Waters

- Waters, Barbara, editor, 2002. *Pure Waters: Frank Waters and the Quest for the Cosmic*. Athens OH: Swallow Press / Ohio University Press.

- Waters, Frank, 1981, 1999. *Mountain Dialogues*. Athens OH: Swallow Press / Ohio University Press.

- Waters, Frank, 1969. *Pumpkin Seed Point*. Chicago: Sage Books, Swallow Press.

- Waters, Frank, 1941. *People of the Valley*. Denver: Sage Books, Alan Swallow.

- Waters, Frank, 1966. *The Woman at Otowi Crossing*. Denver: Alan Swallow.

Technology: Tool Kit and Mindset – Bibliography

The scholars and books listed here have fed my thinking and indicate the context of discernment and analysis on which I draw. A number of books included here postdate the composition of this essay but are included because they significantly extend the discussion.

- Bailey, Lee Worth, 2005. *The Enchantments of Technology*. Urbana and Chicago: University of Illinois Press.

- Berry, Wendell, 1969. *The Long-Legged House*. New York: Harcourt, Brace and World.

- Bookchin, Murray, 1980. *Toward an Ecological Society*. Montreal: Black Rose Books.

- Bookchin, Murray, 1986. *Post-Scarcity Anarchism*. Montreal: Black Rose Books. See the essay, "Towards a Liberatory Technology."

- Ellul, Jacques, 1964. *The Technological Society*. New York: Alfred A. Knopf.

- Fox, Nicols, 2004. *Against the Machine: The Hidden Luddite Tradition in Literature, Art, and Individual Lives*. Washington: Island Press.

- Fuller, Buckminster, 1969, 2008. *Operating Manual for Spaceship Earth*. Zurich: Lars Muller.

- Giedion, Siegfried, 1948, 2014. *Mechanization Takes Command: A Contribution to Anonymous History.* Minneapolis MN: University of Minnesota Press.

- Goodman, Paul, Percival Goodman, 1947, 1960. *Communitas: Means of Livelihood and Ways of Life.* New York: Random House.

- Goodman, Paul, 1965. *People or Personnel: Decentralizing and the Mixed System.* New York: Random House.

- Goodman, Paul, 1970. *New Reformation: Notes of Neolithic Conservative.* New York: Random House.

- Higgs, Eric, Andrew Light and David Strong, editors, 2002. *Technology and the Good Life?* Chicago: University of Chicago Press.

- Hornborg, Alf, 2001. *The Power of the Machine: Global Inequalities of Economy, Technology, and Environment.* Walnut Creek CA: Altamira Press.

- Illich, Ivan, 1973. *Tools for Conviviality.* New York: Harper and Row.

- Illich, Ivan, 1977. *Toward a History of Needs.* New York: Pantheon Books. See the essay, "Energy and Equity."

- Kohr, Leopold, 1957. *The Breakdown of Nations.* New York: Routledge, Kegan and Paul.

- Kohr, Leopold, 1977. *The Overdeveloped Nations: The Diseconomies of Scale.* New York: Schocken Books.

- Marsh, Peter, Peter Collett, 1986. *Driving Passion: The Psychology of the Car*. Boston: Faber and Faber.

- McLuhan, Marshall, 1951, 2002. *The Mechanical Bride: The Folklore of Industrial Man*. Berkeley CA: Gingko Press.

- McLuhan, Marshall, 1962. *The Gutenberg Galaxy: The Making of Typographic Man*. Toronto: University of Toronto Press.

- McLuhan, Marshall, 1964. *Understanding Media: The Extensions of Man*. New York: McGraw-Hill.

- Mumford, Lewis, 1934, 1962. *Technics and Civilization*. New York: Harcourt, Brace and World.

- Mumford, Lewis, 1967. *The Myth of the Machine, Volume I: Technics and Human Development*. New York: Harcourt, Brace and World.

- Mumford, Lewis, 1970. *The Myth of the Machine, Volume II: The Pentagon of Power*. New York: Harcourt, Brace and World.

- Nearing, Helen and Scott, 1954. *Living the Good Life: How to Live Sanely and Simply in a Troubled World*. Harborside ME: Social Science Institute. Reprinted by Schocken Books, New York, in 1990.

- Nelson, Benjamin, 1969. *The Idea of Usury: From Tribal Brotherhood to Universal Otherhood*. Chicago: University of Chicago Press.

- Olson, Robert, David Rejeski, 2005. *Environmentalism & the Technologies of Tomorrow*. Washington DC: Island Press.

- Papanek, Victor, 1972. *Design for the Real World: Human Ecology and Social Change*. New York: Random House.

- Perrin, Noel, 1979. *Giving Up the Gun: Japan's Reversion to the Sword, 1543-1879*. Boston: David R. Godine.

- Polanyi, Karl, 1944, 1957. *The Great Transformation: The Political and Economic Origins of Our Time*. Boston: Beacon Press.

- Rifkin, Jeremy, 1980. *Entropy: A New World View*. New York: Viking Press.

- Rothenberg, David, 1993. *Hand's End: Technology and the Limits of Nature*. Berkeley CA: University of California Press.

- Schivelbusch, Wolfgang, 1986. *The Railway Journey: The Industrialization of Time and Space in the 19th Century*. Berkeley CA: University of California Press.

- Schivelbusch, Wolfgang, 1988. *Disenchanted Night: The Industrialization of Light in the Nineteenth Century*. Berkeley CA: University of California Press.

- Scott, Stephen, Kenneth Pellman, 1990. *Living Without Electricity*. Intercourse PA: Good Books.

- Smith, Merritt Roe, Leo Marx, 1994. *Does Technology Drive History? The Dilemma of Technological Determinism.* Cambridge MA: MIT Press.

- Snyder, Gary, 1969. *Earth House Hold: Technical Notes & Queries.* New York: New Directions.

- Snyder, Gary, 1980. *The Real Work: Interviews & Talks 1964–1979.* New York: New Directions.

- Stein, Matthew, 2000. *When Technology Fails: A Manual for Self-Reliance & Planetary Survival.* White Rive Junction VT: Chelsea Green.

- Tenner, Edward, 1996. *When Things Bite Back: Technology and the Revenge of Unintended Consequences.* New York: Alfred A. Knopf.

- Umble, Diane Zimmerman, 1996. *Holding the Line: The Telephone in Old Order Mennonite and Amish Life.* Baltimore: Johns Hopkins University Press.

- Winner, Langdon, 1977. *Autonomous Technology: Technics-out-of-Control as a Theme in Political Thought.* Cambridge MA: MIT Press.

- Winner, Langdon. 1986. *The Whale and the Reactor: A Search for Limits in an Age of High Technology.* Chicago: University of Chicago Press.

- Wright, Ronald, 2004. *A Short History of Progress.* Toronto: House of Anansi Press.

The Evolution of Environmental Education – Bibliography

- Condon, E. U.: review of *The Idea of a World University*, "Bulletin of Atomic Scientists, October 1967.

- Harman, Sidney, 2003. *Mind Your Own Business: A Maverick's Guide to Business, Leadership and Life.* New York: Doubleday. At a number of points in this book, Sidney Harman writes about the impact his association with Friends World College had on him, both as a member of the Board of Trustees and as its second President.

- Jerome, Judson, 1969. "Friends World College: Report on Evaluation Visit, September 16 -17, 1969." This report was prepared for the New York State Board of Regents and can be accessed at http://files.eric.ed.gov/fulltext/ ED043294.pdf

- Mitchell, Morris, 1967. *World Education – Revolutionary Concept.* New York: Pageant Press.

- Taylor, Harold, 1964. "The Idea of a World University." Saturday Review," November 14, 1964. http://www.unz.org/ Pub/SaturdayRev-1964nov14-00029

- Zweig, Michael, edited by Harold Taylor, 1967. *The Idea of a World University.* Carbondale IL: Southern Illinois University Press.

In the Ruins of a Faith-Haunted World

1. Dylan quotation transcribed from a BBC radio interview, probably from the mid-1960s, and printed with the

BBC identification in a Woody Guthrie tribute sheet I
happened to see some years back and cannot further
identify. I photocopied the section quoting Dylan for my
file. I have searched for the BBC interview but have been
unable to track it down.

2. Ibid.

Tracking Down Ecological Guidance

1. Wissler, Clark, 1926. *The Relation of Nature to Man in
    Aboriginal America*. New York: Oxford University Press.

2. Sauer, Carl Ortwin, 1967. *Land and Life*. Berkeley CA:
    University of California Press.

3. Blakney, Raymond, trans., 1957. *Meister Eckhart: The
    Essential Writings*. New York: Harper

4. Teilhard de Chardin, Pierre, 1970. *Activation Energy*.
    London: Collins.

5. Lovelock, James E., 1979. *Gaia: A New Look at Life on Earth*.
    New York: Oxford University Press.

6. Berry, Thomas, 1988. *The Dream of Earth*. San Francisco:
    Sierra Club Books.

7. Berry, Thomas and Brian Swimme, 1992. *The Universe
    Story: From the Primordial Flaring Forth to the Ecozoic Era; A
    Celebration of the Unfolding of the Cosmos*. San Francisco:
    HarperCollins.

8. Berry, Thomas, 1999. *The Great Work: Our Way Into the Future*. New York: Bell Tower Books.

9. Hocking, Brian, 1965. *Biology or Oblivion: Lessons from the Ultimate Science*. Cambridge MA: Scheckman.

10. Commoner, Barry, 1971. *The Closing Circle: Man, Nature, and Technology*. New York: Alfred A. Knopf.

11. Commoner, Barry, 1976. *The Poverty of Power: Energy and the Economic Crisis*. New York: Alfred A. Knopf.

12. Leopold, Aldo, 1966. *A Sand County Almanac*. New York: Oxford University Press.

13. Fox, George, 1924. *Journal of George Fox*. London: J. M. Dent.

14. Cobb, Edith, 1977. *The Ecology of Imagination in Childhood*. New York: Columbia University Press.

15. Brown, Peter G., Geoffrey Garver, Keith Helmuth, Robert, Howell, and Steve Szeghi, 2009. *Right Relationship: Building a Whole Earth Economy*. San Francisco: Berrett-Koehler.

16. Boulding, Kenneth, 1966. "The Economics of the Coming Spaceship Earth." www.eoearth.org/view/article/156525/ Kenneth Boulding is famous for saying, "Anyone who believes that exponential growth can go on forever in a finite world is either a madman or an economist." www.goodreads.com/quotes/627148-anyone-who-believes-that-exponential-growth-can-go-on-forever

Epilogue: Down to Earth With an Eye on the Future

1. Dreby, Ed, and Judy Lumb, editors, 2012. *Beyond the Growth Dilemma: Toward an Ecologically Integrated Economy*. Caye Caulker, Belize: Quaker Institute for the Future.

2. Ciscel, David, Barbara Day, Keith Helmuth, Sandra Lewis and Judy Lumb, 2011. *How On Earth Do We Live Now? Natural Capital, Deep Ecology, and the Commons*. Caye Caulker, Belize: Quaker Institute for the Future.

3. Hall, Charles A. S. and Kent Klitgaard, 2011. *Energy and the Wealth of Nations: Understanding the Biophysical Economy*. Secaucus NJ: Springer. www.esf.edu/EFB/hall/

4. Ibid.

5. http://8020vision.com/2011/10/17/energy-return-on-investment-eroi-for-u-s-oil-and-gas-discovery-and-production/ and http://ftalphaville.ft.com/2012/05/02/983171/marginal-oil-production-costs-are-heading-towards-100barrel/

6. Heinberg, Richard, 2012. "Don't Worry, There's Plenty of Oil. www.postcarbon.org/blog-post/1083449-don-t-worry-there-s-plenty-of-oil

7. Kamm, David, 2012. "Energy Expert Says Oil Production Has Peaked. www.news-press.com/article/20120826/BUSINESS/308260019/Energy-expert-says-world-s-oil-production-has-peaked?odyssey=mod|newswell|text|Homes

8. Hansen, James, 2012. "Game Over for the Climate." www. nytimes.com/2012/05/10/opinion/game-over-for-the-climate.html

9. McKibben, Bill, 2012. "What NASA's Blue Marble Photo Reveals About Climate Change." www.motherjones.com/ environment/2012/02/bill-mckibben-nasa-blue-marble-photo-climate-change

10. http://www.worldenergyoutlook.org/

11. http://climatechange.worldbank.org/sites/default/files/

12. www.climateanalytics.org/sites/default/files/attachments/ publications/Turn%20down%20the%20heat%2011-16-12. pdf

13. Tainter, Joseph, 1990. *The Collapse of Complex Societies.* New York: Cambridge University Press.

14. Beck, Ulrich, 1999. *World Risk Society.* Cambridge UK: Polity Press.

15. Mythen, Gabe, 2004. Ulrich Beck: *A Critical Introduction to the Risk Society.* London: Pluto Press.

16. Tainter, Joseph A. and Tadeusz W. Patzek, 2012. *Drilling Down: The Gulf Oil Debacle and Our Energy Dilemma.* New York: Springer, Copernicus Books.

17. Boulding, Kenneth, 1965. "Earth as a Spaceship". www. quakerinstitute.org/?page_id=482

18. Hansen (2012) op. cit.

19. McKibben (2012) op. cit.

20. Korten, David C., 2010. *Agenda for a New Economy: From Phantom Wealth to Real Wealth*, 2nd Edition. San Francisco: Berrett-Koehler

21. Ferguson, Charles, 2012. *Predator Nation: Corporate Criminals, Political Corruption, and the Hijacking of America.* New York, Random House.

22. There are a variety of social and economic analysts working in this area and a growing number of books on these themes. Here is a sample:

    - Brown, Peter G., Geoffrey Garver, Keith Helmuth, Robert Howell, Steve Szeghi, 2009. *Right Relationship: Building a Whole Earth Economy.* San Francisco: Berrett-Koehler.

    - Catton, William R., 1982. *Overshoot: The Ecological Basis of Revolutionary Change.* Urbana IL: University of Illinois Press.

    - Costa, Rebecca D., 2010. *The Watchman's Rattle: Thinking Our Way Out of Extinction.* Philadelphia: Vanguard.

    - Coyle, Diane, 2011. *The Economics of Enough: How to Run the Economy as if the Future Matters.* Princeton: Princeton University Press.

- De Villers, Marq, 2012. *Our Way Out: First Principles for a Post-Apocalyptic World.* New York: Random House.

- Dietz, Rob, Dan O'Neill, 2013. *Enough is Enough: Building a Sustainable Economy in a World of Finite Resources.* San Francisco: Berrett-Koehler.

- Gilding, Paul, 2011. *The Great Disruption: Why the Climate Change Crisis Will Bring on the End of Shopping and the Birth of a New World.* New York: Bloomsbury.

- Heinberg, Richard, 2011. *The End of Growth: Adapting to Our New Economic Reality.* Gabriola Island BC: New Society Publishers.

- Homer-Dixon, Thomas, 2006. *The Upside of Down: Catastrophe, Creativity, and the Renewal of Civilization.* Washington DC: Island Press.

- Jackson, Tim, 2011. *Prosperity Without Growth: Economics for a Finite Planet.* London: Earthscan.

- Lewis, Michael and Pat Conaty, 2012. *The Resilience Imperative: Cooperative Transitions To a Steady-State Economy.* Gabriola Island BC: New Society Publishers.

- Rifkin, Jeremy, 2011. *The Third Industrial Revolution: How Lateral Power is Transforming Energy, the Economy, and the World.* New York: Palgrave Macmillan.

- Turner, Chris, 2011. *The Leap: How to Survive and Thrive in the Sustainable Economy.* New York: Random House.

- Victor, Peter, 2008. *Managing Without Growth: Slower by Design, Not Disaster.* Cheltenham UK: Edward Elgar.

23. See Rocky Mountain Institute www.rmi.org/

24. Bradford, Travis, 2006. *Solar Revolution: The Economic Transformation of the Global Energy Industry.* Cambridge MA: MIT Press.

25. Scheer, Hermann, 2007. *Energy Autonomy: The Economic, Social and Technological Case for Renewable Energy.* London: Earthscan.

26. Fullbrook, Edward, editor, 2004. *A Guide to What's Wrong with Economics.* London: Anthem Press.

27. Fullbrook, Edward, editor, 2007. *Real World Economics: A Post-Autistic Economics Reader.* London: Anthem Press.

28. Jacobs, Jane, 1984. *Cities and the Wealth of Nations: Principles of Economic Life.* New York: Random House.

29. Cunningham, Storm, 2002. *The Restoration Economy: Immediate & Emerging Opportunities for Businesses, Communities, and Investors.* San Francisco, Berrett-Koehler.

30. Hutchinson, Francis, Mary Mellor, and Wendy Olson, 2002. *The Politics of Money: Towards Sustainability and Economic Democracy.* London: Pluto Press.

31. Huber, Joseph and James Robertson, 2010. *Creating New Money: A Monetary Reform for the Information Age.* London: New Economics Foundation. www.neweconomcs.org.uk

32. Robertson, James 2012. *Future Money: Breakdown or Breakthrough*. Totnes, Devon UK: Green Books.

33. Hallsmith, Gwendolyn and Bernard Lietar, 2011. *Creating Wealth: Growing Local Economies with Local Currencies*. Gabriola Island BC: New Society Publishers.

34. Lewis, Michael and Pat Conaty, 2012. *The Resilience Imperative: Cooperative Transitions to a Steady-State Economy*. Gabriola Island BC: New Society Publishers.

35. Orlov, Dmitry, 2013. *The Five Stages of Collapse: Survivor's Toolkit*. Gabriola Island BC: New Society Publishers.

About the Author

Keith Helmuth is a founding trustee of Quaker Institute for the Future, serving as its first Board Secretary and Coordinator of Publications. He is a co-author of three books: *Right Relationship: Building a Whole Earth Economy, How on Earth Do We Live Now? Natural Capital, Deep Ecology, and the Commons*, and *Paths of Faith in the Landscape of Science.* He is a co-editor of two books: *It's the Economy, Friends: Understanding the Growth Dilemma*, and *Fuelling Our Future: A Dialogue About Technology, Ethics, and Public Policy.* He has been writing for publication and public presentation for more than forty years.

After university, he managed academic bookstores in Iowa City, Iowa, Syracuse, New York, and New York City. In 1967 he joined the faculty of Friends World College where he helped establish the College's Independent Studies Program and served as the Program's first Coordinator. He and his wife, Ellen, spent a year working with the College's East Africa Program.

From 1972 through the late 1990s, Keith and Ellen, along with sons, Eric and Brendan, operated a farm and market garden business in the Saint John River Valley of New Brunswick. During this time Keith and Ellen worked with community development projects, including a farm market, a credit union, a gristmill cooperative, a homemaker service project, and an employment-training agency. Keith also worked with the Public Participation Division of the Man and Resources Programme (Canada), and in the same capacity with the Saint John River Basin Board. He was a local community representative in the founding of the Valley Solid Waste Commission and continues to serve on its advisory committee. In 1990 he was the Canadian Quaker delegate to the World Council of Churches Convocation on Justice, Peace, and the Integrity of Creation in Seoul, Korea.

After retiring from farming in 1998, the Helmuths spent ten years in Philadelphia where Keith returned to the bookstore business as manager of Penn Book Center on the campus of the University of Pennsylvania. While in Philadelphia he worked closely with the Quaker Eco-Witness project of Philadelphia Yearly Meeting, and with Friends Committee on National Legislation in Washington DC. He helped found Quaker Institute for the Future in 2003. He served in a consulting capacity with Quaker International Affairs Programme (Ottawa) from 2005 to 2010. In 2008 Keith and Ellen returned to New Brunswick where they are again active with the Woodstock Farm Market Co-operative, the Sustainable Energy Group, and with the Community Garden project of Transition Town Woodstock.

About the Cover

Gordon Hammond's drawing depicts the Eastern White Pine that was once a landmark of North Hill Farm near Speerville, Carleton Country, New Brunswick. North Hill Farm was the homestead of Keith and Ellen Helmuth and their sons, Eric and Brendan for almost three decades.

Standing on an open hillside at the head of the farm lane, this great tree was shaped and reshaped by the direct force of the prevailing winds of over its long life. In the late 19th century the farm was owned by Thomas Flemming, the father of James Kidd Flemming, the 14th Premier of New Brunswick. The story has it that when James Kidd was a boy the family had three books: the Bible, Webster's Dictionary, and a life of Abraham Lincoln. The future Premier sat under the great white pine reading and rereading these three books.

David Folster featured the North Hill Pine in his 1987 book, *The Great Trees of New Brunswick*. In 1994, a fierce October storm split the tree and took it down.

CPSIA information can be obtained
at www.ICGtesting.com
Printed in the USA
FFOW05n1715190515